EXECUTIVE EMPLOYMENT LAW

EXECUTIVE EMPLOYMENT LAW

A Handbook for Minnesota Executives

V. JOHN ELLA

MILL CITY PRESS

Mill City Press, Inc.
2301 Lucien Way #415
Maitland, FL 32751
407.339.4217
www.millcitypress.net

Printed in the United States of America.

ISBN-13: 9781545634028

ACKNOWLEDGMENTS

Thank you to my law partner Craig W. Trepanier who originally developed Chapter 7 – Tips for Departing Executives – as a handout for clients after seeing so many executives unnecessarily get in hot water. Craig also co-drafted the Executive Employment Agreement that I have attached as an appendix. Craig is a phenomenal executive-law attorney with a tenacious ability to draft and dissect contracts. This book would not have been possible without his contributions. I would like to thank our Office Manager Joni L. Spratt for her tireless support. Thanks to attorney and editor Kent Dolphay. Thanks also to the intrepid law clerks who worked on this project, Anna M. Koch (JD 2018) and Austin J. Spillane (JD 2018). Acknowledgements to Seymour J. Mansfield and Marshall H. Tanick who taught me executive law in different ways. Thank you to the following Minnesota attorneys who, as experts in their field, reviewed legal content: Scott A. Becker (employee benefits and tax) and Alan Goldfarb (immigration and international issues). Finally, I would like to acknowledge the encouragement and support of my wife, Natasha M. Merz, and my father, who inspired me to be a lawyer.

TABLE OF CONTENTS

DISCLAIMER

This book is not legal advice and should not be relied upon as legal advice. You should contact an attorney to obtain advice with respect to any particular issue or problem.

INTRODUCTION

Welcome to *Executive Employment* Law. This is a handbook for Minnesota executives like you to assist you in furthering your career. As you continue climbing the corporate ladder, you will inevitably encounter a situation that implicates employment law. Your company might be facing a potential merger, you might be offered stock options for the first time, you might bump into a glass ceiling, or you might decide to start your own competing business. Keep a copy of this book in your home office.

This is also a rule book. The business world may seem like a Hobbesian jungle, but the law imposes boundaries on employment relationships. If necessary, courts will step in to resolve workplace disputes. It is therefore important to be familiar with the practical and technical aspects of employment law. Lifetime employment with a single corporation is mostly a thing of the past. You must act in the best interests of your employer, but at the same time you also need to maintain your personal brand and manage your own career. This book also offers tips and real world scenarios from my experience to provide insight to situations you might face. Finally, if you are involved in hiring and firing decisions, the tips in this book will also assist you in responding to employment law issues raised by employees who fall within your managerial responsibility.

I have represented thousands of CEOs and other executives negotiating employment agreements, reviewing severance agreements, and litigating employment disputes. I spent ten years at one of the largest employment defense firms in the country representing Fortune 500 corporations and other companies on the management-side of employment law matters. In my experience, certain scenarios occur over and over and there are proven ways for you to maximize your position when faced with these situations. This book brings you the benefit of this experience to help you meet the challenges of a successful executive career.

CHAPTER 1

THE CORNER OFFICE – WHAT MAKES "EXECUTIVES" DIFFERENT

Americans have conflicting views of business executives. Executives are sometimes perceived as overcompensated and greedy. Yet, American popular culture also recognizes how vulnerable executives are to sudden layoffs or corporate changes outside their control. Actor Michael Douglas epitomized this zeitgeist in several of his movies including *Falling Down*, *Disclosure*, and *Wall Street*. Americans also lionize the accomplishments of entrepreneurs like Steve Jobs and Mark Zuckerberg and look for wisdom from corporate leaders like Jack Welch and Warren Buffet. Some business leaders move into politics, like Mitt Romney and Donald Trump; and some, like Bill Gates, take a philanthropic bent.

Many notable Minnesota executives have risen to the top of the ranks with characteristic Midwestern modesty. Former Medtronic CEO Bill George made a second career of exhorting business students to find their "true north" and calling out business leaders who had lost their moral compass. Similarly, Harvey Mackay of the Mackay Envelope Company has taught many executives to ethically "swim with the sharks." Carlson Company Chair Marilyn Carlson Nelson and several members of the Dayton family (of Target Corporation fame), among hundreds of others, have made a huge impact on the state through personal and corporate philanthropy. Minnesota, like anywhere else, has had its share of corporate scandals recently as well, including a massive pyramid scheme; a kerfuffle regarding back-dated stock options; and a hearing aid company whose president was found guilty of self-dealing at the expense of the company's absentee owner.

A smart executive should be prepared for the unexpected and look for ways to protect herself, whether through a contract, political maneuvering, or in rare situations the threat of a lawsuit. Executives are not only compensated in more complex ways, they are also more likely than rank and file employees to be offered a severance when their employment ends. It is commonly understood that the more money you earn, the more money you will be paid upon termination. One theory for this is that the people making the decision to authorize severance payments are themselves high-level executives who may unconsciously be thinking, "there, but for the grace of God, go I." According to this theory, it is in the interest of these decision-makers to perpetuate the system of golden parachutes, because next time they might be the ones getting downsized. Another explanation is that executives are much more likely when entering into the employment relationship to have negotiated a contract which obligates the company to pay severance on the back end. Yet another factor is that executives are better able to negotiate for themselves and may have a personal relationship with the decision-makers. They may have inside information about how the employer makes decisions, what others have received in the past, or skeletons in the closet. Finally, there is the possibility that a departing executive poses a competitive threat and the employer has tied the payment of a severance to the executive's compliance with a restrictive covenant. You cannot take these factors for granted, however. You need to advocate for yourself in times of transition and retain an outside advocate as well. To paraphrase F. Scott Fitzgerald, the rich are different than you or me because they obtain counsel.

What is an "Executive"?

According to an article in *Lawyers Weekly*[1], "there are three types of entities in the workplace: employers, employees, and executives." What is an "executive?" The term definitely includes "C"-level officers like CEOs and Presidents. It includes other "C*x*Os" as well, including CFOs, COOs, and the like. It may encompass anyone with "Vice President" on their LinkedIn profile and perhaps anyone with managerial responsibility. Executives are likely to have a college degree and perhaps an MBA or other graduate degree and, even if they are not in the top one percent, they are more highly compensated than the average American and have more complicated compensation arrangements. For employment law purposes, the term can also apply to professionals, like doctors and lawyers. At its outer edges it can be said to include anyone who might be offered an individualized severance agreement, which these days is a significant portion of the workforce.

Female Executives and Executives of Color

Women are still confronted with different challenges in the corporate world. Despite a renewed movement to address pay inequity, glass ceilings, paid family leave, sexual harassment and chauvinism, some women might still feel that the board room is overly male dominated. Strong legal protections exist to address these issues. Minnesota's Women's Economic Security Act (WESA), which was signed into law in May of 2015, authorized millions of dollars to help women in the workplace and female entrepreneurs. Female executives, however, may face difficult choices about how and when to explicitly exert their rights under the law, when to address improprieties politically or privately or, in the words of Sheryl Sandberg, when to "lean in." These factors continue to create complicated and subtle career choices for women. At times it can be helpful to discuss these questions confidentially with legal counsel before it is too late to avoid a career-altering lawsuit or public confrontation.

Non-white executives in Minnesota also face an insular corporate culture. A 2016 survey by the *Star Tribune* revealed that 60% of professionals of color in the Twin Cities were planning to leave the state in the next three to five years due to a perception that the region is "cliquey" if you were not born here.[2] The article cited a survey that the Twin Cities ranks first in overall professional talent retention among the 25 largest U.S. metro areas, but 14th for retention for professionals of color.[3] Minnesota corporations are taking steps to improve issues of inclusion, however. The rules and guidelines in this book apply even more so to women and executives of color—the law provides protections from discrimination, but these protections must be wielded strategically for optimal long-term career prospects.

The Minnesota Corporate Landscape

The Twin Cities Metropolitan Area is home to a number of famous American corporations. In many recent years, on a per-capita basis, Minnesota boasted more Fortune 500 headquarters than any state other than Connecticut. UnitedHealth Group currently tops the list, with over $200 *billion* in revenue in 2017. Polaris Industries, Inc. and Securian Financial Group were the newest Minnesota companies to make the Fortune 500 list in 2018. Target Corporation is a retail giant second only to Walmart, and electronics retailer Best Buy calls Minnesota home as well. U.S. Bank by itself establishes Minneapolis as a financial center, along with Ameriprise, Thrivent Financial, and major operations of Wells Fargo. Minnesota is a world leader in the food and agri-business sector thanks to companies like General Mills, Cargill, Land O' Lakes, and Hormel. It is also a global center for excellence in health care with the Mayo Clinic, Medtronic, UnitedHealth, and the University of Minnesota. 3M and Ecolab are examples of Minnesota companies investing in research to develop new industrial technologies. Several global companies maintain their North American headquarters in Minnesota such as Pentair and Allianz. The annals of corporate history in Minnesota also include companies founded in the state that have been acquired or no longer exist, such as Honeywell, Northwest Airlines,

Norwest Bank, St. Jude Medical, Valspar, and St. Paul Companies. As these corporate giants have grown and, in some cases, moved or been acquired, they have spun off talented executives who have started new companies of their own. Medtronic, in particular, has created a significant cluster of medical technology companies in the Twin Cities, sometimes known as "Medical Alley."

Minnesota law has both contributed to the state's economic success and been shaped by it. For example, Minnesota's law regarding unfair competition has been influenced by many court decisions involving the med-tech industry.[4] Minnesota's corporations law is unusually protective of minority shareholders and has led to some significant legal precedents. At the same time, a liberal political tradition in the state has created a regulatory climate similar to California with a number of pro-employee legal protections and unique statutes regarding such topics as requirements for rescission provisions of waivers of discrimination claims, limits on drug and alcohol testing of employees, and protections against termination of manufactured sales representatives. There is a rich and dense body of statutory law and common law in Minnesota and executives working in the state should be familiar with it.

The future is bright for executives in Minnesota. There is no reason to think that the golden age of the American executive is over. The C-suite is increasingly diverse, with many Fortune 500 companies being run by women, minorities, and international executives. In the United States, the rule of law has helped minimize (but not eliminate) corruption, discrimination, and cronyism to a point never before seen in history. This means that the 21st century economy increasingly rewards pure talent, and the most talented individuals will be rewarded the most. But this also means that understanding and using the legal system is more important than ever. The same trends of increased competition, faster technology, and expanding globalization will continue to challenge business leaders.

CHAPTER 2

"IT'S A DEAL"–EXECUTIVE CONTRACTS AND EMPLOYMENT AGREEMENTS

Maxim: It is almost always in your best interest to have an employment contract. Unless you are a tenured professor, a member of a union, or a civil servant, your default employment status under American jurisprudence is likely "at-will." This means that you can be fired for any reason, or no reason at all, so long as it is not for an illegal reason, such as your race or religion. At-will employment is not just a concept. No matter how well you have performed in the past, or how many years of loyal service you have devoted to your employer, without a contract, you can be discharged without warning. Nor is there is any legal requirement in this country for an employer to offer you a severance payment upon termination. Do not enter an executive employment relationship, no matter how rosy things seem, without considering the cold reality that it could end at a time not of your choosing.

If you have an employment contract, the situation is much different. The employer will be bound by the terms of the contract. For example, if the contract says you will be employed for a year and you are terminated prior to that date, you are entitled to what you would have been paid for the duration of the contract. (Courts almost never require companies to keep employees employed, regardless of the contractual language. Instead, courts award monetary damages in the event of a breach, measured by what the employee would have earned.) Another way of achieving the same result, therefore, is to provide that, in the event of termination, the executive will receive a payment, commonly referred to as a "severance" payment.

Monetary compensation addresses some, but not all, problems associated with an involuntary termination. Often the amount of severance you negotiate is less important than protecting your career going forward. How your separation is characterized can matter. Money buys you time to find your next gig. Enough money might allow you to start a business. Executives should also be concerned about reputation and appearance, as well as not burning bridges with their previous colleagues, potential references, and future networking contacts. Executives also need to be mindful of what restrictions a contract might place on their future ability to work.

So, if you are one of the small percentage of American workers offered an employment contract, that is a good thing. If you have not been offered a contract, but you are in discussions about a new, high-level job or promotion, it is probably in your best interest to propose a written contract. If you cannot secure a formal employment contract, consider writing an e-mail setting forth your understanding of the terms of your hire. Under certain circumstances, this could be admissible evidence of a unilateral contract or a legally enforceable promise. If your new boss sketches out the terms of your lifetime employment on a cocktail napkin, keep the napkin in a safe place.

What a contract actually says matters. A strong contract, from the perspective of the executive, would provide for a severance payment in the event of a termination for any reason. Typically, however, most employment agreements have a loophole that excludes severance if the executive is terminated for "cause." In that situation, the definition of "cause" makes a huge difference. An example of a narrow definition might be "conviction of a felony." That would mean the executive could not be terminated while he or she was arrested, indicted, or even until the trial was over or if he or she pled guilty to a gross misdemeanor. (Remember, the company could actually fire the executive anytime it wants. It would, however, have to pay monetary damages.) A broader definition of cause such as "any act which the company, in its sole discretion, deems to be misconduct or a failure of the executive to perform his duties" may appear only slightly better than no contract at all. Even watered-down language can create a potential issue for litigation, however, which can be a leverage point for severance discussions. If you are presented with a proposed contract, review the terms with an attorney and, if appropriate, communicate suggested changes.

Joining a Large Company

Many sectors of the American economy are becoming more concentrated as very large corporations dominate their market. According to the U.S Census Bureau, for the first time in history, Americans are more likely to work for a large employer than a small one.[5] If your job offer is coming from a large company, be prepared for resistance to any proposed changes cloaked with the excuse that "this is our standard contract and we cannot modify it for you, because then we would have to make changes for other executives." This position only holds water to the extent you are a not a valuable candidate. Most companies will usually entertain slight modifications or pushback. You may not in fact have leverage, however, so you need to guard against pushing too much in a contract negotiation and losing out on the opportunity altogether. Outplacement professionals relate that corporate employers used to hire candidates with 6 or 7 out of 10 desired attributes, but now they are looking for a 10 out of 10. If you are a 10, use your leverage.

Publicly-Traded Companies

It should be clear throughout this book that there is a key distinction between public companies and non-public companies. A "public" or publicly-traded company is one whose stock is traded on a public exchange such as the New York Stock Exchange or NASDAQ. The benefit of being able to raise capital on an exchange comes with many trade-offs for businesses in the form of increased regulatory burdens. There are fewer public companies in the U.S. than there used to be, but they are generally larger and more successful, and there are opportunities for highly remunerative careers with these giant corporations.

Executives in public companies can benefit from the ability to receive stock options and to exercise the options without actually paying for the option (by means of a "cashless" exercise). Public companies have robust legal, HR, and compliance teams and are generally much more careful when it comes to executive contracts and employment law.

Publicly-traded companies have transparency requirements. They are subject to regulation by the Securities and Exchange Commission (SEC) and must disclose certain information about executive compensation. The SEC issued expanded requirements in 2006 which included a mandatory "Compensation Disclosure and Analysis." In 2009, the SEC issued another set of new requirements for proxy statements including a discussion of compensation policies as they relate to "risk management and risk taking" and a disclosure with respect to the background of directors and officers. Although the SEC disclosures themselves are the responsibility of securities counsel, the clear implication is that compensation policies ought not overly induce "risk taking." But exactly what that amorphous term means is less clear.

Joining a Private Company

A different dynamic arises when negotiating an employment opportunity with a smaller, privately-owned company. Founders of successful businesses tend to be Type-A personalities. Often, they have never had to answer to anyone. When a business grows large enough such that the founder decides to bring in a new president (perhaps with a fancy MBA) to take the business to the next level, the incoming president should insist on a contract. Otherwise, he or she will be at the mercy of an owner who might not relinquish control easily. In our experience, sometimes the owner in this situation may be too arrogant, or too impecunious, to hire an attorney to prepare or review a contract for the company. This can actually result in the owner agreeing to unusually generous, or perhaps confusing and contradictory terms.

Approaching the Owner for a Piece of the Action

Sometimes one person owns the business and another person runs the business. A key employee who has become critical to the business (either because the owner does not want to do the day-to-day work himself, or cannot), may at some point approach the owner, who he perhaps perceives as his friend or partner, and ask for a piece of the action. This could take the form of a raise, promotion, contract, equity or partial ownership. Sometimes this works out and sometimes it does not.

On one occasion, I prepared a draft contract for a client who considered himself a key employee. He presented the proposal to the owner and the owner immediately became offended and fired him. I have only had this happen once, but it supports a **Maxim: "Ownership is like Royalty."** Under the law, owners have all the power. They can choose to run the company into the ground, shut it down, or fire everyone, like King Joffrey in *Game of Thrones*. They have the legal right to make bad decisions. They may act friendly to loyal executives, but internally they view themselves differently. Approach them like you would a monarch, with flattery and patience. Allow them to arrive at the conclusion that it is their idea to offer you a piece of the action.

Acquisition by Private Equity Fund

As the cost of taking a company public has increased and wealthy investors seek a return on capital, many U.S. companies are being taken over by private equity funds. Existing executives at a take-over target may justifiably dread new ownership in this context. Private equity funds often look to cut costs and drive profit. Lay-offs often follow such an acquisition. As unpredictable as working for a family-owned company can be, once outside buyers come into the picture, any pretense of loyalty is gone. Usually, private equity funds are looking to grow the company and sell it again in a few years, or possibly go public. They may also be looking to chop up the company and sell off a division. Your company may also be lumped together with other businesses with little in common other than ownership by the same financial group for purposes of Human Resources or other support. If you are senior management, you may be answering to ownership in New York or Chicago that does not seem to care about the people or the history of the company in the way that the founders did. Often, you will receive a new employment agreement from an out-of-town law firm with a new non-compete clause. In this case, you should consult with an attorney before committing to the new regime.

Minority Shareholders in Closely-Held Companies

If you are a minority owner (owning some, but less than 50%) of a closely-held corporation or limited liability company and an employee at the same time, you have more rights than a non-owner employee. Under Minnesota law, "closely-held" generally means fewer than 30 owners, although the definition is elastic. By definition, a minority owner does not have voting control over the direction of the business, including decisions about her own employment.

In Minnesota, a minority shareholder can sometimes claim an "expectation of continuing employment," and even monetary damages for termination of employment, but not if agreements expressly state otherwise. In addition to the concern about your employment, if you are terminated, you may have a dispute over receiving fair payment for the redemption of your shares and you may have other equitable claims for minority shareholder oppression. These disputes are referred to as business divorces by attorneys and are just as messy as marital dissolutions. In many states, including Minnesota, shareholders owe each other a duty to be "fair." Few other aspects of the American legal system, require fairness. But shareholders can go to court and cry, "that's not fair!", like a kindergartner, and have their grievances heard.

The key to avoiding expensive litigation in this area is to put well-drafted membership control agreements and buy-sell agreements in place that set forth how a departing shareholder will be bought out and how the company will be valued, along with employment agreements for each owner/employee. In the absence of well-written contracts, a dispute about the business may turn into a free-for-all where everything is up for grabs. Sometimes, the business itself can be destroyed in the ensuing litigation. Issues facing employees who are also minority shareholders are discussed in further detail in Chapter 8.

Selling your Company and Becoming an Employee

Former business owners often become employees after being bought out by a larger entity. In this situation, the selling owner must negotiate not only a price for the business but also an employment contract. When someone creates their own small business and sells to a national conglomerate, it can be unsettling to wake up as an employee the next morning. For example, many small town pharmacists and eye doctors who used to own their own practices are now working for national chains. The owners of the fictional funeral home Fisher & Sons in HBO's *Six Feet Under* faced similar pressure from the Kroner Company. Even Ted Turner went from being a mogul to an employee of Time Warner when he sold his stake in Turner Broadcasting. Keep in mind that moving from being a small business owner to an employee can mean higher income, but also a loss in freedom and flexibility. The doctor played by Eddie Murphy in the remake of *Dr. Doolittle* turned down a lucrative offer to purchase his medical practice for this reason. As discussed elsewhere in this book, non-competes related to the sale of a company are more likely to be enforceable, and for longer periods of time, than run-of-the-mill employment non-competes.

Executives as Independent Contractors, Consultants, and "Executive Temps"

In a different scenario, an executive might, voluntarily or involuntarily, leave a high-level position with a Fortune 500 corporation one day and decide to be a self-employed "consultant" the next. That person has transitioned from employee to business owner and faces a whole different set of concerns and risks. Many employees coming out of corporate downsizing move into self-employment for various reasons, including lifestyle and an opportunity to be their own boss. An increasing percentage of Americans are considered "independent contractors," in part because employers are shying away from the cost of health care and benefits and also because independent contractors can be more easily added or dropped from the budget if business conditions change. The authors of an article in *Harvard Business Review* made the claim that a rising number of executives at the very highest level are acting as "supertemps" and belong to a growing "free agent nation."[6] Short-term contracts are easier to negotiate than long-term employment contracts, because they are more like a fling than a marriage.

Use of Executive Recruiters

Executive recruiters can be extremely helpful in helping you to land a position with a new company. Recruiters are almost always paid by the employer, rather than the candidate. Typically, recruiters retained on a contingency fee receive 20-25% of your first-year compensation (recruiters retained full-time by the employer can receive 30-33% of your total first-year compensation). Recruiters, therefore, owe their duty to the hiring company, not you. Some of them act as though they have loyalty only to the commission. Be guarded when working with a recruiter. For example, you should not hide the fact you have a non-compete, but don't let the recruiter assume it will be an obstacle. It is good to develop a relationship directly with individuals at the hiring corporation instead of filtering all communications through the recruiter; but don't try to cut the recruiter out of their commission. Don't say negative things about the corporation to the recruiter that might get back to the company, and be polite in all e-mail communications. I have seen offers rescinded because the executives acted out after they thought their offers were finalized. On the employer side, always make sure to do your own background check, including a simple Google search, instead of assuming the recruiter will discover all the skeletons in the candidate's background. Before signing an employment agreement, meet with an executive law attorney to make sure you understand the terms, even if you do not plan to negotiate for further changes.

Why Contracts?

Just as contracts are usually a good thing for the executive, it is often not in the interest of an employer to offer an employment contact. So, why do companies ever offer employment agreements? First, there is a mutual need to set forth the basic terms of the job in writing, even if the employment is at-will. This may be in the form of an offer letter. If the employer requires a non-compete agreement or other restrictive covenant, by definition the employer will have to provide a contract. Once you add in the possibility of stock options, bonuses, change-in-control provisions, and other complications, it soon makes sense to have a formal employment agreement consolidating all of this information in a single document. At the same time, the best talent will demand protections in the form of a contract, so having an agreement may be mutually beneficial. Whether the contract provides for a severance or term of employment, however, depends on the bargaining position of the incoming executive as well as the sophistication of the employer. Many executives who are recruited from secure positions, or have critical skills and a proven track record, will not accept a new offer without some type of protection, and can afford to say "no" if the prospective new employer refuses to provide it.

Change-in-Control Provisions

Change-in-control (CIC) clauses provide for additional job protection, severance payments, or the accelerated vesting of stock options in the event the company is taken over or acquired by new ownership. Among other things, a change-in-control clause will allow an executive to concentrate her energies on finding new capital, merger candidates, or a potential buyer, without fearing the consequences of her success. Use this excuse to

11

ask for a CIC provision if you are assigned responsibility for any of these types of goals or hear rumors of a potential sale.

The definition of "change in control" should be specifically stated and may include a majority change in equity ownership of the corporation, the purchase of all or substantially all of the assets of the corporation, or a change in majority control of the board of directors. The "effective date" of a change in control should also be clearly defined, as I have been involved in arbitrating a dispute over this issue. Executives might find themselves pink-slipped immediately prior to a CIC, whether in an effort to avoid the parachute payment, in a last ditch effort to clean house, by coincidence, or at the request of the new owners, even if they have not officially taken control. For this reason, it might be beneficial to define the effective date of a CIC for severance purposes as being 60 days prior to the effective date of a transaction such as a merger, acquisition, public offering, or sale of assets.

Most CIC clauses define a change in control, in part, as a change in the ownership (sometimes referred to in legal documents as "beneficial ownership") of the securities or voting shares of the company representing some percentage of all voting power. From the executive's perspective, the number should be as low as possible, perhaps 20% or even 15%. For publicly-held corporations, 33% or 35% is more common. For small, privately held companies, the trigger is usually 50%. Generally, the larger the company, the smaller the percentage of stock that will be necessary to constitute a CIC. Sometimes application of these clauses can be complicated, depending on the nature of the transaction from a securities law perspective. For example, venture capital or distressed company financing may result in debt that is convertible to equity, such as preferred stock. This can confuse the question of what constitutes "ownership."

A high-level executive in a very large corporation may be the head of a billion-dollar division of the company, but if that division is sold off to a competitor without changing the "ownership" of the company as a whole, termination of the executive's employment may leave him without recourse to a CIC clause. If you are a division head, consider asking to include the sale of your department, division, or product line as a definitional trigger.

Change-in-control clauses may be categorized as either "single trigger" or "double trigger." A single trigger clause, which is rare, automatically pays benefits to the executive upon the change in control if he chooses not to remain with the corporation. A double trigger only pays benefits if there is a change in control and the executive is involuntarily terminated by the new owner within a certain time period following the effective date of the change in control.

Change-in-control provisions provide for payments, referred to as "golden parachutes," of up to two to three times annual compensation and the acceleration of stock options or other compensation. Change-in-control provisions have also been used as anti-hostile takeover devices known as "poison pills" because they may too expensive for the acquiring company to swallow. If a parachute payment exceeds three times the executive's annual compensation, it may not be tax deductible to the company and may subject the executive to a 20% excise tax pursuant to § 280G and § 4999 of the Internal Revenue Code. See Chapter 3 for more discussion on potential tax consequences of receiving a golden parachute after a change in control.

The use of change-in-control clauses is not necessarily limited to executives in Fortune 500 companies. Any employee of any company, even one that is small and privately held by a few shareholders, or even one owner, can ask for this type of protection. I have seen them used with regard to professions ranging from golf course manager to laboratory pathologist.

Before you accept a position with a closely-held company with one major shareholder, it might make sense to inquire what would happen if that person should suddenly pass away. Ask who would inherit ownership of the company. I have seen more than one case involving an owner who inherited his or her spouse's company and made radical changes in management. It may be feasible to obtain CIC protection with a clause that defines "change in control" as "the inheritance or transfer by operation of law of a controlling interest of the shares to a third party", in addition to the traditional provision regarding the "sale" of a controlling interest.

Typical Executive Contract Provisions

Executive contracts can have lots of bells and whistles, some of which are good for the executive, some of which are standard or "boilerplate," and some of which are less desirable. Here is a walk-through of some common contract provisions:

The Introduction

The introduction, perhaps starting with several "Whereas" clauses, sets forth certain background assumptions and the reasons for forming the agreement. It should include an identification of the "Parties", including the exact name of the legal entity (corporation, LLC, etc.) that will be the employer, and the effective date of the agreement. Some courts have held that statements in a "Whereas" clause are not part of the actual contract.

Term

The parties must determine whether the employment contract is designed to alter the at-will employment relationship. Keep in mind that the "term" of the <u>contract</u> may, or may not, be different than the "term" of <u>employment</u>. Poorly-drafted agreements blur these two concepts. Provisions for renewals, automatic renewals, extensions, and notice requirements can also create confusion and must be reviewed carefully. Executive contracts are sometimes, but not always, designed for the specific purpose of providing a guaranteed duration of employment. Where the contract is meant to preserve the at-will relationship, the agreement should clearly state that the executive remains at-will and can be terminated, or can quit, for any reason at any time. One clean approach to drafting is to expressly state that the employment itself is at-will, but that the reason for termination will determine the form, timing, and amount of any severance payments.

A contract altering the at-will relationship can be structured in many ways. The most common is that the executive will be employed indefinitely and may only be fired for "cause", as defined by the contract. Again, the definition of "cause" is very important. The executive will prefer a narrow list of specific examples such as:

- Poor performance
- A material breach of any of the executive's obligations under the agreement
- The repeated failure or refusal to perform or observe his or her duties, responsibilities and obligations
- Loss of a professional license
- Any dishonesty or other breach of duty of loyalty
- Use of alcohol or other drugs in a manner which affects the performance of the executive's duties, responsibilities and obligations
- Conviction of a felony or of any crime involving theft, misrepresentation, moral turpitude or fraud
- Commission of any other willful or intentional act which could reasonably be expected to injure the reputation, business, or business relationships of the company
- The existence of any court order or settlement agreement prohibiting the executive's continued employment

It is in your interest to ask for a written notice and cure provision. This device requires the company to provide written notice of a breach or other basis for cause and allows the executive a period of time to fix or "cure" the problem before termination occurs. In practice, employers often forget they have contractually agreed to such a provision before firing the executive. In this situation, you may be able to negotiate additional severance, if not save your job.

An employment agreement may also provide employment for a defined term, such as one year. The set term contract commonly provides that the executive may be terminated prior to the end of the term "for cause" also referred to as "just cause," as defined by the contract and as discussed above. A common variation on the above types of contracts allows the employer to terminate either "for cause" without a penalty or without cause but subject to a "buy out" of a set amount of compensation and benefits. So-called "evergreen" contracts renew automatically unless terminated for cause or proper advance notice is given.

Title and Duties

An executive contract should clearly set forth the executive's title, duties, responsibilities and position. Executives sometimes measure their status based on who they report to. It used to be more common for the CEO to also serve as chair of the board of directors. A trend in large, publicly-held companies is to recommend that these positions be separated in certain situations and that the chair position be given to an outsider to increase oversight and avoid total control such as that given to former Disney Chairman Michael Eisner, who was stripped of his chairmanship in 2004. Nowadays, the former CEO might ascend to an executive chairman position to allow space and a transition for a new CEO, as in the case of outgoing 3M CEO Inge Thulin in 2018.

Titles can be important, and companies might be more flexible, creative, and generous with titles than they are with compensation. This is the age of the Chief "Something" Officer. Microsoft at one point had seven "CFOs," one for each division, and General Electric had more than 50 Chief Executive Officers at one time.[7] The use of CxO titles outside the traditional CEO, CFO and COO triumvirate continues to proliferate in small companies as well, including but not limited to, an increase in positions such as Chief Technology Officer, Chief Information Officer, Chief Knowledge Officer, Chief Privacy Officer, Chief Legal Officer, Chief Development Officer, Chief Learning Officer, Chief Marketing Officer, Chief Restructuring Officer, Chief Academic Officer, Chief Accounting Officer, and Chief Security Officer, among others.

An employment contract may include a clause governing or restricting the ability of the executive to hold other employment or board positions, sometimes referred to as a "Full Time and Effort" clause. A guarantee of facilities, support, staffing, or capital might be included in a contract for a CEO or COO in a turn-around situation to assure them that they will receive sufficient resources and support to do the job.

Compensation

Employment agreements set forth the executive's compensation and benefits, including base salary; bonus and incentive pay; signing bonuses, if any; and deferred compensation plans. The contract should identify the exact amount of salary in annual or monthly terms and note that applicable deductions and withholdings will be made from salary. It may identify the method and timing of payment of salary, such as bi-weekly or monthly, and state the basis for potential salary increases. Compensation is discussed further in Chapter 3.

The method for determining and providing annual bonuses, commissions, or incentive pay should be clearly defined. Any incentives tied to business or customers brought in or originated by the executive should include a regular tracking provision so there are no surprises or disputes at the end of the year.

"Make-whole payments," also known as an "inducement awards," "golden hellos," or simply a "signing bonus" are designed to compensate the executive for whatever he or she is leaving on the table at their previous employment.

Deferred Compensation

In addition to a 401(k) or standard pension plan, the executive may be entitled to participate in special retirement plans such as a Supplemental Executive Retirement Plan (SERP), a "top hat" plan or other qualified or nonqualified arrangement designed to defer taxation. A "top hat" plan is an unfunded, non-regulated plan maintained for providing deferred compensation to a select group of management or highly-compensated employees.

Clawbacks

Clawback provisions, which place stock grants, bonuses, or incentive payments at risk of being rescinded in the future, have become a standard provision in many executive contracts. 73 Fortune 100 companies said they had claw-back provisions in 2009 compared with only 18 in 2006, according to an executive compensation research firm that studied the issue. Over half of the S&P 1500 companies reported using clawbacks as of 2012. In 2017, Wells Fargo announced it was clawing back over $75 million in compensation paid to top former executives after a scandal involving alleged unauthorized bank accounts. Employers can also assert clawbacks if an executive breaches a restrictive covenant. Clawbacks have complicated tax implications for executives. Contractual clawback provisions should therefore be avoided, if possible.

Other Benefits

Other employee benefits and perquisites could include a signing bonus; training and educational stipends; holidays; vacation; personal time off; a car allowance; a smart phone; a laptop; paid parking; paid internet at home; medical and dental benefits; paid accounting and financial planning services; short- and long-term disability benefits; life insurance; relocation or moving expenses; housing; assistance with the sale of a home; participation in retirement, pension, or related plans; and payment of dues for professional organizations, trade associations, or country club memberships. (Paid country club memberships have lost popularity. In 1998, 54% of small to medium company CEOs had their country club memberships paid by the company. In 2002, the number was down to 8%.) The use of "loans" by employees of publicly-held companies was curtailed by the Sarbanes-Oxley Act.

Restrictive Covenants

Contractual provisions that limit conduct by the executive that could be potentially damaging to the employer are referred to as "restrictive covenants." For instance, an executive might be asked to sign agreements governing assignment of inventions, confidentiality, trade secrets, non-competition, non-solicitation, non-disparagement, or non-recruitment. In such cases, the employer and executive may enter into either a separate agreement, or may incorporate restrictive covenants into an individualized employment agreement. Post-termination violation of restrictive covenants may result in the loss of, or obligation to pay back, severance payments or include clawback clauses, resulting in the loss of stock options or bonuses. Examples of restrictive covenants include the following:

> - Non-compete
> - Non-solicitation
> - Non-disclosure
> - Non-disparagement
> - Non-recruit
> - Non-circumvention
> - Non-inducement
> - Non-raiding
> - Non-tampering

Among other restrictions, an employer may require a "non-disparagement" clause pursuant to which an executive agrees that he or she will not, during the term of employment or thereafter, make disparaging comments regarding the employer. The employee may seek reciprocal protection against employer disparagement.[8] There is further discussion of non-disparagement clauses in Chapter 10. Chapter 6 describes other types of restrictive covenants in greater detail.

Indemnification

The executive employee may seek contractual indemnification provisions by the employer beyond that required by state law, or the maintaining of Directors and Officers (D&O) insurance coverage.

Personal Guaranty

Where the employer is small, thinly capitalized, or a start-up, or in similar circumstances, the executive may seek a guaranty of the performance of the contract by the individual owners or the parent corporation.

Return of Property

Employment contracts typically require that, upon termination, an executive return an employer's confidential information and business records, as well as any phones, laptops, flash drives, keys, and key cards. In this age of cloud computing, it is incumbent upon employers and executives to also delete information that may be on their personal e-mail account or non-employer computers. Employers may also want to confirm that executives have discontinued access to cloud-based storage accounts and provided passwords to social media accounts belonging to the company, such as LinkedIn or Facebook.

Termination by the Executive

- **Resignation**. Employment contracts typically provide that an executive may resign upon giving a specified number of weeks, or months, of notice to an employer; but in that event, receive no severance compensation.
- **Good Reasons Clause**. A "Good Reasons" clause offers powerful protection to the executive, allowing her to declare a breach and claim liquidated compensation and benefits, where the executive's title, salary, benefits, authority, or other material conditions are materially diminished. It might be said that the

hallmark of a platinum level "executive" contract as distinguished from a mere "employment" contract is the inclusion of a "good reasons" clause. The CEO of US Airways reportedly collected over $4 million after resigning pursuant to this type of clause in 2004.

"Good reasons" may include:

- Diminution in status, authority, or responsibility;
- Reduction in cash compensation, equity compensation, or benefits;
- Change in control;
- Failure of acquirer to assume obligation of employment contract;
- Distant relocation of executive's working place;
- Other customized grounds, such as curtailment of staffing support, facilities, or working capital or onerous travel requirements.

(A difference between an employment-law attorney and an executive-law attorney is whether they know the definition of a "Good Reasons" clause.)

Death

An employment contract terminates upon an executive's death. Although less common, an executive may seek a payout to his or her estate, either an amount based on former compensation or funded with a life insurance death benefit, such as split-dollar, or key man insurance.

Disability

Employment contracts terminate if an executive becomes totally disabled from performing the job. Most companies provide only insurance disability benefits in these circumstances, although some executives seek to augment this with severance payments. You should maintain your own, private disability insurance as a back-up.

Arbitration

The parties may agree in advance that any disputes will be resolved by arbitration and not in the courts. Arbitration clauses are almost always enforceable. Despite good intentions, however, arbitration can sometimes be both more expensive and slower than conventional litigation and is not necessarily a panacea for resolving disputes. Litigation in the normal district court system is like a baseball game – technically there is no set ending. Some cases have gone up to appellate courts and back down again multiple times over the span of a decade. Arbitration is more like a football game – you can expect it be completed by a certain date and appeals are generally not allowed. Arbitration also offer greater confidentiality, as proceedings in court are generally open to the public. Certain employees in the securities industry are subject to mandatory arbitration as required by the Financial Industry Regulatory Authority (FINRA). Arbitration is discussed further in Chapter 12.

"Boilerplate" Clauses

- **Fees and Expenses**: A contract may provide that attorney's fees and legal expenses incurred in enforcing the contract may be provided to a prevailing party.
- **Reimbursements**: A contract may provide for reimbursement of any reasonable business-related expenses.
- **Merger:** A merger clause provides for the integration of prior negotiations, documents, or agreements into one final contract.
- **Modification**: Typically, an employment contract provides that it may only be modified by a writing, signed by all parties.
- **Nonwaiver:** Executive contracts often provide that the employer's occasional waiver of certain executive conduct will not constitute a waiver of the employer's right to challenge that conduct at a later time.
- **Successors and Assigns:** Executive contracts typically provide that an executive's contractual rights are not assignable. An employment contract may also specify the obligations of any successor employer with regard to the contract. It may be important to the executive that any successor or acquirer of the company be required to assume the obligations to the executive under her employment agreement. It may also be important to the company to be able to assign its rights to enforce restrictive covenants.
- **Choice of Law:** The contract should specify which state law governs the contract. Although most states have similar law with regard to the enforcement of contracts in general, this provision can have significant implications with regard to the enforceability of non-competes, which are statutorily invalid in California, for example.
- **Forum Selection:** A forum selection clause governs where a legal dispute to enforce the agreement would be brought. Generally, the forum is a state or federal court of a specific state.

- **Severability:** The contract should provide that contract provisions are severable. That means that if one section is declared invalid by a court the rest of the provisions still apply.
- **Signatures and Counterparts:** Authorized parties must sign the contract. A "counterparts" provision simply means that the parties can sign different copies of the same agreement separately and at different times or places instead of meeting to sign the same document at the same time.

A sample Executive Agreement is reproduced as Appendix I.

CHAPTER 3

"SHOW ME THE MONEY" – EXECUTIVE COMPENSATION

"Show me the money!" – Jerry McGuire

Compensation is the good news aspect of executive law. Salary is an obvious component of any executive's compensation package. Executive law attorneys generally do not negotiate the amount of compensation like a Jerry Maguire-type sports agent shouting, "Show me the money." (A recruiter may play a significant role, however.) The discussion about how much you receive will sometimes start with how much you are currently making or were making in a previous position, although many states and cities now limit the right of a prospective employer to inquire into earnings history.[9] The employer may have a set salary band or know what others in the same position are already earning. Large employers will already have compensation plans in place and compensation experts who monitor the market. At the end of the day, negotiating your base salary is not significantly different than haggling over a hand-woven rug in a Moroccan marketplace—try to get the largest number possible.

The true opportunity for a large upside results from other types of compensation: equity (which means ownership), bonuses, and commissions. Generally, the higher the level of the executive, the larger component of his pay that is incentive-based. The contractual terms of all of these types of compensation devices are critical.

One of my earliest executive-law cases was on behalf of a client who had been a high-level officer in a privately-owned company. He had an option to buy stock in the company for hundreds of thousands of dollars, but he had to exercise the option within a few weeks of his termination of employment or it would expire. After he was let go, he sent a check. He quickly got cold feet and realized he did not want to use his own money to invest in a minority ownership of the privately-held company that had just fired him.

Based on the language of the contract, we were able to rescind the agreement and get his money back a year later, with interest, which ended up being a better return than he would have had in the stock market. At that time, in the 1990s, it seemed like any stock option was free money. But an option to purchase part of a privately-held company is not at all the same as a stock option with a publicly-traded company.

"Say-on-pay" shareholder approval of executive compensation continues to be a trend in the area of executive compensation for public companies, whether by corporate governance or legislation. One of the first requirements of shareholder approval for compensation and severance packages was voluntarily adopted by Lucent Technologies in 2004. In 2012, the shareholders at Citigroup rejected a $15 million pay package for the bank's chief executive, Vikram Pandit. Although the vote was only advisory it led to a lawsuit by shareholders. In 2018, shareholders of Walt Disney Co. voted down a non-binding endorsement of compensation for CEO Robert Iger who was to receive a salary of $3 million plus stock worth up to $142 million.[10]

The Dodd-Frank Act includes a non-binding say-on-pay provision and a requirement that companies disclose the ratio of the chief executive's compensation to the median pay package at the company. These provisions only impact a tiny number of American executives and it remains to be seen whether they will exert any downward pressure on mid-level salaries and privately-held companies.

National Trends in Executive Compensation and Public Opinion

1980s and 1990s — Stock Options are King

In the 1980s, *Wall Street*'s Gordon Gekko famously uttered, "Greed is good." The nation experienced an increasing number of corporate mergers and acquisitions, leading to the invention of devices like the "poison pill" and "golden parachute." In 1984, Congress imposed a 20% excise tax on golden parachutes under Sections 280G and 4999 of the Internal Revenue Code in response to the first wave of public concern. The '80s arguably also saw the demise of the company man (or woman), the beginning of the end of defined compensation company pensions, and the rise of the 401(k), a tax provision which was passed in 1978 and started becoming a popular employer offering in about 1982.

Those at the top of publicly-held corporations saw their compensation rise through the 1990s bull market. The ratio between the lowest-paid employee and the highest-paid employee expanded, despite predictions of shareholder revolt and demands for increased board oversight. A theory, cited by some observers at the time and since, was that compensation committees, which rely on comparators, usually conclude that *their* executive ought to be paid at least more than "average," leading to a continuous upward spiral. This is known as the "Lake Wobegon" effect after the fictional Minnesota town where "all the children are above average." Stories in the business media about excessive executive compensation became a regular feature starting at this time. Now, each year, when compensation is disclosed as part of annual SEC filings, *The Wall Street Journal*, *The New York Times*, and *The Star Tribune* publish surveys of how much top managers are paid.

The biggest cause in increased compensation was the use of stock options and other forms of equity compensation. This, in turn, was spurred by a 1993 law limiting the tax deductibility of executive salaries over $1 million, unless it could be demonstrated that the extra pay was linked to performance. Stock options, especially at tech companies and "dot coms," became a national obsession.

2000-2007 — Enron Bursts the Bubble

Trends toward greater and more creative forms of executive compensation were dampened, but not extinguished, by the emerging regulatory environment and other reactions to scandals involving Enron, Worldcom, Tyco, Adelphia, Arthur Andersen, Global Crossings and other companies at the beginning of the 21st Century. The generous lifetime severance, golf club memberships, and other benefits bestowed upon Jack Welch, former CEO of General Electric, which came to light in his divorce, cast a similar shadow on benefits for outgoing executives, as did the furor over excessive pay for Richard A. Grasso, former Chairman of the New York Stock Exchange. In 2004, these matters moved into the realm of criminal court with prosecutions of Martha Stewart, Dennis Kozlowski, John Rigas, Jeffrey Skilling, Andrew Fastow, Bernard Ebbers, and others. In the wake of these scandals, especially for publicly-held companies, new restrictions and public disclosure requirements as well as sensitivity to shareholder reactions, caused boards of directors to start to take a more skeptical view of long-term employment contracts for top management, particularly terms relating to substantial stock options and equity compensation.

In 2005, Congress passed the Bankruptcy Abuse Prevention and Consumer Protection Act which included restrictions on retention and severance payments to executives in companies reorganizing in bankruptcy. In 2006, stock option backdating scandals erupted around the country, including one involving the CEO of UnitedHealth Group, who resigned and paid back over a hundred million dollars. The canard of "pay for performance" during this time period resulted in tighter limits on bonuses and greater restrictions on stock grants as well as new legislation. The most salient examples of these limitations were the Sarbanes-Oxley Act and implementation of Section 409A of the tax code.

2008-2012 — The Great Recession

The downward popularity of Wall Street executives, bankers, and business executives in general, which started with Enron, fell off a cliff shortly after the collapse of Lehman Brothers in September of 2008. Although it allowed Lehman Brothers to fail, the United States Government felt compelled to directly intervene in a number of other large companies, including AIG and General Motors through the Troubled Asset Relief Program (TARP). A number of large banks also participated in the Capital Purchase Program (CPP) which came with strings attached in the form of compensation limitations. In late 2009 and early 2010, when some of those institutions had begun to recover but most of the country had not, public mood soured. The White House openly criticized executive bonuses, appointed a "pay czar" for companies receiving government bailouts, and proposed new punitive taxes for compensation in the banking industry. As the hangover from the bank bailouts set in and unemployment persisted into 2011 and 2012, the Occupy Wall Street movement again put executive pay for the "1 percent" into the national spotlight. White collar crime also saw a resurgence as Bernie Madoff and Tom Petters were convicted of running multi-billion dollar pyramid schemes.

2012-2016 – The Great Flattening

The last term of the Obama Administration was characterized by low growth, low interest rates, a relatively flat stock market, and increasing agitation by sectors of society that had been left behind by globalization and automation. Corporate profits, however, grew significantly, in contrast to small businesses. The share of GDP generated by the *Fortune* 100 biggest companies rose from about 33% in 1994 to 46% in 2013.[11] Market disruption created new opportunities for some in the tech sector and gig economy, such as Uber, Lyft, and Airbnb. Tax inversions led to some U.S. corporations like Medtronic to move their headquarters overseas. As Obamacare changed the healthcare industry, health insurers and healthcare providers struggled to adapt.

2016-2018 – Polarization

Many voters who supported Donald J. Trump in the 2016 presidential elections were middle class Americans who felt left out by the fast moving, winner-take-all modern economy which rewards education and knowledge but produces fewer manufacturing jobs. Executives and those facing the "executive law" concerns and opportunities dis-cussed in this book are more likely to be working in large urban areas with dynamic economies that did not support Trump. But his election was yet another example of public resentment over compensation flowing to an elite few. It remains to be seen how President Trump's policies will be reflected in the area of executive pay.

Taxes and Laws Regulating Executive Compensation

The federal government, many states, and even the European Union, have attempted to limit excessive executive compensation several times over the years. Some of the more notable pieces of legislation include the following:

Sections 280G and 4999 of the Internal Revenue Code (1984)

You may have wondered why some executive employment agreements state that the executive will receive a parachute payment of "2.99 times" her base compensation. Section 280G of the tax code prohibits companies from taking a corporate tax deduc-tion for certain compensation payments contingent on a change in control and Section 4999 can penalize executives (officers, shareholders, and other "highly-compensated individuals") with a 20% excise tax. A couple of definitions are important here. First, a payment contingent on a change in control may include bonuses, severance pay, stock options, and many other forms of compensation. This is known as the "parachute pay-ment." "Base compensation" is the executive's average annual compensation from the corporation for the five years preceding the year in which the change in control occurred. A parachute payment in an amount that is more than the base compensation is consid-ered an "excess parachute payment." But the "safe harbor" under these provisions of the tax code is any amount less than *three times* the base compensation.

This can be confusing, so hold on. If the parachute payment is less than three times the base compensation (say 2.99 times base compensation) the executive does not incur an excise tax. But if the amount is three times base compensation or more, the exec-utive must pay the 20% excise tax on the entire amount that is more than one times base compensation, otherwise known as the excess parachute payment. The 20% tax must be paid in addition to a person's standard income and payroll taxes. Similarly, if the parachute payment is more than three times the base (i.e. outside the safe harbor), the corporation loses its corporate tax deduction on the entire amount paid that is more than one times the base compensation.

Because the potential tax consequences are so dire, employers often try to limit the amount of the parachute payment definitionally in the change-in-control agreement or severance agreement, or provide that the employee waives any compensation that exceeds 299% of their base amount, sometimes known as a "299 waiver." Payments for services performed *after* a change in control are not part of the parachute payments so companies sometimes try to claim that a payment for a non-compete should not be included in the calculation of the parachute payment. Note that if the company agrees to pay the executive for the amount of the excise tax she will incur, known as a "gross up," that amount also is included in the parachute and is itself subject to the excise tax.

Section 162(m) of the Internal Revenue Code (1993)

Section 162(m) of the Internal Revenue Code prohibits publicly-held corporations from deducting more than $1 million per year in compensation paid to each of certain "covered" executives: the CEO and the three highest-compensated officers excluding the CEO and CFO. Commissions and "performance-based" compensation are excluded from the limit.

The Sarbanes-Oxley Act (2002)

The Sarbanes-Oxley Act, sometimes known as "SOX", was signed into law in 2002 by President Bush, who referred to it as the "most far-reaching reform of American business practices since the time of Franklin Delano Roosevelt." The Sarbanes-Oxley Act only applies to "public" companies and their employees. This includes any company whose stock is publicly traded on an exchange such as the NYSE or NASDAQ, on the over the counter or pink sheet market; any company that has filed a registration statement to issue securities in the future; and any entity that is required to file reports with the SEC under 15 U.S.C. § 78c(d). If you do not work for a publicly-traded company (or a company that is about to go public) you do not have to worry about SOX.

SOX has received criticism for imposing excessive compliance costs on public companies. Corporate boards of directors are especially burdened with oversight requirements under SOX which, according to *Business Week*, led to an increase in average director pay to $216,000 from $129,000 in 2003, and pushed some director compensation above $ 1 million.[12] Certain corporate governance provisions of SOX, like codes of ethics and complaint hotlines, are here to stay, however, and have even been voluntarily adopted by many private companies.

While the Act primarily implicates companies, it also has a direct impact on their executive officers, which may include "the president, any vice president in charge of a principal business unit, division or function (such as sales, administration or finance), any other officer who performs a policy-making function, or any other person who performs similar policy-making functions" per Exchange Act Rule 3b-7.

The key points affecting individual executives in terms of compensation, personal liability, and personal obligations are the following:

- *Certification:* The Act requires that the Company's CEO and CFO certify that certain annual reports and other SEC filings do not contain untrue statements of material fact or omit the stating of any material facts, along with certain other representations. This leads directly to the forfeiture provision discussed below. The onus placed on CEOs, and especially CFOs, has led to a shortage of experienced executives willing to take on these roles in a public company, which in turn leads to offers of greater pay or benefits. The incoming officer may also seek written assurances that the company is already in compliance with SOX before accepting employment.

- *Forfeiture of Bonus and Incentive Compensation:* CEOs or CFOs can be forced to forfeit or reimburse the company for any bonus or other incentive-based or equity-based compensation received in the past 12 months, or any profits if the company is required to prepare an accounting restatement due to material non-compliance as a result of misconduct by the corporate officers. In 2009, the SEC filed a lawsuit in the District of Arizona against the CEO of a publicly-traded automotive parts retailer, seeking a return of more than $4 million under Section 204 of SOX even though there was no allegation that the CEO himself personally participated in the non-compliant reporting and a federal judge declined to dismiss the claim.

- *Unfitness:* The Act broadens the definition of "unfitness" for officers and directors under the Securities Act of 1933 and the Securities Exchange Act of 1934. Certain executives who have been involved in improprieties may therefore be barred from serving as officers or directors in public companies. Sections 305 and 1105 of SOX have made it easier for the SEC to enforce the permanent disbarment of officers and directors who have violated antifraud statutes.

- *Blackouts:* In direct response to what occurred at Enron, executive officers are prohibited from buying, selling or otherwise transferring stock during pension fund blackout periods.

- *Prohibitions on Loans:* Companies may not make certain loans to executive employees, including "directly or indirectly extending or maintaining credit, arranging for the extension of credit, or renewing the extension of credit, in the form of a personal loan to any of its directors or personal officers." This applies to outright loans for home purchases, artwork, or anything else. It does not apply to travel advances, company credit cards if used for proper purposes, cashless exercise of stock options or 401(k) loans. The SEC has declined to provide official guidance on this section. As a result, therefore, in 2002 a group of 25 leading U.S. law firms took the unusual step of issuing a 13-page memorandum (the "402 Consensus Memo") setting forth their consensus views on various interpretative questions under Section 402. One consensus position was that the cashless exercise of stock options would not fall under the 402 provision, and that position has not been challenged.

- *Disclosure Obligations:* Officers and directors must disclose changes in beneficial ownership (including the purchase or sale of stock) under Section 16 of the Securities Exchange Act of 1934 and file a Form 4 within two business days after the transaction occurs. Many companies now require an intent to sell notice in advance, so that this two-day deadline can be met. In any case, the company should have a system in place to assist the executive with this filing on a timely basis.
- *Whistleblowing:* Employees of public companies who complain of or provide evidence of fraud to supervisors or any federal regulatory or enforcement agency can seek protection against retaliation from the U.S. Department of Labor (DOL) or a private lawsuit.

Section 409 of the Internal Revenue Code (2004)

Section 409A was another statutory outgrowth of the Enron implosion and has significant implications for the taxation and timing of executive compensation. The provisions of 409A are very complex. You should consult a knowledgeable accountant and tax attorney with regard to its interpretation and application. At a minimum, they should be on the lookout for any provision for deferred payments which might be affected by this code section.

Six-Month Waiting Period: This provision requires any deferred compensation payment that is made on account of separation from service to a "specified employee" of a public company be delayed at least six months. The definition of "specified employee" includes: any 5-percent owner; any 1-percent owner with annual compensation of more than $150,000; and any officer with annual compensation of more than $145,000, but is limited to a number of employees equal to the lesser of: 50 employees, or the greater of three employees or 10 percent of the employees. This definition mimics that of a "Key Employee" found in Section 416(i) of the Internal Revenue Code.

Public Company: The definition for this purpose is <u>broader</u> than that used under the Sarbanes Oxley Act and includes companies listed on foreign stock exchanges or their subsidiaries.

Deferred Compensation: Section 409A imposes a 20% excise tax (payable by the executive) on certain forms of deferred compensation and requires immediate taxation of the deferred amount in the year that the right to the payment vests (even if the payments have not yet been received by the executive). Although the primary financial burden of non-compliance falls on the executive, the employer must timely report and withhold on the amounts included in income under Section 409A and has certain reporting obligations regarding the 409A compliance failure.

"Deferred compensation" includes any compensation to which a "service provider" has a legally-binding right if such compensation will, or could be, paid in any year after the year in which the right arises. Possible examples include:

- Supplemental executive retirement plans, excess benefit plans, and salary and bonus deferral arrangements
- Annual and long-term bonus and other incentive arrangements
- Some severance pay arrangements, depending in part on whether payments are deferred more than a year from when the executive would have otherwise been entitled to them
- Certain equity-based compensation (including discounted stock options and stock appreciation rights, non-discounted stock options and stock appreciation rights with additional deferral features, restricted stock units, performance units and phantom stock)
- change in control agreements

Safe Harbor: Generally, severance payments paid only in the event of involuntary termination and not exceeding the lesser of twice the executive's annualized compensation for the prior calendar year or $490,000 falls within a safe harbor provision.

Exceptions: The most common exception is the short-term deferral exception. This exception generally exempts from Section 409A amounts that, in all possible circumstances, will be paid by the 15th day of the third month following the end of the taxable year (of the employee or the employer) in which the right to the compensation is vested. Other exceptions include vacation pay, sick leave, disability pay and death benefits; medical and health savings accounts and tax-free medical reimbursement plans; qualified retirement plans and certain foreign plans; incentive stock options, employee stock purchase plans meeting the requirements of Section 423, restricted stock, and certain standard non-qualified stock options and stock appreciation rights.

The Bankruptcy Abuse Prevention and Consumer Protection Act (BAPCPA) (2005)

The BAPCPA placed restrictions on retention bonuses for senior managers who remain with a company through Chapter 11 bankruptcy. A bankruptcy judge may only approve such a bonus if it is essential to retaining an employee who has a better job offer and the employee's services are essential to the business.

The Emergency Economic Stabilization Act (EESA), as amended by the American Recovery and Reinvestment Act (ARRA) (2008 and 2009)

The EESA and ARRA required the Secretary of the Treasury to issue standards governing executive compensation for executives at financial institutions that received assistance under the Troubled Asset Recovery Program. Executive compensation for these companies was subject to review by a special master.[13] The program has largely expired, but some of its impact lives on in litigation.[14]

European Union Bank Rules (2010)

European Union regulations cap bonuses for some banking industry executives at 100% of salary, unless 65% of the bank's shareholders approve an increase to 200% of salary.

The Affordable Care Act (2010)

The Affordable Care Act (ACA) provides that a covered health insurance provider may not deduct any compensation paid to an applicable individual in excess of $500,000.[15] The $500,000 limit applies to both publicly-traded and privately-held employers and all employees, directors and independent contractors. It is not limited to officers whose compensation is reportable on an annual proxy filing or any other smaller group of key employees.

The Dodd-Frank Act (2010)

The Dodd-Frank Act imposed clawback requirements requiring publicly-traded companies to develop a compensation recovery policy to claw back incentive-based compensation of executive officers when the company's financial statements are found to contain material errors. These requirements are broader than the clawback provisions under SOX. The SEC also adopted pay ratio rules as required by Dodd-Frank. These rules are designed to provide investors with information regarding the compensation of a company's CEO as compared to the median compensation of that company's employees. The rules took effect on January 1, 2017.

Section 162(q) of the Internal Revenue Code (2017)

As a result of the #metoo movement, Congress added a provision to the Tax Cuts and Jobs Act of 2017 stating that no deduction shall be allowed for any settlement payment related to sexual harassment or sexual abuse if such settlement payment is subject to a non-disclosure agreement.

Nuts and Bolts of Executive Compensation

Executive compensation can be packaged in many different forms, such that, as Forrest Gump might have stated, "they are like a box of chocolates, you never know what you're gonna get."

Salary

Salary is the bedrock of compensation. Most non-hourly workers, except those on a pure commission, earn a salary. But salary has been steadily shrinking as a proportion of compensation for CEOs of public corporations. For *Fortune* 500 executives, salary typically makes up a small portion of the pie. A number of famous CEOs have declared that they will take only one dollar in annual salary compensation, including Mark Zuckerberg at Facebook, Meg Whitman at Hewlett Packard, Larry Ellison at Oracle, Larry Page of Google, and John Mackey of Whole Foods.

Exemptions from Wage and Hour Laws

Most executives, as that term is used loosely in this book, are exempt from having to be paid overtime. In fact, executives, professionals and other high-wage earners work longer hours than low-wage workers. According to *The New York Times*, "it is now the rich who are the most stressed out and the most likely to be working the most."[16] American professionals now spend more time on their laptops and less time with their families than hourly employees. There are five so-called "white collar" exemptions to overtime under federal law: administrative, executive, professional, computer professional, and outside sales.[17] Readers of this book will likely fall within one or more of these exemptions. Note that while most exemptions require the employee to be paid a salary, being paid salary alone does not make one exempt. The actual duties of the position must also be considered under the law.

Equity

An executive who holds stock in a company has an ownership stake in the company's performance. If the company does well, the stock goes up and the executive is worth more money. Equity awards are supposed to motivate the executive to work on behalf of the company. This theory has lots of critics. Some point out that executives are motivated by stock price and quarterly earnings at the expense of long-term growth. In a closely-held company, the executive will have difficulty liquidating the value of any growth in the value of the stock, unless he is able to sell it, the company goes public, or there is some other realization event. Nevertheless, equity will always remain a huge part of executive compensation. The most straightforward means of acquiring equity is to be a founder of a company, or to buy in as a shareholder or partner.

Stock Grants

Stock grants are another means of obtaining equity with an existing enterprise. Sometimes an important executive receives a small portion of stock immediately when he agrees to join a small company as a president or CEO just to have some "skin in the game." Usually, however, there is a waiting period (restriction) for ownership in the stock to vest.

In private companies, an executive contract may provide for stock options or a phase-in of equity position or ownership, in return for services or at a heavily-discounted price, as well as control positions as an officer or director of the business. Depending on state corporate statutes, private equity ownership in a closely-held business may create shareholder rights as well as special fiduciary duties for the executive as shareholder, including an expectation of continued employment unless expressly disclaimed.

Restricted Stock

"Restricted" stock is stock that is issued but subject to a restricted period before it can be sold, and is forfeited if the executive leaves or is terminated before that time. Restricted stock is cleaner than a stock option. It is the same as if your uncle gives you stock in a company. Once you get it, you own it and you do not pay a price to buy it. The catch is that you do not receive ownership of the stock until a specific date in the future, and only if you are still employed as of that date. For example, many executives are dismayed to learn that if they are involuntarily terminated 23 months into a two-year restricted stock period they get nothing. Depending on the circumstances, a claim can be made that the timing was intentional and in bad faith. But some states, including Minnesota, do not recognize the covenant of good faith and fair dealing in employment contracts.

Phantom Stock and Stock Appreciation Rights

Phantom stock and stock appreciation rights (SARs) are different terms for the same thing. SARs are a way to award an employee with growth in the value of a company without giving the employee actual ownership. It is important to understand that SARs are completely a creature of contract. Phantom stock can be a useful tool for situations where the shareholders of a privately-owned company do not wish to provide the executive true ownership or voting power in the company, but want them to share in the gain of the stock price.

Awarding phantom stock agreements or SARs to an executive may be favored by the owners as they carry no ownership or voting rights or fiduciary duty obligations as would be accorded to shareholders, but may be satisfactory to executives because of financial rights to participate in gains upon the sale of the company or repurchase at an appreciated price.

Issues to consider when presented with SARs include the following:

- What does the agreement actually say?
- How is the initial base price determined?
- How will the company, and therefore the SARs, be valued at the time of payment? By book value, multiple of earnings, appraiser, or some other method?
- What happens in the event of a change in control?
- Are you being presented with a non-compete or restrictive covenant in exchange for the SARs?

Stock Options

A stock option is the right to buy certain stock at a certain time at a certain price, known as the "strike price." Stock options are granted pursuant to carefully-drafted plans for key managers and officers. Stock options form an important component of a company's overall compensation system for at least three reasons. First, options are used to attract and retain talented management personnel by providing them with a method of obtaining a long-term equity stake in a corporation. Second, linking an employee's compensation to the company's performance is considered an excellent way to moti-vate high-level executives. Third, options grants may have significant tax advantages for the corporation or the employee.

Compensatory stock options fall into two categories: incentive stock options (ISOs) and non-qualified stock options (NSOs). ISOs are stock options which satisfy certain requirements of the Internal Revenue Code (Code). NSOs, which do not qualify under the Code, are both more simple and more common. Each has differing tax treatment and statutory requirements. By statute, incentive stock options, unlike non-statutory options, must terminate upon the executive's separation. Most non-statutory stock options pro-vide the same limitation by grant agreement. Thus, without contractual protections, unvested options will be forfeited at termination and vested options must be exercised immediately. "Hurdle" options are a type of premium stock option commonly used in the United Kingdom, Australia and New Zealand.[18]

Stock options are often issued in "tranches." For example, tranche one is issued in year one and vests in four equal parts over four years. Tranche two is issued in year two and also vests over four years.

What about an ESOP?

An ESOP, or employee stock ownership plan, is a tax-qualified retirement plan cov-ering all full-time employees under which the employer holds company stock in trust in the employee-participants' names, unlike ISO's or NSO's. ESOPs are subject to the Employee Retirement Income Security Act of 1974 (ERISA) and are highly regulated as an employee group plan. Some confusion has arisen from the idea that "ESOP" might stand for "executive [or employee] stock *option* plan."

- *Valuation and Taxation of Stock Options*

Placing a current value on unvested stock options is difficult. For example, it is unclear whether a grant of stock options which have not yet vested and could poten-tially be worth nothing is sufficient consideration for a covenant not to compete. This challenge arises in other contexts as well, including family law and estate planning in addition to employment law and corporate law. For example, executives who possess stock options may need to place a value on them in a divorce, but courts have some difficulty determining whether options are marital property if they are compensation for future performance. On the other hand, unexercised stock options have value that was determined at the time of issue and could be easily calculated at any future date depending on the actual stock price without considering the option.

Taxation of stock options depends on whether they are qualified or non-qualified options. ISOs (qualified options) allow employees, provided certain rules are met, to defer taxation until they sell the shares and to pay tax at the capital gains rate rather than at the ordinary income tax rate. Employees are generally not taxed until they sell the stock. At that point, they pay tax on the difference between the sale price and what they paid for it. The company does not receive a tax deduction.

Employee recipients of NSOs (non-qualified options), on the other hand, pay ordinary income tax on the spread between the price they paid for each share when they exercise their options and the fair market value at that time. The company receives a deduction for the amount of the spread. If the employee holds the stock instead of selling it immediately, any additional gain is taxed as capital gain.

Therefore, a terminated employee will not necessarily know if he or she would be better off with cash or options as part of a severance package and should consult with a tax planning professional before making any decisions.

- **Relevant Documents**

Stock options are governed by several documents, typically a "plan," an "agreement" (or "grant(s))" and sometimes "amendments" to the agreement. An executive may have one or both of these documents for each of several different stock option grants from various years.

The plan is typically adopted, often on an annual basis, by the board of directors on behalf of the company, and may authorize the distribution of options, establish a compensation committee, or set forth other terms. The agreement is a specific contract, entered into pursuant to the plan, between the company and the employee and will contain information regarding the grant, the strike price, vesting and exercise period, as well as conditions regarding termination, disability, or a "change in control" of the company. The agreement or plan will also indicate if the options are qualified or non-qualified.

- **Stock Option Agreements Do Not Generally Alter the At-Will Employment Relationship**

Courts have generally held that a stock option agreement, on its own, does not convert an at-will employment relationship into an employment contract for a specific term, even where the stock options are granted over a period of years. If the agreement or contract specifically states that the employee can only be terminated "for cause", however, a contract might be inferred. Generally, most well-drafted agreements specifically state that the at-will employment relationship is not altered, but that all rights to stock options will be extinguished only if the employee is terminated "for cause." Thus, the motive for termination may become an important issue, even in an "at will" relationship.

- ### *Stock Options at Termination*

Executives who shrewdly negotiate stock options when their careers are on the rise may sell themselves short when they are shown the door and asked to sign a severance agreement. If this happens, they should be aware that they may be able to renegotiate the terms of existing stock option agreements and that their employer might even be willing to provide severance pay in the form of additional stock options.

The employee's first concern when facing termination is that the window of time in which to exercise previously-vested stock options, the "exercise period," suddenly ends soon after the date of termination. In some cases, the plan may allow up to a year, but most allow anywhere from one month to 90 days, depending on the reason for the termination.[13] **WARNING:** Some public companies do not have any grace period and there are stock options which cannot be exercised after termination. In other words, an executive may have fully-vested options which are not under water which she has not bothered to "exercise." If she is suddenly fired, it is too late. The options vanish. Know what your plan provides and regularly exercise options upon vesting if you work for one of these companies, even if you think your employment is secure.

Termination of employment will restrict the employee's ability to wait for the stock price to rise to a certain level and may not allow enough time to wait out a cyclical downturn. For example, if the stock is "under water" (less than the strike price) for the entire 30 days, the options are worthless to the employee. Thus, extending the exercise period might be an important goal for a terminated employee in crafting a separation agreement. As a technical matter, however, ISOs can only be held by continuing employees. Thus, when an employee is terminated, ISOs must be "swapped out" for non-qualified options to effectuate such an extension. Another important alternative to extending the exercise period, and a favorite of executives everywhere, is to simply reprice the options at a lower strike price. In all of these situations, the company's attorneys will need to closely review any proposed changes.

An even greater concern of terminated executives is that, due to their departure, they will lose out on valuable future vesting of stock options under one or more stock option agreements. These are options which have already been "granted" but are not yet "vested." In this situation, the employee may be able to negotiate the "acceleration" of the vesting of certain stock options before he or she leaves the company.

Qualified stock option plans, or ISOs, are typically subject to strict guidelines which cannot be modified without risking the tax benefit status of the plan. Qualified stock option plans can sometimes be converted to non-qualified stock option plans in order to provide additional flexibility in crafting a severance plan. The downside, that the compensation would no longer be considered part of a qualified plan for tax purposes, may be compensated for by the ability to modify the terms of the plan. This conversion may be accomplished by inserting a clause in the severance agreement referencing the number of shares, the date of the grant, the exercise period and strike price.

Renegotiating stock options can be an effective and creative way of bolstering severance pay in the event of a layoff or downsizing. It is important to remember that there is no guarantee what options will be worth, however, as it depends entirely on the future price of the stock. In the event of a major stock market downturn, stock options may become less valuable and less significant. In fact, in many cases it may be preferable for the employer to offer additional money, as severance in lieu of lost stock option opportunities, by reducing the value of the options to cash. Furthermore, although stock options offer some advantages over cash when crafting an executive severance package, employers may be reluctant to award options to executives who are leaving the company because of the effect on remaining employees, both in terms of morale and in terms of allocating limited amounts of stock. After all, options are supposed to motivate and reward employees for future performance. In fact, some employers may simply refuse to discuss the possibility.

An employer may also be reluctant to make any alterations to a stock option plan which must be approved by the company's board or compensation committee or may have to be reported to the SEC. These reports are open to the public and often followed by the financial media. Ex-employees, especially former statutory insiders, should also be aware of reporting obligations under § 16 of the Securities and Exchange Act of 1934 whenever they receive stock or stock options as part of a severance package.

Ultimately, determining whether or not modifications can be made to a stock option agreement will require looking at the terms of the plan itself to determine whether the employer (usually a special committee of the board such as the compensation committee) has the discretion to modify post-termination entitlement and whether there are any implications under § 16 of the Securities and Exchange Act of 1934, applicable stock option rules under the Internal Revenue Code of 1986 (e.g., § 422 if an incentive stock option is involved), or other applicable laws and regulations.

"Premium" stock options are part of a trend in equity compensation exemplified by IBM which announced that its executives would only receive "premium price" stock options. This means that the stock price must go up by at least 10 percent in order for the executives to cash in. Among other things, this lowers the amount that a company would have to expense under the financial Accounting Standards Board rules.

Profits Interest

A limited liability company (LLC) has the ability to grant an executive a "profits interest" which is an interest in the future profits and assets of an LLC. The recipient of the profits interest becomes a member of the LLC, which can create an expectation of continued employment under Minnesota law. The member may not have the right to vote or participate in corporate governance matters, however. Properly structured, the grant of a profits interest does not result in taxable income to the recipient until at such time he sells his interests. Once an executive receives a grant of a profits interest, he may no longer be considered an employee of the LLC for tax purposes and may have to pay self-employment tax. In some cases, however, the executive can receive a profits interest in the holding company LLC and be an employee of a subsidiary.

Bonuses and Commissions

Employers offer commission and bonus arrangements for several reasons. First, they provide an incentive for employees to work harder or sell more. Second, bonuses are useful in recruiting talent. Third, these types of plans allow fairness among workers — employees are hard-pressed to complain about disparities in compensation based on objective criteria. (This is another example of "pay for performance.") Fourth, such plans help share the risk and can protect the employer on the downside. In other words, if the employee does poorly, the employer is not required to pay as much to the employee. (On the other hand, if the employee does extremely well, even though the employer may be required to pay a large of amount of money to the employee, presumably it will receive an even greater amount in revenue with which to pay the employee.) Poorly drafted bonus or commission plans, however, work contrary to these goals and create unnecessary uncertainty and liability.

If you are presented with a written bonus or commission plan, challenge the plan with various scenarios. What happens if you leave or you are terminated mid-year? What happens if you perform extremely well or not very well? The most important aspect of a commission or bonus plan is to define *how* the commission or bonus is calculated. Objective criteria are preferable to subjective criteria. For example, a commission based on sales can be easily tracked and determined. Similarly, bonuses for hitting revenue goals, recruitment targets, or billable hours can be measured in a neutral, mathematical fashion. Objectivity avoids uncertainty and litigation. A good tip is to create a mechanism to keep track of commissions or other metrics during the life of the plan. This helps avoid end-of-the-year disputes regarding which customers or sales are properly credited to the employee. An incentive plan may also include a mechanism for the possibility of shared commissions when two or more employees collaborate.

A frequent source of disputes with commission plans is whether a departing employee should get paid for a sale that has been consummated but is still in the "pipe-line." A vague contract can cause litigation. To avoid problems, the plan should state clearly, for example, that the commission is not "earned" until the product is shipped, *and* the company receives payment. Companies typically allow for charge-backs, returns, offsets, or credits if they apply to the industry. If the plan allows for draws against commissions, make sure the system is laid out clearly.

It is common practice to require an employee to be employed on a certain date in order to receive a bonus, and these provisions have been specifically upheld in many states.[19] It is also common for bonus plans to have a statement that the bonus is "discretionary" when it is not. If the plan has specific criteria and the employee meets them, the company generally cannot refuse to pay simply because it changed its mind. Substantive changes must be communicated prospectively. It is appropriate, however, to have a statement allowing the company sole discretion to interpret the plan. Finally, some plans have a "cap" on bonuses. These are generally enforceable if clearly stated in the contract, but unpopular when implemented.[20]

Bonuses and commissions are creatures of contract, either express or unilateral. The potential for litigation arises when an employee is involuntarily terminated shortly before the payment date and alleges that he was fired in "bad faith" specifically to avoid payment under an "employed by a certain date" clause. Such claims can succeed under narrow circumstances.[21] See Chapter 12 for more information about claims for unpaid wages, commissions, and bonuses.

CHAPTER 4

"I HAVE TO QUIT" OR "I THINK I'M GOING TO BE FIRED" – NAVIGATING ROUGH WATERS

Maxim: **Don't quit!** That is often the first piece of advice I provide executive law clients. If you are in a miserable work situation or you think you are going to be fired, quitting may have powerful emotional appeal. However, resigning takes away most of your leverage under the law. Once you quit, you have given up much of your power to extract severance or other terms from your former employer. Generally, an employee who voluntarily resigns cannot claim wrongful discharge under any of the various theories, such as discrimination, or whistleblower retaliation. There is an exception to this rule known as constructive discharge. The constructive discharge theory requires the employee to prove that the conditions were intolerable and she was forced to quit. Although this can be shown in some cases, it is a high hurdle for plaintiffs.

Be Prepared

You should set up a home office with certain information, even if you are not expecting to change positions in the near future. First, you should keep a paper copy of any employment agreements, non-competes, stock option grants, bonus plans, and performance reviews in a safe place at home, or store everything on a personal cloud-based document management system. Second, you should have a home computer with a non-work email to communicate with your friends, legal counsel, and potential new employers. Work email is the property of your employer, and you should not use it for any of these purposes without expecting your company to access and read them. You should not keep any confidential, proprietary, or competitive business information in your home office or non-work email. Make sure you are able to access your professional contacts and be able to change your LinkedIn profile from home in the event of a sudden transition.

Every executive ought to be mindful of a few key considerations before change is thrust upon them. You should understand whether you are an employee, an independent contractor, sole proprietor, minority shareholder, partner, or some combination thereof, and what that means from a legal, tax, and liability standpoint. As noted, these categories can morph throughout one's career. They can also overlap. For example, business owners are often also employees of their own company. And independent contractors may work for years for a single large company while running their own "business" for employment law and tax purposes. You need to know if you are an at-will employee or whether you have contractual protection from being terminated without cause. If you have a contract, know whether it provides for severance and whether it has a change-in-control or good reasons clause.

Consider whether the customer and client contacts you have developed are actually yours or are your employer's. You should know whether you are subject to a covenant not to compete or non-solicitation agreement in the event you were to leave one employer for another or go off on your own. Your employer may consider your list of personal contacts a trade secret that belongs to the company. Similarly, you should be aware up front whether any intellectual property you develop in your occupation belongs to you. If you have signed an "assignment of inventions clause" or "work for hire agreement," the patent or copyright on your work product may belong to someone else.

It's Not Working Out

If you are in an intolerable work situation, instead of just quitting, consider meeting with a lawyer. A lawyer can run interference, especially where the employer also would like to end the relationship, but has not pulled the trigger due to potential legal claims. A potential legal claim exists whenever an employee is a member of a "protected class" based on race, sex, age, disability, religion, sexual orientation, or marital status, which pretty much includes everyone. It also comes into play when the organization knows that the boss is the problem and the employee is upset. (*See* Toxic Boss Syndrome, below) It also arises when the executive has a contract but the company does not want to pay the severance. Sometimes employers will park an executive in an empty office with nothing to do, or assign projects beneath their status, in order to wait them out and force them to quit.

When the employee tells her boss or HR that she would like to leave, the employer can often characterize this as a quit. When a lawyer calls, however, he can communicate with the company's lawyer, in a non-emotional transactional context. He will typically start the call with, "we both know this is not working out. What can we arrange in terms of an exit package?" Companies often appreciate this approach, as it is less messy than a termination or a miserable status quo.

Taking Leave

If your workplace situation is so intolerable that it is causing medical symptoms, or you simply cannot go to work while you are waiting for your lawyer to work things out, consult your doctor. He or she may sign a doctor's note entitling you to leave under the federal Family Medical Leave Act (FMLA). This Act allows you up to twelve weeks of leave, during which time you can negotiate the terms of your departure. (Note that some executives may be considered "key employees" who are not protected by the act, and not all employers fall under the act. Also note that a doctor's note stating that you are "stressed out" or experiencing psychological issues such that you cannot return to work will be placed in your medical records and could constitute a pre-existing condition should you apply for disability insurance in the future.)

There are other alternatives to FMLA leave. I urge executives in limbo to try to let go of some of their emotion. Once you know you are leaving, your boss or the company should not be in your head. Use up your vacation. Don't stress about impossible goals. Let your lawyer worry about negotiating a severance package.

Toxic Boss Syndrome

If you complain about your boss or any higher level executive, unless you have video evidence of him stealing money or worse, do not expect the company to take your side against his. **Maxim: A company will circle the wagons when faced with a claim or accusation by an employee**. This is the nature of large organizations. You are on the outside and they are on the inside. You may have delusions that the detailed descriptions of your boss's incompetence, unreasonable expectations, leering glances, poor decisions, and excessive vacation schedule you emailed to HR and the Board of Directors will prompt the organization to investigate, fire him, and put you in his place, but it doesn't usually happen. (The rash of #metoo terminations in 2017 was an exception to this rule.) If you become enough of a thorn in their side, or have the evidence, the company may pay you to go away. And, if it gives you any solace, your terrible boss may, in fact, be investigated, disciplined, demoted, or even fired; but that will probably only happen after your claims are fully resolved and you are long gone.

Under Investigation: Responding to Accusations of Wrongdoing

High-level executives who find themselves accused of wrongdoing, either criminal or civil, need to develop a responsive strategy immediately. If you are accused of criminal activity, you should retain a criminal law attorney. If you are under investigation for sexual harassment you need to cooperate.

Employers are generally required to indemnify employees for claims resulting from actions the employee took in the course and scope of his or her duties. Indemnification may be required by contract, by Minn. Stat, § 181.970, the Minnesota Business Corporations Act, Minn. Stat § 302A.521; the Minnesota Limited Liability Company Act, Minn. Stat. § 322B.699 or § 322C.0408, or similar laws of another state and may be covered by Directors and Officers liability insurance.

Executives with Substance Abuse Issues

If you are struggling with addiction to alcohol or drugs, there are several aspects of the law which may help to protect both you and your career. First, alcoholism may be considered a "disability" under the Americans with Disabilities Act for which an employee may be entitled to an accommodation (and protected from discharge). Second, in Minnesota, testing of employees for drugs or alcohol is limited by the Drug and Alcohol Testing in the Workplace Act,[22] and an employee cannot be terminated for testing positive the first time without being allowed an opportunity to attend and compete a treatment program. Third, if you are a medical professional, you may be eligible to participate in Minnesota's Health Professionals Services Program (HPSP).[23]

CHAPTER 5

GOING TO THE COMPETITOR: NON-COMPETES, NON-SOLICITATION CLAUSES, AND OTHER RESTRICTIVE COVENANTS

The use of non-competes is on the rise. Once, they were reserved for the most senior executives. Now, recent surveys suggest that roughly one in five American employees works under the strictures of a non-compete agreement.[24] Litigation surrounding non-competes has exploded, nearly tripling since 2000.[25] Disputes regarding non-competes that get settled before they go to court are also increasing.

Non-competes are the bane of executives. Sometimes they are viewed as leg irons, and executives will whisper rumors to each other of former co-workers who got out or beat the non-compete in court. On the other hand, I have met scores of well-informed executives who insisted that non-competes are unenforceable because Minnesota is a "right to work state." That is both a myth and a misnomer. "Right-to-work" is a term that refers to labor unions and has nothing to do with non-competes. There are two states where non-competes are not enforceable: California and North Dakota. In most of the rest of the country, depending on the details, a properly drafted and signed non-compete will prevent you from competing. In short, it is not true that non-competes are unenforceable. Non-competes are commonly and routinely enforced in Minnesota. (Note: non-competes for brokers in the financial sector may be subject to the "Broker Protocol." See Chapter 13 for more information.)

If You Are Presented with a Non-Compete to Sign

Maxim: TAKE NON-COMPETES SERIOUSLY. If you are presented with a non-compete agreement to sign, take it seriously. Study it. Do not just sign it without reading it and assume you will never have to worry about it. Understand what it says and discuss it with a lawyer. Assume that things do not work out and you have to leave this employer. Would you be able to earn a living? Would you be able to maintain your career? Would you be able to keep your client or customer relationships? What if a better opportunity comes along? Would you be barred under this agreement from taking it?

Non-competes are standard fare in many industries. If you refuse to sign you may forfeit your job offer, or your job. What options do you have? You may be able to negotiate a carve out or modify the language. These types of discussions can be awkward. A new or potential employer may not get a warm and fuzzy feeling from a candidate who wants to negotiate a non-compete with an eye toward her next opportunity. Some employers, however, are reporting that job candidates are becoming more savvy and experienced candidates are refusing to sign non-competes. Negotiating and narrowing the terms of proposed non-competes is becoming more common as their use increases and awareness of their significance spreads. It is helpful to engage an executive law attorney for this type of negotiation. (Executive-law attorneys representing individual employees rarely draft the first version of employment contracts, non-competes, and severance agreements. A good executive-law attorney is skilled at reading and interpreting what the company has proposed and recommending edits that protect the individual executive.)

The Law of Non-Competes

Each state has a different body of laws regarding non-competes and restrictive covenants. Indeed, the law among the states varies more in this area than most. In Minnesota, non-competes are allowed and enforced on a regular basis. Under Minnesota law, however, non-competes are considered "disfavored." What does this mean? It means that judges will enforce agreements that are supported by "consideration" (more on that later), that are well-drafted, and that are "reasonable." Among other things, though, it also means many Minnesota judges are perfectly happy to throw out a non-compete that is poorly drafted by the employer or contains typographical errors. Indeed, one Minnesota court opinion famously referred to non-competes as vestiges of "industrial peonage without redeeming virtue in the American enterprise system."[26]

To be enforceable in Minnesota, a non-compete agreement must be necessary to protect a "legitimate business interest." It must be reasonable as to both temporal duration and geographic scope. Generally, in Minnesota, a non-compete lasting longer than two years is considered unreasonable unless it is in connection with the sale of a business. The majority of non-competes are one year in duration, or sometimes less. Years ago, the geographic restriction, such as a 100-mile radius from Minneapolis, was quite important as well. These days, many companies are engaged in business across the country or around the world, so restrictions against competing anywhere in the country may be considered reasonable.

Perhaps the most important aspect of Minnesota law is the requirement that the non-compete be supported by adequate *consideration*. "Consideration" means the employee must receive something of value in exchange for their agreement to not do something. In Minnesota, an offer of employment can be sufficient consideration for a non-compete. An offer to continue employing someone, however, is *not* adequate consideration under Minnesota law.[27] In other words, if you start a job on Monday and are asked for the first time to sign a non-compete on Tuesday, it probably is not enforceable under Minnesota law. Companies can enter into enforceable non-competes with existing employees in exchange for other types of independent consideration however, such as a cash payment, stock options, or a promotion and raise.

> **TIP:** If you were sent a non-compete to sign but everyone seems to have forgotten about it, you may want to wait until someone follows up. It is incumbent on the employer to make sure this document is executed timely, not you.

If you are Currently Under a Non-Compete

If you have signed a non-compete and you get an offer from a competitor what should you do? First, consider whether your potential new job would actually pose a competitive threat to your current employer. You should know enough about the industry to have a gut instinct as to whether the proposed move would be threatening to your old employer or be perceived as threatening. In some of these situations, both sides may eventually agree after discussion that there is no actual threat posed (because the companies are not true competitors, or because you are moving to a new field, or any other factual reason).

Second, if there is some overlapping competition and potential for harm, consider whether a "carve-out" makes sense. A carve-out is a specific agreement that allows you to leave your current employer and go to work for a new employer, so long as you agree for a certain time frame not to do certain things, like call on particular clients, work on specific projects, or work in a particular geographic area.

As litigation over non-competes has increased, it is becoming more common to settle these disputes early. Employers know that enforcing non-competes is expensive and there is significant uncertainty as to how any particular judge will rule. Non-compete disputes are amenable to settlement because there are multiple variables that can be negotiated including time and duration, geographic limitations, customer restrictions (even if the original agreement was a blanket non-compete), and payment of money by the new employer to the old employer.

It is possible to ask your current employer for a waiver, carve out, or letter of understanding. It happens all the time. But what if your employer just says no? Consider the best case, the status quo, and the worst case scenarios. A best-case scenario is that you are able to work out a deal without burning bridges and take a more interesting job with better compensation and even better prospects. Status quo is that you don't ask, or you do ask but are not able to work out a deal and you stay where you are. But the worst case scenario is that your employer interprets your request as disloyalty, eventually terminates your employment, and still insists on enforcing your non-compete.

Scared yet? Don't worry. You can also challenge the agreement in court. There are many permutations to these negotiations, but consider that I have worked with hundreds of positive-energy individuals who have challenged non-competes. These are entrepreneurs who know in their hearts that they will succeed, and will not allow anything, including a non-compete, to stop them on their path to success. Sometimes they go to court and lose the first round. Sometimes they spend money to fight the non-compete and lose, and have to sit out an entire 12 months. Sometimes they win. Often, they cut a deal. But, invariably, the process ends (after all, no non-compete lasts forever) and they move on, unencumbered by their old employer or the chains of a restrictive covenant, to start their own business or join a new one. Win or lose, they rarely regret taking on the fight. These individuals amaze me; and if this sounds like you, go for it. Fight the non-compete and don't look back.

What Happens if You Don't Reach a Deal?

If you accept a position that might be barred by a non-compete, your previous employer will probably send you a cease-and-desist letter "reminding" you of your obligations. This opens a space for negotiations. If negotiations don't work, the old employer may sue. This starts with a summons and complaint that is personally served on you or someone at your house. Service of a summons and complaint means a lawsuit has commenced. Usually one of the claims in these cases is breach of contract. In most breach of contract claims, the plaintiff (the party suing) is seeking money. In non-compete cases, however, the plaintiff (your old company) will quickly, after the lawsuit is commenced, schedule a hearing with a judge and bring an emergency motion for a temporary restraining order, temporary injunction, or preliminary injunction. These are all variations of a motion asking a judge to order you to not violate your agreement, which often means an order to not work for the competitor. If you lose this motion, you cannot take on the new job lest you be held in contempt of court. More on this later, but as you can see, the stakes are high.

Challenging the Agreement in Court

If you cannot work out an amicable arrangement because your intentions are directly competitive to your old employer, the only remaining option is to challenge the enforceability of the restriction head-on. For this, you will need to see an attorney, but here are some guidelines as to what to consider. First, determine what state laws apply to the interpretation and enforcement of the agreement. Typically, the agreement will have a "choice of law" provision setting forth which state's laws will govern. This may or may not be the same state where you work. If you work in a state like California, the choice of law provision may not be enforced by the court because it conflicts with the public policy of the state where you live.

Types of Restrictive Covenants

"Restrictive covenant" is a broad term that includes any provision in a contract with an employee that restricts the employee's behavior, actions, or speech; including but not limited to, non-competes, non-solicitation provisions, and non-disclosure clauses. In many cases, what we think of as a "non-compete agreement" is actually a bundle of various restrictive covenants. Here, are some of the most common forms of restrictive covenants:

Non-Competes

Although often used as a catchall term (generally, and in this book), including other types of restrictive covenants, "non-compete" technically has a specific meaning. A non-compete clause prevents a former employee from entering the same line of business as her former employer, regardless of whether the employee actively solicits the former business's clientele. In this way, it is the broadest form of restrictive covenant. As we will see, many courts tend to disfavor non-competes for this reason.

Non-Solicitation of Customers

Employment agreements containing restrictive covenants often contain a clause prohibiting the employee from "soliciting" former customers, either in lieu of or in addition to, a pure non-compete agreement, especially if the employee worked in a sales capacity. When it comes to enforcing non-solicitation clauses, a debate can arise as to whether a former employee under such a restriction actually "solicited" the customer in question. The employee may claim that they did not solicit the customer; but, rather, the customer sought them out and they merely responded to the customer's overture. This begs the question of what the term "solicit" actually means. The Minnesota courts have addressed this only on a few occasions. While the courts have relied on the facts of each case to determine whether the customer was solicited, they have been unified in agreement that, as a principle of law, such non-solicitation covenants may be enforceable. In fact, they may be preferred over pure non-competes because they are narrower, allowing the former employee to continue working in the same industry, and more obviously tailored to protect a legitimate business interest of the former employer—customer goodwill. If a former employee is subject to both a non-compete and a non-solicitation provision, in some circumstances, the employee can settle the dispute with the former employer by agreeing to the non-solicitation provision while being allowed to otherwise compete in the marketplace.

The waters also get murky when it comes to pre-existing client or customer relationships. New York law, for example, protects such relationships if the customer was not serviced during the employment relationship.[28] The question in Minnesota seems to be whether the employer has a legitimate interest in protecting relationships that first existed with the employee. This requirement is discussed later in the chapter.

To add further confusion, many non-solicitation clauses purport to protect not only "customers" but "prospective customers." One might think that everyone is a "prospective" customer. These clauses can be enforceable, but "prospective customer" should be defined in a way that allows the former employer to objectively show that the former employee was actively courting the customer while employed.

Non-Solicitation of Employees

An increasing number of restrictive covenant agreements also include a clause that prohibits an employee from directly or indirectly soliciting for employment, or hiring, the company's other employees for a period of time. This clause is sometimes also referred to as an "anti-raiding" clause or "anti-recruitment" clause. While there are few Minnesota cases where the court explicitly analyzes non-solicitation of employees covenants, there are general legal principles of restrictive covenants[29] that provide guidance.[30]

Non-Disclosure Agreements

Almost every employment contract with any restrictive covenants includes a covenant restricting the disclosure of trade secrets, confidential information, and other proprietary business information. This is an important and understandable requirement of almost every competitive business. "Confidentiality" agreements, or non-disclosure agreements, potentially cover a wide category of information. Non-disclosure agreements are a contract, and in Minnesota require adequate "consideration" (discussed below) just like other restrictive covenants.[31] Employees who take company property including confidential information may also, separately, face liability under common law, the Minnesota Trade Secrets Act, or the Defend Trade Secrets Act. Because trade secrets laws require the holder to take reasonable steps to protect the alleged trade secret, employers use non-disclosure agreements, in part, as evidence to show they are actively safeguarding the information.

Assignment of Inventions

An assignment of inventions clause is a provision that ensures that anything you invent while on the job belongs to your employer, not you. Minnesota and a handful of other states have specific legal requirements that must be followed in order for an assignment of inventions clause to be valid and enforceable. For instance, in Minnesota, inventions that do not utilize the employer's time or resources in any way cannot be assigned by clause.

The Minnesota Assignment of Inventions Statute, Minn. Stat. § 181.78.

Subd. 1. **Inventions not related to employment.**

Any provision in an employment agreement which provides that an employee shall assign or offer to assign any of the employee's rights in an invention to the employer shall not apply to an invention for which no equipment, supplies, facility or trade secret information of the employer was used and which was developed entirely on the employee's own time, and (1) which does not relate (a) directly to the business of the employer or (b) to the employer's actual or demonstrably anticipated research or development, or (2) which does not result from any work performed by the employee for the employer. Any provision which purports to apply to such an invention is to that extent against the public policy of this state and is to that extent void and unenforceable.

Subd. 2. **Effect of subdivision 1.**

No employer shall require a provision made void and unenforceable by subdivision 1 as a condition of employment or continuing employment.

Subd. 3. **Notice to employee.**

If an employment agreement entered into after August 1, 1977 contains a provision requiring the employee to assign or offer to assign any of the employee's rights in any invention to an employer, the employer must also, at the time the agreement is made, provide a written notification to the employee that the agreement does not apply to an invention for which no equipment, supplies, facility or trade secret information of the employer was used and which was developed entirely on the employee's own time, and (1) which does not relate (a) directly to the business of the employer or (b) to the employer's actual or demonstrably anticipated research or development, or (2) which does not result from any work performed by the employee for the employer.

Minnesota Non-Compete Law in Depth

Many issues in employment law are governed, either by federal law or by general common law, in a similar manner across the country. The law regarding non-competes, however, varies significantly from state to state. We look first at Minnesota law.

Contract Law

A non-compete agreement must generally satisfy the elements of a contract to be enforceable. The formation of a contract requires an offer, acceptance, and consideration.[32] "Consideration" is the *quid pro quo*. If both sides to a contract do not agree to provide something of value, it is not a contract but merely an unenforceable promise.

Non-competes are different from other contracts in that a judge will also look at the agreement to determine if it is reasonable. Under Minnesota law, restrictive covenants are generally "disfavored" and must be narrowly construed.[33] Minnesota courts, however, have upheld restrictive covenants where they meet certain requirements in addition to the traditional requirements that are necessary in forming a valid contract. In a case called *Bennett v. Storz Broadcasting Co.*, the Minnesota Supreme Court outlined the test that courts should apply when considering restrictive covenants that relate to employment contracts entered into by wage earners. The court stated that:

> The test applied is whether or not the restraint is necessary for the protection of the business or good will of the employer, and if so, whether the stipulation has imposed upon the employee any greater restraint than is reasonably necessary to protect the employer's business, regard being had to the nature and character of the employment, the time for which the restriction is imposed, and the territorial extent of the locality to which the prohibition extends.[34]

The Non-Compete Agreement Must Be Accepted by the Employee

In non-compete litigation, an issue that frequently arises is whether the agreement was provided to the employee at the appropriate time and whether the employer provided the employee with appropriate consideration. Whether the agreement is provided at the inception of the employment relationship, during the course of the employment relationship, or at the termination of the employment relationship, the employee must accept the non-compete agreement for the non-compete agreement to be enforceable.

Under Minnesota law, an employee's conduct constitutes acceptance if a reasonable person would understand it as such.[35] While signing the agreement is the most obvious— and certainly the safest—way of demonstrating acceptance, spoken words and actions may sometimes be considered acceptance.

Unsigned Non-Competes

Under Minnesota law, if two parties clearly agree that there will be no binding contract until there is a signed agreement, an unsigned agreement is not enforceable.

Absent a clear indication that signatures are necessary to form a contract, an unsigned written agreement may be enforceable if there is evidence that the parties accepted the document as a binding contract.[36] A binding contract may arise even when the parties contemplate entering into a formal written agreement at a later date, provided that there is clear evidence that the parties' correspondences otherwise satisfy the requirements of a contract.[37]

Outside of Minnesota, there is limited case law regarding the enforceability of unsigned non-compete agreements. Courts in other states have sometimes upheld unsigned non-competes when language in the employment contract acts to explicitly incorporate the non-compete into the terms of the job offer.[38] Several courts in other states have taken the position that continued employment after being made aware of the non-compete could be held as sufficient acceptance to make not signing the agreement irrelevant.[39]

Even if there is not a valid non-compete, this does not preclude the possibility that the employer can sue for breach of loyalty. In one case, the court held that the employee did not sign a non-compete agreement with the former employer, but the former employer was not required to have a non-compete agreement with the employee in order to prevent her from soliciting business from one of its customers during the employee's employment with the former employer.[40] There is more to say about this in the next chapter.

The Non-Compete Agreement Must Be Supported by Consideration

As a contract, a non-compete agreement must be supported by consideration to be enforceable.[41] Ultimately, the adequacy of consideration for a non-compete agreement depends upon the facts of each case.

- ### At the Inception of Employment

Where an employer requests that the employee sign a non-compete agreement at the inception of the employment relationship, the offer of employment itself is adequate consideration for the non-compete agreement.[42] In order for the offer of employment to provide the employee with adequate consideration, the employer must provide the employee with an opportunity to inspect the agreement and not just merely provide notice that the employee will be required to sign a non-compete agreement.

- ***Mid-stream***

Where an employer requests that the employee sign a non-compete agreement after the inception of the employment relationship, or during the course of the employment relationship, the employer must provide the employee with independent consideration for the non-compete agreement to be enforceable.[43] Various courts have recognized wage raises,[44] bonuses,[45] promotions,[46] stock options,[47] substantial training,[48] and access to confidential information[49] as adequate independent consideration. For each of these, the benefit must be new (i.e., the training must not be a pre-existing obligation of the employer) and in actual consideration for the non-compete (i.e., a pay raise given to all employees cannot be consideration for an individual's non-compete).[50]

In a few cases, Minnesota courts have held that the continuation of employment may provide adequate consideration, such as in at-will employment situations where it is clear that the employee knew of the addition of the non-compete and continued to work for the employer. This is especially true when there is evidence that the non-compete was discussed and the employee received benefits. Similarly, if a non-compete was clearly negotiated prior to the beginning of employment but signed after, a court may consider it as part of the original contract and require no additional consideration.

- ***As Part of a Severance Agreement***

A non-compete agreement may be (and often is) requested and required for an employee to receive a larger severance package or termination benefit than the employee is already entitled to. In such cases, the additional severance pay is usually adequate consideration.[51]

Protection of Legitimate Business Interest

A non-compete agreement must protect a legitimate employer interest in order to be enforceable under Minnesota law. There are two broad types of legitimate employer interests that a restrictive covenant may properly protect. The first interest is trade secrets or confidential information, and the second interest is the employer's goodwill.[52]

- ***Confidential Information and Trade Secrets***

Minnesota courts have uniformly held that protection of confidential information is a legitimate employer interest for obtaining a non-compete agreement.[53] It is important to note that the information an employer seeks to protect does not need to rise to the level of a trade secret to be a legitimate employer interest, if the covenant is properly written.[54]

Examples of confidential information or trade secrets typically include customer information, pricing, marketing strategies, financial information, new product development, unique manufacturing methods, and technical information.

- ***Good Will***

Minnesota courts have uniformly held that protection of good will is a legitimate business purpose for requiring employees to sign non-compete agreements. Good will is frequently found "where the services have been such a character that the employee's name carries with it the good will of the employer's business," or where an employee "comes directly in contact with customers" who "may be attracted to him personally and are likely to go with him should he enter the service of a competitor."[55]

In determining whether the employer has a legitimate interest to enforce a non-compete agreement, Minnesota courts consider the nature and character of the employment relationship. An employer has a "legitimate business interest in protecting customer relationships that it has spent years developing and nurturing."[56] In order to justify enforcing a non-compete, the employee must have had personal contact with his former customers that would be sufficient to affect its former employer's goodwill.

Minnesota courts are less inclined to find a compelling employer interest in good will when a customer terminated the relationship with the former employer prior to the employee's departure. Since the employer has already lost the customer's contract, the transaction cannot be undone by enforcing a non-compete, nor is it clear that an employer would face any additional loss.

- ***Training***

Specialized training of its employees may be part of establishing the employer's goodwill with clients.[57] Where an employer invests substantial time, effort, and money in training its employees in areas necessary for success in their job, the investment in that training by the employer could potentially provide a legitimate reason for enforcing a covenant not to compete. Courts have reasoned that the knowledge and skills of the employee, such as a sales representative, enhance the reputation of the company. Courts have been more inclined to find this true where the industry itself is specialized or requires reasonable expertise.

The Non-Compete Agreement Must Be No Broader Than Necessary

Under Minnesota law, the general rule is that a non-compete agreement must not be broader than necessary to protect the employer's interests.[58] The scope of a non-compete is measured by its geographic restrictions, duration, and substantive terms. Each of these is discussed in detail below.

Moreover, Minnesota courts tend to construe the language used to describe the extent of the restriction quite narrowly. Where the language of non-compete agreements is challenged as overly broad or unreasonable, Minnesota courts will engage in intensive fact-finding to determine whether the challenge is appropriate. Where the court turns to the facts to determine whether the language of the non-compete agreement is overly broad, the practical burden is on the proponent of the restriction to prove its reasonableness.

Minnesota courts have adopted the blue-pencil doctrine. This means that, in some cases, courts in Minnesota may decide to modify or "blue-pencil" a non-compete agreement that is overly broad. Courts are permitted to blue-pencil an unreasonable agreement by reducing the scope, duration, or geographic limits of the agreement to the minimum extent necessary to make it reasonable. There is more about blue-penciling below.

- ### *Substantive Scope*

The substantive scope of a non-compete agreement will differ greatly from one agreement to another, from one employer to another, and from one industry to another. The scope of some agreements is very broad and will prohibit any form of competition by the employee without specifically outlining what activities are prohibited. Other non-compete agreements will specifically prohibit the employee from working for, owning, operating, or assisting a competitor. Finally, some agreements are narrower in scope and will only prohibit the employee from soliciting the employer's customers (or the subset of customers that the employee worked with, or about which the employee gained confidential information). Ultimately, the general rule is that the substantive scope of the agreement must be reasonable and necessary given the legitimate business interests that the employer is trying to protect with the agreement.[59]

Minnesota courts are more likely to find that a restriction against the solicitation of the employer's customers is reasonable as contrasted with a restriction that prohibits the employee from working for a competitor or staying in the same industry, especially when the employee already had experience in the same industry prior to joining the employer and where there is a large competitive market with numerous customers to be pursued. The rationale is that, as long as the employee does not divert or steal away his former employer's customers, he should be allowed to earn a living in the same industry.

- **Geographic Scope**

The geographic scope of a non-compete agreement must be reasonable. Courts generally uphold geographic limitations when they are limited to areas necessary to protect the employer's interest.[60] As an astute reader may by now guess, the court's analysis depends heavily on the particular facts of each case, which may involve weighing the geographic scope against the other restrictive elements of the non-compete.

The geographic scope should be directly related to either the employer's business territory or the territory served by the former employee. Thus, in the case of a hair stylist, an agreement not to work within a 10-mile radius of her former employer may be reasonable.[61] In the case of a travelling salesman, a reasonable geographic scope may extend to the states where he does regular business and has established customers.[62]

Further, a broader geographic scope may be more reasonable when other aspects of the non-compete are carefully tailored. Thus, for example, a clothing salesman may reasonably be restricted from selling in an eight-state region because that was his former territory.[63]

In some cases, the geographic scope of a non-compete agreement will be considered not reasonable. Courts will most frequently find the scope unreasonable when it expands substantially beyond the former employer's existing business footprint. This is especially true when the expanded footprint may be seen as intentionally denying options to the employee that would not result in actual competition with the former employer.[64] Minnesota courts have also been skeptical when the company's business footprint is vastly expanded by including "affiliated companies" that may well have little to do with the employee's work.[65]

Under Minnesota law, global restrictions are generally not enforceable. However, Minnesota courts have occasionally held such restrictions enforceable when the former employer is truly international in nature and the skills or knowledge the employee possesses are particularly valuable or border on being trade secrets.[66] In such cases, the non-compete will have to be quite narrow and tailored in its other aspects.

The absence of any geographic scope in the non-compete agreement may invalidate the non-compete agreement altogether. This is because courts tend to view the geographic scope of the non-compete as a material term. Without such a material term, the agreement is effectively incomplete.[67] While some "incompleteness and imperfection" is permissible in a contract, courts hesitate to enforce agreements that "cannot be consummated without new and additional stipulations between the parties."[68] Since the enforceability of a non-compete rests on its reasonableness, including its scope, the court's reasoning makes a certain amount of intuitive sense.

An employer, however, may argue that a non-compete agreement lacking any geographic scope is intended to operate worldwide. The employer may also encourage the court to blue-pencil the agreement to simply define the geographic scope to some reasonable area, rather than invalidate the entire agreement. While courts are allowed to modify the agreement, courts are not required to modify an overly broad non-compete agreement. A court may decide to strike down an unreasonable agreement altogether. Therefore, a Minnesota employer should not draft the broadest possible non-compete agreement with the expectation that the court will simply narrow the language to make it reasonable.

In some cases, Minnesota courts have applied the blue-pencil doctrine to narrow the geographic scope of a non-compete that did not otherwise define it, although in narrow circumstances. For example, a court has blue-penciled a non-compete for the purpose of a temporary restraining order, even though the court noted its skepticism that such a non-compete would be found reasonable during later stages of litigation.[69]

In one Minnesota case,[70] the non-compete agreement in question did not specify whether the restriction should be measured by driving distance or 'as the crow flies.' In the case, the former employee signed an employment contract that contained several restrictive covenants, including a non-compete clause that forbade her from competing with the former employer by working in or owning another spa or hairstyling business within a five-mile radius for a one-year period following termination of her employment. The parties submitted conflicting evidence regarding the distance between the former employer's salon and the former employee's new salon. The former employer submitted evidence that the driving distance was 4.8 miles and also within a five-mile radius using a straight-line measurement.

The trial court provided that "even if it can be shown that the former employee's business is within five miles 'as the crow flies' it is not clear that this is a reasonable way to measure distance in the context of this case... the ease with which one can travel that distance must also be considered."[71] Ultimately, it appears that, in the absence of a method to measure the geographic restriction, the court will take this as greater latitude to determine for itself what a reasonable scope may be.

In many cases, customer-based restrictions have been found to be an appropriate alternative to a physical geographic scope. In situations involving a narrowly-tailored covenant prohibiting the employee from soliciting former customers (rather than a broad non-competition covenant barring the employee from working for any competitors or otherwise competing against the employer), Minnesota courts have allowed a customer restriction to substitute or complement a geographic restriction.[72] While such an agreement could be quite broad in terms of actual geography, the narrow tailoring to specific clients or customers suggests that nothing would prevent the former employee from going to work literally next door, which is clearly reasonable for the employee.

- *Temporal Scope*

Under Minnesota law, a restrictive covenant will only be enforced for the length of time that is "necessary for the protection of the business or good will of the employer."[73] In order to determine whether the temporal scope is reasonable, the court will consider the nature of the job, the amount of time necessary to find and train a replacement for the employee, and the amount of time necessary for the employee's customers to become accustomed to the employee's replacement.[74] A particular time period is reasonable to the extent that it is necessary to "obliterate the identification between employer and employee in the minds of the employer's customers" or "the length of time necessary for an employee's replacement to obtain licenses and learn the fundamentals of the business."[75]

As a general rule, Minnesota courts tend to find that non-compete agreements lasting one year or less are reasonable in duration.[76] In such cases, courts view even the basic development of client relationships as a reasonable motivation for the one-year duration, giving the employer time to re-develop those bonds.[77]

Minnesota court decisions involving non-compete agreements lasting two years are more mixed. In several cases, Minnesota courts have enforced two-year non-compete agreements. Such cases have involved non-competes that limit the scope to existing customers of the old employer.[78] In other cases, Minnesota courts have refused to enforce two-year non-compete agreements, often reducing them to one year in scope after examining the circumstances. Where an employee's tenure with the company is short, or where her exposure to clients or confidential information is minimal, the courts may refuse to uphold the full two-year duration.[79]

Minnesota courts usually refuse to enforce non-compete agreements lasting three-years or longer. To uphold such an agreement, a court must be convinced that such a unique relationship exists between the employee and existing customers as to require three years to sever the connection between the employee and employer in the customers' minds.[80] Alternatively, an employer would have to demonstrate that a full three years was needed to train a replacement such that the new employee was "fully incorporated into the business routine."[81]

Where a non-compete agreement is given in connection with the sale of a business, Minnesota courts are willing to enforce longer agreements than typical in the employer-employee context.[82] Courts tend to worry less about issues of bargaining power and whether the individual entering into the non-compete will be able to find new employment. As such, five year—or longer—non-competes may be found reasonable.

Even in the sale of business context, however, Minnesota courts will carefully scrutinize the duration of the non-compete agreement and may shorten its duration accordingly.[83] As we have already seen, the courts will weigh such factors as the burden placed on the individual under the non-compete and the effect on the public interest, and weigh these factors against whether the buyer can secure his own goodwill with customers in that time frame.[84]

The Non-Compete Agreement Must Not Be Unreasonably Burdensome to the Employee

Under Minnesota law, a non-compete agreement must not be unreasonably burdensome to the employee.[85] Courts have expressed doubt about restrictive covenants that arise "not so much to protect the business as to needlessly fetter the employee."[86] This is something of a catchall of all the previously mentioned factors. The courts, in determining the enforceability of a non-compete agreement, balance the employer's business interest against the employee's right to earn a livelihood.[87]

The Non-Compete Agreement Must Not Be Harmful to the Public

A non-compete agreement may not be harmful to the public under Minnesota law.[88] For example, a non-compete that fostered a monopoly may be held invalid as "injurious to the public."[89]

Restrictive Covenants in the Sale-of Business Context

The Minnesota Supreme Court has held that restrictive covenants are viewed differently in the business-to-business context.[90] Minnesota courts apply a "more lenient" standard when considering non-compete covenants between businesses than between an employer and employee.[91] This is understandable, given that the policy concerns that exist in an employer-employee relationship are generally considered not as problematic between two business entities. While the legal standard for evaluating non-compete agreements between businesses is "more lenient," the non-compete agreement must still be reasonable to be enforceable.

For example, a non-compete agreement is often given in connection with the sale of a business. The owner selling her business may agree not to begin immediately competing with her old company, given that much of what is being bought is the reputation and goodwill of the existing business. In such cases, courts have held non-competes of five or more years to be reasonable when, had the context been between an employer and employee, they most likely would have not.[92] Of course, courts may still find the non-compete unreasonable and subsequently invalidate or blue-pencil it.

Restrictive Covenants for Independent Contractors

Minnesota law suggests that non-competes and other restrictive covenants can be valid and enforceable against independent contractors and indeed the post-employment consideration requirements for such contracts may be more lax.[93] Companies should be wary of agreeing to such provisions, however, as they may be used to show that the relationship is not truly that of an independent contractor.[94]

Potential Defenses to a Non-Compete Under Minnesota Law

You may at this point be thinking, "so far, so interesting ... but is it actually possible to get out of a non-compete?" The answer is yes—in certain circumstances. The following is a non-exhaustive list of common potential defenses that can be used to overcome a non-compete agreement.

Loopholes and Typographical Errors

The first thing to look for as a defense to a non-compete agreement is the language of the written contract itself. Drafting errors can easily destroy the intended impact of non-compete provisions, often to the advantage of the employee. The terms of an employment agreement must be internally consistent and free of ambiguities. Courts construe ambiguities against the drafter of a contract and in favor of the non-drafter—the employee.[95] Typos are therefore fertile ground for establishing a defense to a non-compete. A lawyer can help you find potential loopholes in your non-compete.

Lack of Consideration

As discussed above, the second-most common defense to a non-compete, at least in Minnesota, is the lack of consideration. If the agreement was signed after the first day of employment, it may not be enforceable unless the employer provided additional consideration in the form of a payment or raise.

Expiration or Termination

An employment agreement must directly address the events that trigger the commencement of a non-compete provision and provide for the survival of the restriction even after the agreement expires in order for the non-compete to be enforceable. Silence as to the triggering event or survival after expiration may mean the non-compete expires, and is therefore unenforceable, on an earlier date, or that it is extinguished upon termination of the employment agreement.

For example, failure to identify a specific triggering event for a non-compete provision may lead to the running of the non-compete period during an employee's employment with a company after changing positions internally or signing a new contract with the same company. In one case, the triggering event was poorly defined as the termination of a particular employment contract, so an employee who received a new contract for a different position in the same company was later able to avoid his non-compete upon leaving.[96] In another case, the non-compete started upon expiration of the two-year employment agreement. The employee kept working after the first two years, but when he later left and the employer tried to enforce the non-compete, a court found that it had expired.[97]

Material Breach of a Contract

In standard contract law, one party cannot assert a breach of contract if that party breached the contract first. Thus, if an employer breached the employment agreement before the non-compete was allegedly violated, a former employee may have a defense. It is important to emphasize that the employer's breach must be a meaningful breach of a material term of the contract.

At-will employees—those without contractual terms of their employment—may have a tough time proving a meaningful breach, as any non-compete signed is generally considered ancillary to their employment agreement.[98] There is some case law that suggests Minnesota courts may be sympathetic to an employee who has his salary or duties drastically altered without negotiation, as these factors are clearly on his mind when agreeing to the non-compete.[99] This area remains murky.

Selective Enforcement

If an employer attempts to enforce a non-compete agreement in Minnesota, the attorney for the ex-employee will often attempt to demonstrate that the employer has not consistently enforced its non-compete agreements against other similarly-situated employees in the past. This defense, often called "selective enforcement," is relevant on two levels. First, the failure of the employer to consistently enforce its non-compete agreements arguably may operate as a waiver of its right to enforce the agreement against other employees. Second, the employer's failure to enforce the non-compete agreement in the past may serve as evidence that the restrictions contained in the agreement are not truly necessary to protect the employers' legitimate interests. While the defense has worked on occasion,[100] in practice it can be difficult to establish. At least one court has said that a company is free to decide which contracts it seeks to enforce.[101] Thus, while employers are wise to draft narrowly tailored non-compete agreements and consistently enforce them, the failure to prosecute every breach of a non-compete agreement may not prove fatal to future enforcement activity.

Other Similarly-Situated Employees Were Not Required to Sign Non-Competes

In one Minnesota case, a company required its outside salespeople to sign a new non-compete in order to participate in a new compensation plan. One salesperson, however, was allowed to participate in the new plan without being required to sign. When the company attempted to enforce the non-compete against a different employee who later left for a competitor, the court held that it was invalid because "absolutely no distinction was made between signers and non-signers."[102]

Failure to Identify Consideration – Statute of Frauds

An old English legal principle known as the "statute of frauds" (codified in Minnesota law) requires, among other things, that for an agreement which cannot be performed within one year of its making, the consideration must be expressed in writing. In one legal dispute, a company was unable to enforce its agreement containing a 24-month non-compete because the agreement did not expressly state the consideration.[103] The agreement also contained a so-called "integration clause" stating that the agreement contained the entire agreement between the parties, which blocked the company from using other written documents to demonstrate the consideration.

Superseded by Subsequent Agreement

If an employee signs a separation agreement after termination, the severance agreement may void an earlier non-compete if it contains an integration clause stating that it is the "entire agreement" between the parties or if it has a merger clause stating that the severance agreement "supersedes all previous agreements." In one case, for example, an employer was denied injunctive relief to enforce a non-compete because a subsequent settlement agreement contained a merger clause stating, "there are no other agreements or promises other than what are contained in this Agreement."[104]

Unassignable Contracts

Generally, employers can assign the right to enforce a non-compete agreement to a new company that acquires its assets if the contract includes a successors and assigns clause.[105] If the contract does not contain such a clause, however, a change in control at the corporate level may invalidate a non-compete.[106]

Waiver

Under Minnesota law, courts have held that a party may waive—voluntarily give up—a known right, even without the presence of consideration. A party that waives conditions of a contract cannot assert non-performance of those conditions by the other party. As is often the case, it is best to secure a waiver in writing. Waiver by words and actions may be difficult to prove, but if your direct supervisor assured you when you left that the non-compete was not a problem in terms of your new job, and two months later the company sues you, your supervisor's assurance might be a defense.

Equitable Estoppel

Minnesota courts have the power to apply a doctrine called equitable estoppel, which bars ("estops") a party from making a legal claim that contradicts its prior conduct. A party may raise a defense of equitable estoppel if it can prove that it reasonably relied upon the promises or actions of the other party, and that harm will come if estoppel is not applied.[107]

In certain respects, estoppel is similar a fraud defense, except that there is no knowledge or intent requirement. Thus, an employer who conveys in error, but in good faith, the limits of the non-compete, may be barred from arguing a different position in court if doing so could lead to harm for the employee who was found to have taken certain actions in reliance upon the employer's words or conduct.

Unreasonable, Overly Broad, or Lack of Legitimate Protectible Business Interest

An employee can always go into court and argue that a contractual restriction is overly broad or not necessary to protect a legitimate business interest, as discussed above, based on the facts of the case. The goal in this situation is usually to get the judge to "blue-pencil" the agreement.

Blue-penciling

As discussed, when a Minnesota court finds a non-compete unreasonably broad, the court can opt to modify or blue-pencil" the agreement by reducing the substantive scope, duration, or geographic limits of the agreement to the minimum extent necessary to make it reasonable.[108] Litigation over the "blue pencil doctrine" is often the heart of a lawsuit interpreting a non-compete agreement under Minnesota law. Even if the agreement is supported by adequate consideration and is designed to protect a legitimate employer interest, the court can still strike down portions of the non-compete agreement that are deemed unreasonable. Minnesota courts may not always choose to "blue-pencil" a non-compete agreement, however; a court may instead choose to invalidate the agreement altogether. In particular, where the court fears that it could not blue-pencil the agreement without re-writing it whole cloth, it may err toward invalidation.[109]

Unclean Hands

In cases where the former employer is seeking an "equitable" remedy (such a court injunction to enforce the non-compete) instead of monetary damages, the former employee may be able to assert the doctrine of unclean hands. The unclean hands doctrine holds that a party that asks the court for an equitable remedy must have acted equitably in the matter.[110] The equitable defense of unclean hands is premised on the notion that a court will withhold judicial assistance from a party guilty of bad intent or when the remedy sought would lead to an unconscionable outcome.[111] Minnesota case law has long provided that the doctrine of unclean hands only applies when the previous misconduct occurred within the scope of the facts underlying the current lawsuit.

Thus, the bad acts of the former employer that are unrelated to the employee or the employment contract cannot be used in an unclean hands defense.[112]

Unlikely Defenses to a Non-Compete Under Minnesota Law

Wrongful Termination

The Minnesota Supreme Court has held that termination of an employment contract does *not* preclude enforcement of a restrictive covenant, particularly when the employer has not taken "undue advantage" of his right to terminate.[113] However, wrongful termination and bad motives may preclude equitable enforcement of restrictive covenants, leaving the former employer with monetary damages at best.[114] Counterclaims for wrongful termination, unpaid wages, or other wrongful conduct may also provide leverage for settlement negotiations in a lawsuit.

Contract of Adhesion

A contract of adhesion is one in which such a great disparity in bargaining power exists between the parties, with the contract being offered on a "take-it-or-leave-it" basis, that enforcing it would be unconscionable. Accordingly, Minnesota courts sometimes refuse to enforce contracts of adhesion in the consumer context.[115] It would be surprising for a court to declare a non-compete agreement between a business and one of its executives a contract of adhesion, however. Minnesota courts have rarely extended the theory to employment contracts, even when those contracts are of a non-negotiated standard form. Further, an executive is likely to be seen by a court as a competent individual, capable of looking after herself in a business setting.

Fraud in the Inducement

In some cases, fraud in the inducement may be a potential legal defense in non-compete litigation. As the name suggests, fraud in the inducement exists when one party makes a false representation about a material fact to another party, intending for the other party to rely on the false representation.[116] In other words, through a misrepresentation, one party induces the other to act in a certain way. The challenge in demonstrating fraud in the inducement is proving that you *reasonably* relied upon a misrepresentation, even though there was a written agreement. This is generally considered a question of fact.[117]

If You Lose a Court Challenge: Damages and Remedies

Injunctive Relief

Typically, an employer seeking to enforce a restrictive covenant will ask the court for an "injunction." An injunction is an order from the court prohibiting a party from doing something, or occasionally ordering a party to do something. Injunctive relief is considered an "extraordinary" remedy. Lawyers learn that a classic instance where an injunction might be appropriate is if an historic building is about to be destroyed by a wrecking ball. If a lawsuit to challenge the destruction is allowed to take its normal course through trial, which may take a year or more, the building may be destroyed by then and it would be too late. A pre-trial order to preserve the "status quo" is an injunction. Injunctions are considered to be a form of "equitable" relief (a term you will see this used often in this book). Any district court judge has the power to issue an injunction. A "temporary restraining order" or "TRO" is a temporary injunction issued by a judge, often without the other side being present to argue against it. TROs should only last a few days, until the other side has a chance to appear. Most non-compete cases start with a request for a temporary injunction where both sides are present to argue the motion. Chapter 12 has more information about injunctions and litigation.

Lost Profits

If the judge denies a motion for injunctive relief, or if a company elects not to seek injunctive relief, the employer may still seek monetary damages for breach of contract, as in any other civil case. Damages awarded for breach of a non-compete agreement "are measured by the business loss suffered as a consequence of the breach."[118] An employer must prove by a "preponderance of the evidence" that (1) profits were lost, (2) the loss was caused by the breach of the restrictive covenant, and (3) the amount of the lost profits is calculable with reasonable certainty.

In order to determine the amount of lost profits, the plaintiff must segregate the losses due to the defendant's breach of contract from losses due to other factors. The Minnesota Supreme Court has consistently held that the plaintiff has the burden to prove with reasonable certainty the amount of the damages alleged.

In some circumstances, the defendant's gain may be useful in determining the plaintiff's loss. The Minnesota Supreme Court has held that "where an employee wrongfully profits from the use of information obtained from his employer, the measure of damages may be the employee's gain."[119]

In other cases, the plaintiff's application of a profit margin is appropriate. Where there is evidence that sales to certain customers of the plaintiff have decreased after the defendant entered into competition, the defendant admits to doing business with these certain customers, and the defendant offers no evidence to rebut the reasonable inference that the plaintiff's decline in sales to these customers was attributable solely to competition in breach of contract, then the plaintiff can apply plaintiff's profit margin to the amount of the decrease in sales to these customers to determine its damages.[120] It is generally more difficult to prove damages for a new business, as such calculations are speculative and not based on a long record of transactions.

Liquidated Damages

A few non-compete agreements contain a "liquidated damages" clause that places a set value to be paid upon breach of the agreement. This is essentially a pre-determined amount of damages. A liquidated damages clause is considered valid on the assumption that it does not represent a penalty for non-performance, but rather fair compensation for breach-related damages caused by a party's non-performance.[121] Enforcement of a liquidated damages clause is dependent upon the satisfaction of two elements: (1) the fixed amount is a reasonable forecast of just compensation for the harm caused by the breach; and (2) the harm is incapable of accurate estimation or is very difficult to estimate. If the former employee can prove that one of these two assumptions is not satisfied, then the liquidated damages clause may be held invalid.

Attorneys' Fees and Court Costs

Under Minnesota law, the general rule is that a party may not shift its attorneys' fees to its adversary without a specific contractual or statutory authorization. Where there is such a provision in the contract, fees will generally be awarded. Many employment agreements with non-competes include a clause allowing for attorney's fees by the "prevailing party" (either the employer or employee), but sometimes only for the employer, assuming the employer is successful on the merits of the claim.

Interestingly, Minnesota state courts have also held that if a former employer succeeds on a claim of tortious interference (discussed in Chapter 11) against a new employer who hires an employee in violation of the non-compete, the new employer may be forced to pay the former employer's attorney fees incurred in establishing a breach.[122] This is based upon the third-party exception to the fee-shifting rule, since the new employer's tortious interference directly causes the former employer to enter litigation against its former employee to protect its rights under the non-compete agreement.

In order to determine reasonable attorneys' fees, Minnesota courts use the "lodestar method." By this method, the court will determine the number of hours the party reasonably expended on the litigation multiplied by a reasonable hourly rate.[123] Further, Minnesota courts must consider "all relevant circumstances" in making a reasonableness determination. Factors that a Minnesota court may consider are: the time and labor required; the nature and difficulty of the responsibility assumed; the amount involved and the results obtained; the fees customarily charged for similar legal services; the experience, reputation, and ability of counsel; and the fee arrangement existing between counsel and the client.

Non-Compete Laws of Other States

Maxim: The law regarding non-competes varies significantly from state to state. Some states have a statute (a written law on the books) governing non-competes and others rely on common law (past court decisions). In some states, an existing employee can sign an enforceable non-compete in exchange for the employer agreeing to continue to employ him or her. In other states, to be enforceable an employee must sign the non-compete before the job relationship starts or it must be supported with additional consideration such as a monetary payment. Some states will always throw out a non-compete that is too broad or unreasonable, and others will allow judges to modify or narrow the agreement through blue-penciling.

Non-competes and non-solicitation clauses in employment are not enforceable in California or North Dakota (the latter of which is having an increasingly important economic connection with Minnesota companies). In South Dakota, a state statute provides that a non-compete is void unless the agreement specifically complies with an exception. In Illinois, a protectable interest in customers exists only where there are "near permanent" relationships. In Texas, non-competes are enforceable only when ancillary to an otherwise enforceable agreement.

In the majority of states, non-competes are generally enforceable, despite the widespread myth that they are not. Some states presume irreparable harm from a violation of an employment non-compete, making it much easier to get injunctive relief; some do not enforce non-competes where the employee was fired without cause; and some have statutory presumptions regarding the permissible duration of the restriction.

Statute Versus Common Law

A number of states have specific statutes regarding non-competes, others do not. States with non-compete statutes include: Florida, Georgia, Hawaii, Louisiana, Michigan,

Missouri, Montana, Oklahoma, Oregon, Texas, and Wisconsin. States where non-compete law is entirely based on court decisions and case law include: Minnesota, Illinois, Iowa, Nebraska, and New York. A number of states are considering new legislation to restrict non-competes and the law continues to be in flux.

Peculiarities and Oddities

Some states restrict non-competes such that only agreements that prohibit doing business with the established customers of the former employer will be enforced. These states include Oklahoma and Nebraska. Some commentators characterize the law in these states as being limited to "non-solicitation" agreements.

Some states require specific references to particular geographic restrictions. Louisiana requires that each municipality or parish in which the agreement is to be enforced be named in the agreement, and that the employer be actively doing business in those locations. South Dakota requires a limitation "within a specified county, first or second class municipality, or other specified area." In Pennsylvania, unlike most states, an otherwise valid and enforceable non-compete agreement may be deemed unenforceable depending on the manner in which the employee's employment is terminated, i.e., involuntary termination for poor performance may nix any protectable interest of the employer in enforcing the non-compete. Oregon requires non-competes to be provided two weeks prior to starting work.[124] Illinois passed a law in 2017 called the "Freedom to Work Act" that prohibits employers from entering into non-compete restrictions with low-wage employees. "Low wage" is defined as $13 per hour or the minimum wage, whichever is higher.

Utilization of Choice of Forum, Choice of Law, and Consent to Jurisdiction Provisions

Generally speaking, if a Minnesota employer includes a Minnesota choice of law provision in its agreement and sues to enforce the agreement in another state, that state's courts will likely ignore the choice of law provision if it conflicts with the public policy of the forum state (in other words if there is a different result as to enforceability of the restriction). Certainly, a choice of law provision will likely be ineffectual if litigation takes place in a state such as California which does not enforce non-competes at all.

A choice of forum clause, however, may allow the employer to bring an action in a more favorable state, such as Minnesota. Forum selection clauses, once disfavored, have found support in modern courts, with the U.S. Supreme Court summarizing the reason that, when parties have contracted in advance to litigate in a particular forum, more harm than good may come from disrupting what may have figured centrally in the negotiations and affected other terms.[125] Minnesota-based employees of major corporations headquartered in other states should not be surprised to find forum selection clauses in their contracts that remove any litigation from Minnesota.

CHAPTER 6

EVEN IF YOU DON'T HAVE A NON-COMPETE: TRADE SECRETS AND THE DUTY OF LOYALTY

Executives who leave to work for a competitor can run into legal trouble even if they never signed a restrictive covenant. Under the common law duty of loyalty, executives must be careful not to compete with their employer before they have left. Executives must also be mindful of state and federal statutes which govern the documents and records an employee can retain after leaving.

The Employee's Duty of Loyalty

You have probably heard of non-competes, but you may not be familiar with the application of the common law duty of loyalty to employees who leave to compete. Sometimes this principle comes like a rude slap in the face, so you are better off understanding it ahead of time. Duty of loyalty issues arise primarily, but not exclusively, when an employee of a business, while employed, communicates with the business's customers about the possibility of her leaving and taking business with her. Often, this is done without considering the legal consequences of a breach. The employee in breach may be barred indefinitely from seeking business from those customers and by that time it is too late to un-do what has occurred. **Maxim: Beware the Duty of Loyalty.**

If you are planning to leave to start your own business, proceed with caution. If you have a close relationship with customers and you are not subject to a contractual non-compete restriction, you can generally leave your employer and successfully, and legally, solicit those customers for your own new business. After all, this is America. Unfortunately, many budding entrepreneurs find themselves boxed in, having burned their bridges at the old employer and becoming barred from working with former customers because they did not wait until after they quit to solicit them.

Two important points about duty of loyalty claims involving customers: First, **the obligation arises whether or not there is a written employment agreement** and regardless of the employee's title at the company. Second, the timing and sequence of events are crucial. An employee who contacts a customer 15 minutes after she quits is in a more defensible position than one who does so 15 minutes before quitting.

The "duty of loyalty" owed by every employee of a company[126] is different from the similar, but higher, "fiduciary[127] duty" owed by a corporate officer or shareholder. In other words, all citizens of the kingdom owe a duty of loyalty to the king, but only a small circle of elite knights owe the higher fiduciary duty. The concepts are often intertwined, however, and courts sometimes refer to a "fiduciary duty of loyalty."[128]

An "employee's duty of loyalty prohibits her from soliciting the employer's customers for herself, or from otherwise competing with her employer, while she is employed."[129] For example, in one case, an employee left to start her own business. Before doing so, she informed a major customer of her intention and the customer told her that there would probably be some new contracting opportunities. The trial judge dismissed the claim because the employee had not actually "solicited" the customer. The appellate court reversed, noting that "even if the characterization of her conduct as passive were accurate, it would not necessarily shield her from liability."[130] (It also stated, "if prospective customers undertake the opening of negotiations which the employee could not initiate, he must decline to participate in them.") This holding is a further warning to employees who are thinking of leaving their employer—they should avoid discussions with a major customer who is dropping hints that they should leave and start their own business.

The Minnesota Court of Appeals also stated, "Employees who wish to change jobs or start their own businesses, however, should not be unduly hindered from doing so. An employee has the right, therefore, while still employed, to prepare to enter into competition with her employer."[131] This means that, other than contacting or soliciting customers, an employee may take certain steps prior to leaving. For example, he may form a corporation, secure lending, or enter into a lease while on his own time and without using company resources or connections.[132] Another court summed up the situation as follows: "While it is true that an employee may take steps to insure continuity in his livelihood in anticipation of resigning his position, he cannot feather his own nest at the expense of his employer while he is still on the payroll."[133]

An implied condition in every employment relationship is the employee's duty of honesty and faithfulness to his employer.[134] One Minnesota court recognized at least three claims upon which relief can be granted based on a violation of the duty of loyalty: (1) soliciting business of the employer prior to leaving, (2) disclosing or misappropriating information that the employer has treated as a secret, and (3) engaging in serious misconduct, such as embezzlement or referring customers to a competitor.[135]

The duty of loyalty is more elastic than those three categories, however. In one case, the employee was found in breach because he pulled his pants down at a public awards banquet and embarrassed his employer.[136] In another, the employee breached his duty by encouraging a colleague to take and retain a severance check from the company even while rescinding his severance agreement.[137] The Minnesota Court of Appeals has also noted that soliciting other employees to leave can be a breach of duty of loyalty.[138]

The employee's duty of loyalty precludes him from soliciting a former or current employer's customers prior to resignation and from failing to give sufficient notice of an intention to resign.[139] However, there is no precise line between acts by an employee which constitute prohibited 'solicitation' and acts which constitute permissible 'preparation.'[140] Because of the competing interests, the actionable wrong is a matter of degree. Whether an employee's actions constituted a breach of her duty of loyalty is a question of fact to be determined based on all the circumstances of the case. What is required is a balancing of the employer's legitimate interest in having its business advanced by an employee, and the employee's legitimate interest in bettering him or herself in a new business and providing for his or her continuing livelihood.[141]

The question has arisen whether an employee who also holds shares in a closely-held corporation is free to compete once he leaves employment, but before his share ownership is redeemed. One means of resolving this is to have the employee/shareholder tender his shares or give them up (without payment) to make the lack of connection clear.

It is not uncommon for a major customer to ask a key employee of a vendor to join it in an "in-house" position. This can limit or eliminate the work to the former employer and could be seen as a breach of duty of loyalty, but no court has adopted this view where the employee does not start his own business. The situation may be more clear-cut where the employee has arranged to become an independent contractor of the customer before leaving employment.

The duty of loyalty should not be taken lightly. I have watched many clients and parties go through long and painful litigation that could have easily been avoided by an awareness of the rules of the road up front.

Trade Secrets

A "trade secret" means information, including a formula, pattern, compilation, program, device, method, technique, or process, that:

(i) derives independent economic value, actual or potential, from not being generally known to, and not being readily ascertainable by proper means by, other persons who can obtain economic value from its disclosure or use, and

(ii) is the subject of efforts that are reasonable under the circumstances to maintain its secrecy.[142]

This definition is from the Minnesota Uniform Trade Secrets Act (MUTSA). Minnesota as well as most other states and the District of Columbia has adopted a version of the Uniform Trade Secrets Act which uses this definition. The federal Defend Trade Secrets Act of 2016 also contains a similar definition.

True trade secrets are rare creatures and misappropriation (basically theft) of trade secrets is alleged far more often than it is proven. When a former executive leaves to compete head on, however, the old corporation's attorneys will investigate to determine if there is any evidence that he or she took any company property, including electronic data, customer lists, pricing information, as well as true trade secrets, such as the recipe for Coca-Cola.

Most large employers are diligent about having high-level executives sign a non-disclosure agreement, even if they do not require a non-compete, or some document that obligates the executive to maintain the confidentiality of and return all corporate property upon termination. This means that if you take any information, documents, or property with you, you are likely in breach of contract, even if the information does not meet the definition of a trade secret.

Measure of Damages for Misappropriation of Trade Secrets

To prove that a defendant violated MUTSA, the plaintiff must show the existence of a trade secret, the defendant's acquisition, and disclosure or use of the trade secret.[143] MUTSA provides the types of damages that can be recovered in an action for the misappropriation of trade secrets:

Except to the extent that a material and prejudicial change of position prior to acquiring knowledge or reason to know of misappropriation renders a monetary recovery inequitable, a complainant is entitled to recover damages for misappropriation. Damages can include both the actual loss caused by misappropriation and the unjust enrichment caused by misappropriation that is not taken into account in computing actual loss. In lieu of damages measured by any other methods, the damages caused by misappropriation may be measured by imposition of liability for a reasonable royalty for a misappropriator's unauthorized disclosure or use of a trade secret.[144]

Damages for a MUTSA claim must be based in fact, not mere speculation.[145] MUTSA provides for exemplary damages in certain instances of misappropriation.[146]

Inevitable Disclosure

If you are involved in a trade secrets lawsuit, you will inevitably hear someone mention the "inevitable disclosure" doctrine. This is the concept that a certain type of executive, who moves to a certain type of position with a competitor, will "inevitably" disclose trade secrets by virtue of the job description and the nature of the competition between the companies. Companies try to use this theory in situations where the executive does not have a written non-compete agreement to ask the judge to essentially create a non-compete and order that the executive cannot work in that position. The term originated in a case out of the Seventh Circuit Court of Appeals in 1995, *PepsiCo., Inc. v. Redmond*.[147] In that case, the court enjoined (prevented) an executive from leaving PepsiCo to work for another beverage company because he had knowledge of his former employee's business strategy and competitive "playbook." Since then, the doctrine has been applied exceedingly sparingly, especially in Minnesota. MUTSA allows for injunctive relief.[148] So a request for an injunction is not improper on its face. But Minnesota Courts have held that the remedy of a court-imposed non-compete requires the showing of a very high burden and is usually rejected.[149]

Defend Trade Secrets Act

The Defend Trade Secrets Act of 2016 (DTSA) also allows companies to sue for misappropriation of trade secrets. The definitions and remedies under this federal law are very similar to MUTSA, although the DTSA provides plaintiffs with jurisdiction to sue in federal court. MUTSA is perhaps most notable for imposing certain requirements in written contracts. As an executive, therefore, it may be helpful to understand why this particular language is in your employment contract.

Defend Trade Secrets Act – Whistleblower Provision

The DTSA contains a whistleblower provision that allows, under specific circumstances, employees and independent contractors to disclose trade secrets of their employer to a "federal, state or local government official" under seal "solely for the purpose of reporting or investigating a suspected violation of law." The DTSA also allows individuals who file a whistleblower retaliation lawsuit to use trade secret information in their litigation, and to provide the information to their attorney, so long as it is filed under seal.

Defend Trade Secrets Act – Employer Notice Requirement

Not only does the DTSA provide a mechanism for employees to use trade secrets to report suspected wrongdoing or to support a whistleblower retaliation lawsuit, it requires employers to provide notice of these rights in any confidentiality or non-disclosure agreement signed after the Act takes effect.

Specifically, an employer must provide notice of whistleblower protections in its confidentiality and non-disclosure agreements or reference a separate "policy document" with the same disclosures, or it will not be able to seek and obtain double damages and attorneys' fees as a prevailing plaintiff in a DTSA lawsuit. This does not mean a company that fails to include notice language is without remedies to protect trade secrets. That company could still avail itself of Minnesota state law (including double damages and attorney's fees) and could still seek injunctive relief and actual damages under the DTSA.

So, failure to include the notice language does not change or diminish whistleblower protections for a company. It must be emphasized, however, that this federal law states, "An employer **shall** provide notice of the immunity set forth in this subsection in any contract or agreement with an employee that governs the use of a trade secret or other confidential information."

Defend Trade Secrets Act - 18 U.S.C. § 1833(3)

"(A) IN GENERAL—An employer shall provide notice of the immunity set forth in this subsection in any contract or agreement with an employee that governs the use of a trade secret or other confidential information.

"(B) POLICY DOCUMENT—An employer shall be considered to be in compliance with the notice requirement in subparagraph (A) if the employer provides a cross-reference to a policy document provided to the employee that sets forth the employer's reporting policy for a suspected violation of law.

"(C) NON-COMPLIANCE—If an employer does not comply with the notice requirement in subparagraph (A), the employer may not be awarded exemplary damages or attorney fees under subparagraph (C) or (D) of section 1836(b)(3) in an action against an employee to whom notice was not provided.

"(D) APPLICABILITY—This paragraph shall apply to contracts and agreements that are entered into or updated after the date of enactment of this subsection.

"(4) EMPLOYEE DEFINED—For purposes of this subsection, the term 'employee' includes any individual performing work as a contractor or consultant for an employer.

Secret, Confidential, or Proprietary: What's the Difference?

Secret

The rarest type of protected information is that of a "trade secret" which must meet the strict test as narrowly defined in MUTSA and the DTSA. If information *is* found to be a trade secret, MUTSA preempts other non-contract claims for misappropriation.[150] Theft of trade secrets can also result in criminal liability under the Economic Espionage Act[151] or Minnesota law.[152]

Confidential

Minnesota has recognized a common law claim for misappropriation of "confidential information" that does not rise to the level of a trade secret.[153] "Confidential" information is that which an employee knows or has reason to know is confidential.[154]

Courts have also held that an employee may breach their common law duty of loyalty by using confidential information to compete while employed.[155] The duty only exists before the employee terminated employment, but if they took information before resigning they potentially could still face a claim of breach of duty of loyalty. Whether such a claim is preempted by MUTSA is an open question and depends on the facts.[156]

An employer may protect a broad range of information by means of a confidentiality or non-disclosure agreement. The contents of a Hollywood movie script might be confidential until the release of the film, for example, even if it does not meet the requirements of a trade secret. The definition of "confidential" in this context should be specifically set forth in the contract. Contract-based claims are not preempted by MUTSA. Confidentiality agreements must be supported by consideration like any other restrictive covenant, however.[157] Failure to have a confidentiality or non-disclosure agreement in place may also doom an employer's trade secret claim for failure to take reasonable measure to protect trade secrets.

Proprietary

An employee has a general duty to return and not keep property of a former employer, whether or not it is "confidential." In theory, a box of blank copy paper is the property of the employer, as is the office key, corporate credit card and company laptop. Prudent employers include a "return of property" provision in their employment agreements and handbooks. If an employee refuses to return property, the employer may assert a civil claim for "conversion" or possibly "replevin" to get the property back.

Private

A fourth type of protected information under the law is "private" information of an individual. The law of privacy is outside the scope of this book.

CHAPTER 7

"DON'T TAKE ANYTHING!"–TIPS FOR DEPARTING EXECUTIVES

There are ways to avoid liability when leaving an employer. The most common way executives get into trouble is by taking or keeping information or documents from their old employer. The following is a helpful checklist for preparing to leave and compete.

Identify Governing Contracts

You should identify and obtain copies of all your contractual obligations to your employer before your last day of employment (or as soon as possible following your departure). This may sound elementary, but many employees forget that they have signed non-competition agreements during their careers or do not possess copies of their relevant employment agreements. In other cases, the employee may have signed multiple agreements over many years that may impose conflicting or differing obligations. The employee must identify all of these agreements as soon as possible in order to minimize the risk of breaching these agreements. Under most state laws, employees can request access to their personnel record. In response, most employers will furnish the employee with such agreements. Thus, if possible, ensure that you have copies of all offer letters, employment agreements, non-compete agreements, non-solicitation agreements, non-disclosure agreements, company policies regarding confidentiality and trade secrets, the company's code of ethics, the company's employee handbook, and other documents that describe your obligation(s) to protect the company's confidential information or not to compete against the company.

Obtain Legal Advice Before You Quit

If you are subject to a written non-disclosure, non-solicitation, or non-competition agreement, you should seek legal advice before you tender your resignation or accept another job in the same industry. As previously discussed, the laws governing the enforceability of non-compete agreements are complex, nuanced, and vary from jurisdiction to jurisdiction. The enforceability of your non-compete agreement may depend upon many factors, such as the timing of when you received the agreement, whether you received anything extra from your employer for signing the agreement (e.g., a bonus or promotion), the scope of the restrictions contained in your agreement, whether your agreement contains a "choice of law" clause, and whether your new job is in another state. The time to obtain a legal opinion regarding your non-compete agreement is before you quit, so that you can properly understand your risks and plan accordingly.

Comply with Your Contractual Notice Provisions and Other Requirements

If your employment contract requires you to provide advance notice of your resignation, or resign only for certain stated reasons, you should carefully comply with all of your obligations. Among other things, this means providing proper written notice and following the provisions of your contract governing how notices must be given (e.g., hand delivery, certified mail, etc.). Further, with proper planning, you might be able to maximize your eligibility for receiving severance pay, post-employment bonuses and commissions, stock options, or other compensation. Often, employment contracts, commission plans, bonus plans, and stock options will require the employee to provide advance notice of resignation or be employed on a specific date (e.g., December 31st or the last day of the fiscal quarter or year) in order to receive certain benefits.

Follow the Golden Rule

You should treat your employer fairly, honestly, and openly at all times leading up to your departure, even if you are frustrated or upset. A court will be less sympathetic to you if it appears that you have acted unreasonably or dishonestly. Many employees are tempted to lie about whether they are planning to join a competitor. This deception will often backfire and will be used against you if there is litigation. Although you are not required to notify your employer of your future plans (unless your employment contract requires such disclosure), often the best strategy involves voluntarily notifying your employer of your competitive plans and trying to proactively address any concerns of the former employer.

Provide Advance Notice of Your Resignation

To the extent possible, you should provide your employer with adequate advance notice of your resignation. Give the company a reasonable amount of time (generally, at least two weeks, but ideally more if you are in a high-level position) to find and train a replacement. Ideally, indicate that you are willing stay on until the company has been able to find an adequate replacement for you. If it appears that you are ambushing your employer by suddenly resigning, going into competition, and soliciting your employer's workforce or customers, a court is far more likely to consider issuing a Temporary Restraining Order or other injunctive relief against you.

Complete Your Assignments Prior to Resigning

Prior to tendering your resignation, you should do your best to get caught up with your work and complete all outstanding projects in a professional manner. Prepare a written memo to your employer explaining the status of any pending projects and be prepared to fully cooperate with your employer to complete all pending work, or transition the work to another employee, prior to your last day of employment. Even though you may be psychologically focusing on your new job, one of the best ways to avoid a lawsuit is to leave your old job on a positive note and ensure that your employer is not "left in the lurch." This may reduce your employer's suspicions about your departure and potential motivation to sue you. Moreover, if your employer does sue you, a court will be much more sympathetic to your position and legal arguments if your departure was handled respectfully.

Follow All Company Work Rules Prior to Your Last Day of Work

Leading up to your resignation (or last day of work if you have been involuntarily terminated), you should report to work promptly for all shifts, follow all company policies and guidelines, work hard, and be professional. If you are planning to resign, you do not want to give your employer any reason to terminate you before you announce your resignation (or following your notice of resignation, but prior to your last day of employment). As with the previous two guidelines, you also want to leave your employer on a positive note if at all possible.

Quietly Gather Your Personal Belongings

Prior to tendering your resignation, and without drawing too much attention to yourself, you should clean out your office and remove your personal effects, or be in a position to do so on a moment's notice. In the event that your employer escorts you to the door once you resign, you will want to be in a position to grab your personal belongings quickly. The question of whether to retain or remove any other employer information is complex and should be discussed with an attorney. While you generally have a right to retain your individual personnel information (e.g., your individual employment contracts, performance reviews, paystubs, and employee benefits information), it can be very risky to remove or retain copies of any other employer records. This is because employees are generally prohibited from using or disclosing their employer's "confidential information" or "trade secrets", either during or after the employment ends. Employers often take an aggressive stance regarding what types of information are entitled to legal protection as being "confidential" or qualify as "trade secrets."

Document Mistreatment or Unlawful Conduct Before You Resign

If your employer is treating you unfairly, harassing you, breaching its agreements with you, withholding compensation or commissions that are owed to you, or otherwise treating you unfairly, you should seek legal advice regarding these issues prior to resigning. Your lawyer may suggest that you carefully document each instance of such behavior by taking contemporaneous written notes, maintaining a log of events, and calculating amounts owed to you. Retain copies of any e-mails or other documents that help to prove that your employer is treating you inappropriately. In consultation with your attorney, you may wish to report the unfair or inappropriate behavior prior to resigning and give your employer an opportunity to correct the problems. Properly documenting employer wrongdoing, discrimination, harassment, or breach of contract can minimize the risk of a lawsuit against you by your former employer for fear that you will file a counter-suit. Further, retaining evidence of wrongful conduct by your employer can substantially reduce the risk that a court will issue a Temporary Restraining Order or other injunctive relief against you, even if you have signed a written non-solicitation or non-competition agreement. Under the doctrine of "unclean hands," the judge can refuse to grant the former employer an injunction if you have been treated unjustly or unlawfully.

Investigate the Employer's Enforcement of Non-Compete Agreements

You should attempt to find out whether other similarly-situated employees have been required to sign non-compete agreements with your employer. If so, determine whether your employer has enforced those agreements against departing employees in the past. Look for any facts that might help to establish that the company is inconsistent, does not require all similarly-situated employees to sign non-compete agreements, or has not consistently enforced non-compete agreements against departing employees in the past. Because non-competition agreements must be reasonably necessary to protect the employer's legitimate interests (such as confidential information and customer goodwill), evidence that the employer has not consistently required or enforced non-competition agreements can be very persuasive.

Be Prepared to Return All Company Documents and Property

Before resigning, you should carefully gather all business records, customer lists, vendor lists, sales materials, marketing plans, financial information, pricing information, research and development, technical data, letterhead, stationery, business cards, company laptop (if applicable), company cell phone (if applicable), documents, and all other company property that belongs to your employer, so that you can return it to the company on your last day of work. This includes documents and property stored in your home office, filing cabinets, basement, attic, garage, and old briefcases. Remember that most business records are "company property" owned by your employer, even if you were the author or creator. Employees often make the mistake of assuming that just because they created these materials, they are entitled to keep them. Often, this is not the case. You should obtain specific legal advice regarding your situation if you claim ownership of company materials.

Do Not Copy or Download Company Files

You should not download, copy, place on a thumb drive or disk, export, e-mail to yourself, or otherwise take with you, any physical or digital customer lists, vendor lists, sales materials, marketing plans, financial information, pricing information, research and development, technical data, or other documents that belong to your employer. This is the biggest mistake that an employee can make when exiting a company. All of your e-mails, computer records, and paper records can be "discovered" later during a lawsuit. If you copy or disclose this information, you might be sued under a variety of legal theories, including breach of contract, breach of the duty of loyalty, misappropriation of trade secrets, civil theft, conversion, violation of the federal Computer Fraud & Abuse Act, or under other claims. If you have taken such information with you, a court will be more inclined to punish you and find in favor of your former employer, even if you have other valid legal defenses (e.g., invalidity of your non-compete agreement). Further, in our experience, a court is more likely to enforce a contractual non-compete agreement against an employee who has actually taken confidential or trade secrets information with them.

Be Prepared to Disclose Digitally Stored Data to Your Employer

You should determine if company information has been stored on your personal laptop, home computer, or other digital storage media. If so, make sure to save all of this data on the company's main computer server prior to resigning so that you do not possess the only copy. You should probably get legal advice about whether to delete such data from your personal computers or leave it intact. There are advantages and disadvantages associated with each approach. If you leave the information on your home computer, the employer may argue later that you have misappropriated trade secrets. But if you delete the information, the employer might argue that you were attempting to "conceal evidence" related to misappropriation of trade secrets. Usually, the most conservative approach is to find out what files reside on your home computer. When you resign, notify the employer about the existence of these files and offer to delete them (or even have a company IT agent inspect your computer and delete them).

Do Not Destroy Company Files or Evidence

You should avoid suspicious activity on your company computer as well as your personally-owned computers, such as deleting large numbers of files, "defragmenting" your computer, "scrubbing" your computer, or other techniques that may appear as if you are hiding information. If you have done this, or are considering doing so, obtain legal advice immediately. This type of activity can be "discovered" in litigation and is very incriminating. It is very common for the former employer to obtain a court order allowing it to copy your hard drive to be examined by a computer forensics expert. A trained computer forensics expert can easily detect attempts to "wipe out" the hard drive or conceal files. Moreover, a trained expert can often recover deleted files. An expert can determine if you obtained a new hard drive or software. If you are worried about what a computer forensics expert will find on your computer, or you have already engaged in these activities, it is better for you to get serious legal advice before you announce your resignation and/or join a competitor.

Return All Company Documents and Property

On your last day of work, or earlier (if instructed by your employer), you should return all company documents and property, including cell phones, laptops, printers, stationery, credit cards, and confidential or proprietary materials. Create a spreadsheet or cover memo cataloging all of the items that you are returning, and if possible, have a friendly witness (such as a sympathetic co-worker) observe you when you return the company documents and property. If you ship the items back to the company, retain a receipt from the shipping company along with a packing list or spreadsheet itemizing all of the items that you returned. As explained above, in most situations, you should not retain copies of the information that you are returning due to the legal risks involved.

Do Not Search for a Job Using Company Time or Resources

You should not use company resources to look for a new job, plan a new business, or for any other competitive purposes. This includes not using company e-mail accounts, computers, paper, printers, fax machines, copy machines, scanners, telephones, or internet connections. Do not conduct your job search or business planning activities during working hours. Searching for a new job or planning a new business should occur at home during non-working hours, using your own e-mail account, computer, paper, printer, toner, and other resources. Likewise, if you retain an attorney to give you legal advice, you should not use a company-owned computer, e-mail account, or cell phone to communicate with your attorney. This could result in the waiver of the attorney-client privilege. For the same reason, you should not even access your personal e-mail using a company-owned computer or other device, because this may violate computer usage policies and also leave a trace image of the e-mail message on your computer hard drive which can be viewed by your employer.

Do Not Begin Competing or Solicit Customers Prior to Your Last Day of Employment

Regardless of whether you have signed a contractual non-compete agreement, you are legally prohibited from "competing" against your employer prior to your last day of employment. Thus, under no circumstances should you solicit business from your employer's clients, customers, or vendors or otherwise begin to actively compete against your employer until after your last day of employment. Seemingly innocent actions, such as notifying customers and vendors of your impending departure, can be dangerous; so it is best to take a conservative approach and wait to notify anyone of your departure until after your last day of employment. If a customer suggests that you should resign and start your own business or join a competitor (while you are still employed), you should terminate the conversation and not respond to the encouragement or solicit the customer's business (even indirectly). You can violate your duty of loyalty by even continuing the discussion about going into competition if you are still employed by the company.

Do Not Recruit Employees Prior to Your Last Day of Employment

While you are still employed, do not encourage any of your co-workers to leave the employer, join you at your new business, or consider employment with your new employer. You can be accused of violating your duty of loyalty if you recruit or solicit co-workers to resign while you are still employed. Thus, even innocent statements, such as, "I am really impressed by the company I will be joining and know that they are hiring," can result in potential liability and an accusation that you are encouraging co-workers to quit while you are still employed.

Minimize Your Paper and Electronic Trail

To the extent possible, you should avoid creating a "paper trail" or "electronic trail" of your job search, business planning, or related activities. All e-mails, faxes, résumés, cover letters, job applications, cell phone records, credit card receipts, bank statements, travel logs, mileage logs, and other such records that you create will be "discoverable" in litigation, along with everything on your work and personal computer hard drives. This includes e-mails sent from your home computer from your personal e-mail account. While it is difficult to completely avoid creating these documents while looking for another job, simply be mindful that your employer, your employer's attorney, the judge, and a jury might read these documents someday. Thus, be professional, courteous, cautious, and careful when drafting these documents. If you are interviewing with a competitor, it is better that most communications take place over the phone or face-to-face rather than creating an e-mail trail of the position, duties, and potential solicitation of customers or plans to actively compete against your current employer.

Do Not Disclose Sensitive Employer Information During Your Job Search

You should avoid disclosing sensitive marketing data, customer lists, vendor lists, pricing information, profit margins, financial information, sales data, revenue data, or similar information to a competitor of your employer while you are searching for a job. Take care when describing your accomplishments on your résumé, as you might inadvertently disclose financial data, profit margins, business plans, or other sensitive information that your employer deems to be "confidential" or a "trade secret." Avoid identifying customers by name. Do not list actual dollar figures when describing sales, revenue growth, profits, etc. While not all of this information may be entitled to legal protection, a conservative approach will minimize the risk of a lawsuit.

Delay Business Planning Until After Your Employment Ends if Possible

If you are starting your own business, to the extent possible, you should try to delay the incorporation of your business, obtaining a tax ID number, opening a bank account, meeting with an accountant, hiring a graphic designer, leasing office space, or engaging in other business planning activities until the very last moment (ideally, after your last day of employment). This can be difficult, but be aware that if you have engaged in business planning activities for a long period of time while still working for your current employer, even if those activities took place during non-working hours, you could appear to have taken advantage of your employer or acted in an underhanded manner. Further, evidence of these activities will be fully "discoverable" in litigation. Under the law, employees generally can "prepare" to compete while still employed. But there is a fine line between "preparing" and actually "competing." Therefore, postponing your preparatory activities until after your last day of work will minimize the risk of a potential lawsuit.

Do Not Lie About Your Plans

You should not lie about your intentions to go into competition with your employer. This dishonesty will almost certainly be used against you in litigation if you are sued by your former employer. I once represented a company outside of Minnesota that hired an employee with a non-compete in a service business supporting manufacturing plants. When the employee left his old company, they asked him what he was going to do. Out of nervousness, he said he was going to sell insurance, which was not true. A few weeks later they bumped into him wearing the competitor's shirt and cap at a factory as part of the bid-process for a new contract. They sued him within days. It is possible they would not have sued if he had been more forthcoming about his plans. If asked about your intent, either sidestep the question or be truthful and forthright. Ideally, you will approach the company on your own and tell your employer about your plans to join a competitor or start your own business. You probably should get some legal advice and coaching before this conversation because it can be risky and extremely sensitive. Take contemporaneous written notes of any conversations you have with your employer on this topic. In any event, lying will typically not do much good, but will often heighten your employer's distrust and prejudice the judge and jury against you. Lying makes you look guilty and rarely prevents your employer from figuring out your true plans.

Explore Negotiations Regarding Your Competitive Activities

You may wish to consider negotiating an agreement with your employer regarding your departure and which competitive activities will be permitted thereafter. For example, the company might waive portions of a non-compete or non-solicitation agreement in exchange for your agreement to stay away from certain key customers for a period of time, waive a severance package, forfeit a commission, or provide something else of benefit to the employer. An attorney can help guide you (at least "behind the scenes") during these negotiations. You should probably involve your new employer and its legal counsel in these negotiations, as well, to provide a united front.

Request Your Personnel Record in Writing

Following your last day of employment, you should send a written request for a copy of your personnel file under the Minnesota Personnel Records Act. Ask your former employer to mail a copy, at no charge, of your personnel record to your home address. You should request your personnel file following your termination, even if you previously requested the file while you were actively employed. You want to ensure that you have a complete copy, including any new documents that were placed in your personnel file in connection with your departure. Further, the enforceability of non-compete agreements often turns on the timing of such agreements and whether you received anything of value (such as a promotion or raise) in exchange for signing such agreements. Because this information (whether favorable or damaging) is typically included in your personnel file, you and your attorney will need this information in order to respond to a lawsuit if your former employer proceeds with litigation.

Delay the Solicitation of Customers Following Your Departure

Following your last day of employment, you should avoid immediate solicitation of your former employer's customers, vendors, and employees. Attempt to keep a "low profile" for a period of time. You may wish to wait several weeks or months before actively contacting key accounts, even if you have not signed a contractual non-competition or non-solicitation agreement. While your first instinct might be to aggressively solicit your former customers, doing so will provide the strongest motivation for your former employer to sue you. By giving your former employer a fair opportunity to solidify its customer relationships, find and train a replacement, and introduce the replacement to your former customers, a court will be less likely to prohibit you from doing business with these customers in the future on behalf of a competitor. Of course, if you have a written non-solicitation or non-competition agreement, you should also honor the terms of that agreement for the full duration (typically one or two years following your departure), unless you have received legal advice that the agreement is not enforceable, and you are prepared to defend your position in a court of law.

Independently Create Your Own Customer List

Following your last day of employment, but before contacting any customers of your former employer, you should independently gather information about each customer through legitimate, publicly available, alternative sources, such as internet searches, industry publications, trade association membership rosters, purchased customer lists, and the like. Independently prepare your own customer list from scratch prior to making any sales calls. Maintain a printed (and dated) record of all internet search results, research materials, and other evidence to prove how you learned of the customer's identity. Your goal is to prove, through contemporaneous dated records, that you have independently identified these customers after your final day of employment, without relying on your memory of the company's customer list and without using any of your employer's documents or lists. Thus, rather than simply searching for the website of each of your former customers, you should conduct "higher level" searches in various industries that will identify a range of customers (not just the ones you called on). Next, drill deeper to research each particular customer's address, telephone number, e-mail address, and the name of its decision-makers. Print dated records of all of your research results. Ensure that your customer list is not overwhelmingly comprised of your former employer's customers and take care to include names of new prospective customers with whom your former employer has never done business. Understand that many employers claim that their customer lists and/or specific information about their customers (such as the names of decision-makers, contact information, budgets, buying history, quality requirements, order volumes, etc.) constitute "trade secrets." You should attempt to defeat this claim by proving how easy this information can be gathered from legitimate publicly-available sources with minimal effort.

Do Not Engage in Predatory Pricing

When soliciting customers, you should not intentionally "under-bid" your former employer based upon your knowledge of the former employer's pricing. If you intend to under-bid your former employer, have the customer voluntarily provide you with pricing information from your former employer (e.g., bids, quotations, or purchase orders) before providing a quotation or bid. This will help you show that you obtained the pricing information from a legitimate source (the customer) rather than from stolen trade secrets or even your memory. If possible, your prices on various bids or quotations (in the aggregate) should be above, near, and under your former employer in order to demonstrate that you are independently quoting prices. Do not disclose your former employer's pricing or profit margins to your new employer or the customers. If possible, have an independent person or department from your new employer set pricing, at least for a period of time (e.g., 6–12 months) to avoid the appearance that you are engaging in predatory pricing based on your knowledge of the former employer's pricing and profit margins.

Do Not Raid Your Former Employer's Workforce

You should avoid recruiting former co-workers for a period of time (e.g., 6–12 months) following your departure. Even if you have not signed a contractual "no hire" provision, many employers lash out if they feel former employees are "raiding" their workforce. If you have signed a written "no hire" or "anti-raiding" agreement, the risks are even higher, and in most cases, you should honor the agreement for its full term (which might be longer than 12 months), unless your attorney has provided a legal opinion that it is not enforceable and you are prepared to defend your position in court. Be very careful to avoid communications with former employees that could be construed as "recruitment." Keep in mind that even if you have not signed a written non-compete agreement, if your former employer believes that you (or your new employer) are aggressively targeting its workforce, you may force your former employer into a corner and it may retaliate with a lawsuit against you alleging a variety of claims (whether or not they are meritorious). Thus, it is usually advisable to simply move on in your career and have minimal contact with your former co-workers for at least 6–12 months.

Do Not Ignore a Cease-and-Desist Letter

Often, prior to starting litigation against an ex-employee and his or her new employer alleging unfair competition, the former employer will send a "cease-and-desist letter."

You should not ignore the cease-and-desist letter under any circumstances. If you receive such a letter, you should strongly consider retaining legal counsel familiar with non-compete contracts, trade secrets law, and unfair competition theories immediately. Likewise, you should probably cooperate with your new employer and its legal counsel to develop a united front and effective strategy for responding to the letter. Once you have identified your best legal defenses, your attorney can write a letter to your former employer and attempt to negotiate an amicable settlement before needless litigation begins.

Prepare Your Legal Papers Before a Lawsuit Begins

Unfair competition litigation is often hard-fought, intense, and compressed into a very short period of time. Often, the former employer begins a lawsuit coupled with an emergency request for immediate injunctive relief such as a Temporary Restraining Order to enforce the non-compete agreement, avoid the disclosure of confidential information or trade secrets, or otherwise prevent the employee from competing. The lawsuit is often brought against both you and your new employer. The hearing on the TRO motion can take place almost immediately after the lawsuit is filed; sometimes even the same day or within a matter of days. It is critical that you consult a Minnesota non-compete attorney immediately after receiving the "cease-and-desist letter" so that the attorney has time to respond to the letter and prepare for a possible lawsuit. If you and your attorney are caught off-guard, you won't be able to tell your side of the story effectively to the judge. If the judge enters a TRO in your case because you did not have time to present affidavits or a legal brief, it could be difficult to convince the judge to lift the TRO later. You want to win the initial TRO hearing, if at all possible.

Be Mindful of Technology Issues

Modern technology allows work and personal information to be intermingled and stored in multiple locations. Ideally, employees should avoid putting personal information on their work computer, and should use a personal e-mail account for personal communications. Never use a work computer to communicate with your attorney. At the same time, you should avoid putting work information on a personal computer. If given the choice, it may be preferable to own the computer, laptop, and smart phone you use for work purposes, so that you have greater control. Try to follow your employer's Computer Usage Policy. Back up your contacts regularly, assuming you have a right to keep them. Avoid creating a paper or electronic trail. In the event of litigation, the process of "discovery" will allow the other party to search both personal and work computers, as well as e-mails, and in most cases deleted information can be recovered.

95

Once litigation commences or can be reasonably expected, a party has a legal obligation to preserve and not delete relevant information. Always maintain a professional image online, even in private social media. Never criticize your employer online.

Conclusion

Employees face potential legal risks whenever they leave their jobs. These risks are heightened when the employee plans to stay in the same industry, join a competitor, or start a competing business. Executives, officers, directors, and shareholders of closely held businesses face additional exposure due to their unique duties and the substantial competitive damage they can cause. All of these risks are greatly magnified when the employee is subject to written non-disclosure, non-solicitation, and/or non-competition obligations. While the scope of the employee's legal obligations will depend on the unique facts of his or her contractual obligations, work history, and competitive plans, following the guidelines summarized above will likely reduce the risk of litigation regardless of the legal theory alleged by the former employer. Given the high stakes involved in lawsuits alleging unfair competition, disclosure of confidential information, breach of the duty of loyalty, breach of fiduciary duty, and misappropriation of trade secrets, employees should carefully consider these recommendations in consultation with an attorney prior to resigning.

CHAPTER 8

"I STARTED THIS COMPANY"–
EXECUTIVE SHAREHOLDERS IN
CLOSELY-HELD COMPANIES

Executives who also own a non-controlling piece of the company they work for face complicated legal issues when they are forced out of the business. Like many employment law disputes, situations involving oppression of shareholder/employees can be emotional because the employee feels like he is being kicked out of a company he helped start or helped run and perceived himself as being more than merely an "employee." Executives in this situation have powerful rights under the law, however, especially if the company involved is incorporated or organized in Minnesota. In fact, the Minnesota Business Corporations Act (MBCA) has been described as the "among the most liberal" in the country when it comes to protections for shareholders.[158]

Unique Challenges for Minority Shareholders in Closely-Held Companies

Executives at one of the many *Fortune* 500 corporations in Minnesota are part of a large bureaucracy in which no one person makes important decisions without oversight. The officers report to the CEO, who reports to a board of directors, who answer to the shareholders. Rash decisions are less common, legal compliance is baked in at every level, HR departments are involved, public perception is a factor and litigation is generally to be avoided if possible. Privately-held companies, however, may be run at the whim of a president who answers to no one. Anger, control issues, greed, and other emotions can drive owners into expensive litigation when a minority owner and officer is forced out of a company.

Because of the personal nature of close corporations, whether formed by family or other personal relationships, shareholders often find themselves in active roles in the management of the company and dependent on the financial returns provided by the company. This may lead to an expectation of continued employment. Shareholders typically comprise the board of directors and, because the authority to elect board members belongs to those with a majority of voting shares, minority shareholders may find themselves at the mercy of the majority shareholders and those they elect when decisions concerning management, employment, compensation, distributions, and other matters concerning minority shareholders are made. This lack of control can lead to various forms of oppression by majority shareholders. Minority shareholders may be locked into their investment, however, especially if nobody is willing to buy non-controlling shares.

The nature of close corporations has prompted Minnesota law to recognize that minority shareholders are potentially subject to prejudicial treatment from majority shareholders and directors. When a minority owner is unfairly excluded from decisions or deprived of his or her ownership interest in some way (often referred to as "oppression" or a "squeeze-out"), both statutory and common law relief is available in Minnesota. The remedies available are cumulative, such that a party may claim and be awarded damages under multiple provisions and theories. Understanding minority shareholder's rights and applicable remedies is important to avoiding unnecessary minority shareholder disputes and responding appropriately if your rights are violated.

What is a "Closely-Held" Company?

The MBCA, Section 302A.011, subdivision 6(a), defines a close corporation as any corporation with 35 or fewer shareholders, but a court may also find a larger corporation to be closely-held under common law. The Minnesota Supreme Court identified three characteristics that indicate a common law close corporation:

(1) the shareholders are active in the business;
(2) there is no market for a minority interest in the stock; and
(3) dividends are not usually distributed.[159]

Where these factors are established, a court may find that a company is a closely-held corporation, even if it does not fit the statutory definition. "Courts generally identify common law close corporations by three characteristics: (1) a small number of shareholders; (2) no ready market for corporate stock; and (3) active shareholder participation in the business."[160] "[T]he lack of a public market is the dominant characteristic of a common law close corporation."[161]

A "minority" shareholder is one who owns part of a company, but not enough to control decisions of the company, and usually means someone owning less than fifty percent of voting shares or membership units in the company. (The rights and protections of a minority owner of a limited liability company in Minnesota are generally the same as a part-owner of a corporation.) Disputes between partners in a partnership are also subject to the same principles discussed in this chapter, but where two equal partners share 50 percent ownership, the potential for deadlock is even higher and resolution of disputes can be even more difficult.

Shareholder Rights to Examine Documents

Maxim: Get the documents. Often, the first clue that a minority shareholder is being frozen out of decision-making is that they are denied information about the company. The first thing an attorney representing a minority shareholder might do, therefore, is demand certain documentation.

A shareholder of a privately-held Minnesota corporation has the right, upon written demand, to examine and copy, in person or by a legal representative, the following corporate documents:[162]

- the share register;
- records of all proceedings of shareholders for the last three years;
- records of all proceedings of the board for the last three years;
- corporate articles of incorporation and all amendments currently in effect;
- corporate bylaws and all amendments currently in effect;
- financial statements that are required by Minn. Stat. § 302A.463, which means an annual financial statement that has been prepared within 180 days after the close of the corporation's fiscal year. The statement must include a balance sheet as of the end of the fiscal year; and a statement of income for the fiscal year. (If the statements have been audited by a public accountant, then each copy must be accompanied by a report setting forth the opinion of the accountant on the statements. Otherwise, each copy must be accompanied by a statement that the financial statements were prepared with reasonable accounting methods.);
- the financial statements for the most recent interim period prepared in the course of the operation of the corporation for distribution to the shareholders or to a governmental agency as a matter of public record;
- reports made to shareholders generally within the last three (3) years;
- a statement of the names and usual business addresses of all directors and principal officers;

- voting trust agreements;
- shareholder control agreements;
- a copy of agreements, contracts, or other arrangements or portions of them incorporated by reference in the articles of incorporation; and
- other corporate records at any reasonable time only if the shareholder of the privately-held corporation demonstrates a proper purpose for the examination. (A "proper purpose" is a purpose that is reasonably related to the person's interest as a shareholder.)[163]

The privately-held corporation must make these documents available within 10 days of receipt of the shareholder's written demand. If copies of the share register or documents stated above are required to be furnished, they must be furnished at the expense of the corporation.[164] In all other cases, the corporation may charge the requesting party a reasonable fee to cover the expenses of providing the copy. If the records are kept on illegible storage medium and require conversion to a legible format, the costs of conversion are borne by the same party who would bear the cost of copying the records.[165]

Rights and Remedies of Shareholders in Closely-Held Corporations

The Minnesota Supreme Court has noted that minority owners in a close corporation are more vulnerable to abuse than other minority shareholders.[166] Minnesota law thus imposes upon shareholders in a closely-held business a fiduciary duty to act with "the highest standard of integrity and good faith in their dealings with each other."[167] This duty includes loyalty, open and honest dealing, and disclosure of material facts.[168] Officers and directors are expected to uphold these fiduciary duties and may be held personally liable for a breach of such duties.[169] When fiduciary duties are breached, legal and equitable relief is available, as well as punitive damages.[170] A court may also grant attorney's fees for the breach of fiduciary duties.[171]

Judicial Intervention – Mandatory Buy-Out of Shares or Dissolution of the Corporation

Minn. Stat § 302A.751 lists causes of action available to a minority shareholder as:

> ➤ a motion for dissolution;
> ➤ A motion for a mandatory buy-out;
> ➤ dissenter's rights actions;
> ➤ equitable remedies; or
> ➤ shareholder derivative suits.

The remedies under the equitable remedies and buy-out provisions of Section 302A.751 are used most frequently by minority shareholders. Minnesota's Limited Liability Company statutes contain similar provisions. (Minn. Stat. § 322B.833 and Minn. Stat. § 322C.0901)

Minnesota courts have held that "[i]n determining whether to order equitable relief, dissolution, or a buy-out, the court shall take into consideration the duty which all shareholders in a closely-held corporation owe one another to act in an honest, fair, and reasonable manner in the operation of the corporation and the reasonable expectations of the shareholders as they exist at the inception and develop during the course of the shareholders' relationship with the corporation and with each other."[172]

Triggers for Court Intervention

In order to invoke the remedies of Section 302.751, mentioned above, there must be one or more triggering events. Possible triggers include the following:

Director Fraud or Illegal Acts

"[W]here the corporation, its officer or director violates a provision of Chapter 302A by, for example, distributing corporate funds without authorization or improperly issuing stock" judicial intervention is warranted. Minn. Stat. § 302A.467.[173]

Unfairly Prejudicial Conduct

Unfair or prejudicial conduct may also trigger relief from the courts. A "trial court may grant a buy-out motion in its discretion as long as there is at least one uncontroverted incident of unfairly prejudicial conduct by the board of directors toward a shareholder."[174] Courts have held that "unfairly prejudicial" conduct includes that which frustrates the reasonable expectation of shareholders. "[W]e have interpreted the phrase [unfairly prejudicial] to mean conduct that frustrates the reasonable expectations of all shareholders in their capacity as shareholders or directors of a corporation

101

that is not publicly held or as officers or employees of a closely held corporation.[175] All close-corporation shareholders have an obligation not to engage in oppressive or unfair negotiating tactics that may otherwise "conform to the rough 'morals of the marketplace.'"[176]

- ### *Termination of Employment*

Termination of employment is a typical example of unfair or prejudicial conduct.[177] Termination of a shareholder-employee is reviewed using the reasonable expectation standard, which provides that termination is only unfairly prejudicial when the employee has a reasonable expectation of continued employment. In Minnesota, the presumption is that employees are typically at-will. As a result, simply being a shareholder and employee at the same time will not satisfy this standard, but if a shareholder has a written agreement regarding continued employment, such agreement is typically determinative of the employee's reasonable expectation.[178] If there is no written agreement, or the contract is silent or ambiguous regarding the term of employment, a reasonable expectation of continued or even lifetime employment might be inferred based on the parties' conduct and the circumstances.[179] Further, a court may find a reasonable expectation of continued employment if it determines that employment was part of a shareholder's investment.[180]

Factors to be considered in determining whether a shareholder reasonably expected that their investment entitled them to continued employment include:

(1) whether a shareholder's salary and benefits constitute de facto dividends; and
(2) whether procuring employment with the corporation was a significant reason for investing in the business, among others.

The right of minority shareholders to continued employment "is sometimes viewed as an important part of their return on investment."[181] Not all shareholders in closely-held companies are entitled to continuing employment. Shareholder employment agreements that expressly permit termination of employment for "any reason" will block such a claim because they are inconsistent with a reasonable expectation of continuing employment.[182]

Some courts have found that expectations of continuing employment are reasonable only if the expectation is known and accepted by the other shareholders,[183] although other courts have suggested that a reasonable expectation of employment can be based on unspoken associative bargaining.[184]

- ### *Lack of Transparency, Abusive Tactics, and Use of Corporate Counsel*

The Minnesota Court of Appeals has found unfair and prejudicial conduct where the controlling shareholder shouted at a minority shareholder, slammed the door, accused him of incompetence and dishonesty, and threatened to fire his son if he did not resign voluntarily and where he "did everything preparatory in secret, including conferences with lawyers and advance preparation of legal documents."[185]

- ### *Squeeze-Outs and Freeze Outs*

Squeeze-outs occur when majority shareholders of a corporation, through their capability to elect and control all or most of the directors and to determine the outcome of shareholders' votes on other matters, use this great power to give themselves an advantage at the expense of minority shareholders. Squeeze-outs commonly affect the minority investor's cash flow from the venture while attempting to increase the cash flow of the controlling shareholders; at the very extreme end, the minorities' cash flow will be sealed off completely through elimination of their shareholder status. One of the tell-tale signs of an ongoing squeeze-out is the decrease of participation in the decision-making process affecting corporate governance. Another is the poorly justified or unexplained negative changes in cash flows; such as manipulating returns. Examples of manipulating returns include:

- dividend withholdings;
- excluding minority shareholders from company employment and the board of directors;
- appropriation of corporate assets;
- usurping corporate opportunities;
- self-dealing;
- dilution of shares by issuances of stock; and
- withholding information.

Examples of restructuring governance include:

- eliminating cumulative voting;
- amending stock transfer restrictions;
- arrangements relating to corporate meetings; and merging with or being acquired by another corporation.

Minnesota courts have held that majority shareholders did not breach their fiduciary duties by squeezing out the plaintiff when the shareholders' contracts explicitly provided for such right. "[A] written agreement specifically stating that the shareholder may be terminated without cause contravenes a finding that the shareholder had an expectation of continued employment."[186]

"Typical 'freeze out' techniques include terminating the minority shareholder's employment with the corporation or terminating dividends and the minority shareholder's return on his or her investment."[187] Other actions include removal from the board, removal as an officer, denial of notice or participation in shareholder meetings, refusing to provide records, failing to disclose information, and withholding profits.

- ### *Deadlocked Directors*

When directors are deadlocked in the management of corporate affairs and the shareholders cannot break the deadlock, judicial intervention may be necessary.[188]

- ### *Failure to Pay Distributions and Dividends*

Shareholders have a variety of financial rights. These include the right to participate on a pro rata basis in any distributions made to shareholders of a similar class, except as modified by any shareholder agreements.[189] Shareholders have similar rights with respect to the distribution of the remaining assets, if any, upon the dissolution of a business. Those in control of closely-held corporations have a substantive obligation, for instance, not to withhold dividends or use corporate assets preferentially.[190]

Remedies

General Equitable Relief

Minn. Stat. § 302A.751 allows a judge to grant equitable relief to a shareholder who establishes that the directors or persons in control have acted fraudulently or illegally. The scope of "general equitable relief" is very broad. As noted, a shareholder may also be able obtain equitable relief when a director acted in a manner that is unfairly prejudicial towards one or more shareholders, even if it does not rise to the level of fraud or illegality. For the statute to apply, the harm caused to the shareholder must affect his or her capacity as a shareholder or director, but, in a closely-held corporation, the statute also applies to shareholders in their capacities as officers or employees. A similar provision in Minn. Stat. § 322B.833 extends the statutory protection to minority members of Limited Liability Companies. When the statute applies, the court has discretion as to the appropriate remedy. "Equitable relief" can include monetary damages for the loss of employment.

The *Pedro* Case

The three Pedro brothers each owned a one-third interest in the family business, The Pedro Companies, a Minnesota corporation which manufactured and sold luggage and leather products. After working for the company for 45 years, Alfred Pedro discovered an accounting discrepancy of $330,000.

Despite hiring an independent accountant to conduct an audit, the full accounting discrepancy could not be solved. Carl and Eugene Pedro warned Alfred to stop investigating, but when Alfred refused, his two brothers fired him and cut off his pay and benefits. After a lengthy litigation battle, including two appeals to the Minnesota Court of Appeals, Alfred was awarded almost $2 million in compensation for his stock ownership, lost wages, his brothers' breach of fiduciary duty, and attorney fees. *See Pedro v. Pedro*, 463 N.W.2d 285 (Minn. Ct. App. 1990); *Pedro v. Pedro*, 489 N.W.2d 798 (Minn. Ct. App. 1992).

The consequence of this important case is that an employee who is also a shareholder might have a "reasonable expectation" that his employment is not terminable at will and that he can expect to work for the company as long as he chooses as a part owner. If a shareholder's employment is terminated unfairly and unlawfully by his co-owners, he can receive back wages and lost wages until his projected date of retirement, in addition to payment of the fair value of his ownership in the business.

Motion for Mandatory Buyout

Minn. Stat. § 302A.751 specifically references one remedy that a court may grant, at a party's request—an order that the company buy out the minority holder's shares for "fair value." The question of what constitutes fair value is determined by the courts. A court may, upon motion of a corporation or a shareholder, order the sale by a plaintiff or a defendant of all shares held by that party to either the corporation or the moving shareholders, whichever is specified in the motion. Typically, a minority shareholder brings a motion for a buy-out and asks that the corporation purchase the shareholder's shares. "Minn. Stat. § 302A.751, subd. 2, states that if a circumstance warranting judicial intervention is established, the court may "order the sale...of all shares of the corporation held by the plaintiff or defendant to either the corporation or the moving shareholders," at the price set forth in any existing agreements, "unless the court determines that the price or terms are unreasonable under all the circumstances of the case."[191] In rare occasions, the court may order a sale of the entire company.

Valuation Issues

"Fair Value"

Under Minn. Stat. § 302A.751, subd. 2 (2008), the district court may order the sale of all shares of the corporation held by the plaintiff or defendant to either the corporation or the moving shareholders if the court determines in its discretion that an order would be fair and equitable to all parties. The purchase price shall be the "fair value" of the shares. Minn. Stat. § 302A.751, subd. 2. "Fair value" means the pro rata share of the value of the corporation as a going concern. To determine fair value, the [district] court may rely on proof of value by any technique that is generally accepted in the relevant financial community and should consider all relevant factors, but the value must be fair and equitable to all parties.[192]

In a court-ordered buy-out, the purchase price for the shares is the "fair value" of the shares either as of the date of commencement of the action or any other date deemed equitable by the court. "'Fair value' shall be the price unless the parties have established another price for the shares in the corporation's bylaws or a shareholder agreement, which price is reasonable under all circumstances."[193] Under Minnesota law, after the entry of a buy-out order, the corporation has 5 days to provide the shareholder with its determination of "fair value" and other information required by the dissenters' rights provision. If the parties do not agree on a fair value for the shares within 40 days of the entry of the buy-out order, the court determines the fair value of the shares using the provisions of the dissenters' rights statute and may also allow interest or costs.

The MBCA gives the court broad discretion in determining "fair value." The court may take into account "any and all factors the court finds relevant" when determining "fair value." The court may also appoint an appraiser "to receive evidence on and recommend the amount of the fair value of the shares." The Minnesota Court of Appeals has noted that, while a court may rely on an appraiser's recommendation, it may not actually delegate its authority to determine "fair value."[194]

If the court does not appoint an appraiser, determination of fair value develops into a battle of the experts. The analytical methods used by experts vary, but are generally based on common principles of business valuation. "[F]air value, in ordering a buy-out under the Minnesota Business Corporations Act, means the pro rata share of the value of the corporation as a going concern. To determine fair value, the trial court may rely on proof of value by any technique that is generally accepted in the relevant financial community and should consider all relevant factors, but the value must be fair and equitable to all parties."[195] The Minnesota Supreme Court has stated that, "In our application of the extraordinary circumstances exception to avoid an unfair wealth transfer, maximum flexibility can be achieved by taking into account factors relevant to fair value, including whether the buying or selling shareholder has acted in a manner that is unfairly oppressive to the other or has reduced the value of the corporation, whether the oppressed shareholder has additional remedies such as those available pursuant to Minn. Stat. § 302A.467 (1998), or whether any condition of the buy-out, including price, would be unfair to the remaining shareholders because it would be unduly burdensome on the corporation."[196] "[A]bsent extraordinary circumstances, fair value in a court-ordered buy-out pursuant to section § 302A.751 means a pro rata share of the value of the corporation as a going concern without discount for lack of marketability."[197]

Valuation Methods

There are several means of valuing a business. The most conservative is "book value"—the value of any hard assets owned by the company, such as cash on hand, real estate, furniture, computers, etc. Probably the most common valuation is based on a multiple of earnings, often determined as earnings before interest, taxes, depreciation, and amortization or "EBITDA." Potentially the most accurate, if comparisons exist, is to look at what other, similar companies have recently sold for, known as the comparator method. Other factors involved in valuing a company include the nature of the business; the economic outlook of the company, the industry, and the nation or region; its financial condition and book value; the earning capacity of the company; its dividend-paying capacity; any good will or intangible value; whether non-competes are in place; and recent sales of stock, among many others.

Potential Discounts

- #### Minority Interest Discount and Lack of Control Discount

For most valuation purposes, minority shares may be discounted to reflect the decreased value attributed to the shares' lack of control over corporate decision-making. A minority discount can be substantial and often ranges from 15–35% of value."[198] The

Minnesota Court of Appeals, however, has held that a minority discount is improper under the dissenters' rights statute. After surveying a split in decisions from other jurisdictions, the court concluded that the legislature's "evident aim" of protecting dissenting shareholders precluded use of discounts for lack of control. The Minnesota Court of Appeals has also rejected application of a discount for lack of control of shares in a section 302A.751 buy-out.[199]

- ***Lack of Marketability Discount***

"A discount for lack of marketability, (or illiquidity) reflects the fact that investors will pay less for an interest that cannot be freely traded, as it would be if listed on an organized exchange. Jurisdictions also are split on the applicability of a discount for lack of marketability. Several courts have denied application of marketability discounts. Some jurisdictions, however, have permitted marketability discounts."[200]

- ***Key-Person Discount***

A key person discount is applied in some business valuations to reflect the reliance of the business' success upon one individual. At least one Minnesota court has considered the applicability of a key person discount, but did not decide the issue because it held that the shareholder was not a key person and that there were other competent people who could operate the business. However, a key person discount has been upheld in Delaware.[201] The district court explained, however, that the applied discount rate was based on three factors, which were necessary to consider in order to prevent the appellant from receiving a disproportionate amount of damages. The three factors the district court considered in discounting the valuation were: (1) there were no non-compete agreements in place; (2) there were no employment contracts binding the employees; and (3) the market trend on the valuation date was strongly downward. Minnesota generally takes the position that a minority shareholder discount or marketability discount is improper.[202]

- ***Date of Valuation***

According to Minnesota Statute § 302A.751, subd. 2: The purchase price of any shares so sold shall be the fair value of the shares as of the date of the commencement of the action or as of another date found equitable by the court. The valuation date of shares under Section 751 is presumed to be the date of commencement of the action.[203] While the commencement of the action is often the date of valuation of shares, the court has broad equitable discretion to set another date if it feels it is equitably justifiable. Minn. Stat. § 302A.751, subd. 2. Unless equitable considerations are brought to the court's attention, the valuation date of shares is typically the date of the commencement of the action.

The Importance of Written Agreements

Most of the bitter fights that result from shareholder disputes could have been avoided with proper written agreements. **Maxim: Well-drafted corporate documents, including a "Buy-Sell" Agreement and employment agreement, are a "must" for any closely-held business.**

Presumption of Reasonable Expectations

Section 302A.751, subd. 3a provides that written agreements are "presumed" to reflect the parties' reasonable expectations, but this presumption may be rebutted by other evidence, particularly where there are changed circumstances or modified expectations.[204] This law emphasizes the importance of considering the parties' expectations as reflected in the agreements they have signed. Indeed, the law should encourage parties to accurately set forth their expectations and intentions in written agreements relating to their stock and employment with the corporation. If the agreement accurately reflects the parties' expectations and is the product of arms-length negotiations, the agreement is presumptively valid. A shareholder may rebut the presumption that her reasonable expectations are set forth in an agreement by demonstrating that the provision regarding "expectations" is ambiguous, being read out of context, or not the product of an arms-length negotiation.[205]

Agreements to Avoid the Presumption–Employment Agreements

Employers will often require a new shareholder employee to sign an employment agreement stating that he or she is an at-will employee. Executives should be wary of signing an agreement with this type of provision if they can avoid it.

Buy-Sell Agreements

As noted, in most minority shareholder disputes, the remedy is a fair value buy-out of the plaintiff's stock in the corporation.[206] The fair value buy-out is subject to limitation, however, if the parties have created a shareholder control agreement or the corporation's bylaws dictate the sale and purchase of shares.[207] In this instance, the court will often order the sale of shares based on the price and terms set forth in the agreement.[208]

If the court decides that the price or terms of the agreement are unreasonable given the circumstances, then the court can override the contractual valuation.[209] Even when the bylaws of the corporation or a shareholder control agreement exist, the court still has the power to exercise its broad discretionary powers and reject the agreement.[210] The court will examine whether the controlling shareholders used the agreement to manipulate or force a sale.[211] If the enforcement of the buy-out provision frustrates the reasonable shareholder expectations or if the corporation manipulated the minority shareholders, then it is likely that the court will not enforce the agreement.

Minn. Stat. § 302A.751, subd. 2, provides that if a "shareholder control agreement" exists, its terms shall govern the buy-out of a shareholder who brings an action under that section, unless the court determines that those terms are unreasonable. Given the broad scope of matters that may be covered by written agreement of the parties, it appears that chapter 302A does not bar the parties from agreeing to when the shareholder status of a shareholder-employee ends."[212] "[W]hen the parties are governed by a shareholder agreement, shareholder status terminates when the corporation or other purchaser tenders payment for the shareholder's shares that conforms with the terms of the shareholder agreement."[213] "Minnesota courts are required to honor shareholder agreements setting the purchase price of shares, unless the court determines that the price is unreasonable under all the circumstances."[214]

Effect of Oral Agreements

Reasonable expectations are not required to be stated in writing. "[T]he standard of proof when interpreting contracts and determining the elements of a contract claim is preponderance of the evidence."[215] "[W]hen a party asserts that there has been an enforceable oral modification of the terms of a written contract, that party has the burden of proving the modification [of the written contract] by clear and convincing evidence."[216]

Course of Dealing (Implied)

Reasonable expectations can arise from a course of dealing between shareholders and a company.[217] For example, a shareholder might have a reasonable expectation that a certain percentage of a business's profits will be distributed to shareholders if similar distributions have been made for many years.[218] When a contract governs the duties of the parties for a specified term and it has expired, the parties may thereafter enter into a new contract by conduct (continued payment and performance) or otherwise, and they may adopt the provisions of their former contract or agree to modify them.[219]

Dissenters' Rights

The dissenters' rights provisions in Minnesota Statutes sections 302A.471–473 permit a shareholder to "dissent" from certain fundamental corporate changes and obtain payment from the corporation for the "fair value" of the shares. In contrast to section 302A.751, which allows a shareholder to obtain payment for his or her shares by showing a broad range of "unfairly prejudicial conduct," the dissenters' rights statute only allows a shareholder to obtain payment for his or her shares upon the occurrence of one of five enumerated triggering events.[220] Minnesota courts have held that the triggering of dissenters' rights prevents the shareholder from taking action based on any alleged unfairness of the corporate change that gave rise to the rights. In other words, a dissenters' rights action is the exclusive remedy available to a shareholder unless the action dissented from is fraudulent.[221]

CHAPTER 9

WRONGFUL TERMINATION: SEXUAL HARASSMENT, WHISTLEBLOWING, DISCRIMINATION, AND MORE

Executives who are terminated from their employment have the same rights and range of potential legal claims as any other employee in the American legal system. For executives, these "potential" claims can be used as leverage for negotiating a severance, even if the executive does not file a lawsuit for wrongful termination. A complete review of employment law is beyond the scope of this book, but we will touch upon some of the more common types of claims.

Sexual Harassment

In 1979, Catherine MacKinnon published "Sexual Harassment of Working Women," arguing that sexual harassment is a form of sex discrimination under Title VII of the Civil Rights Act of 1964. In 1980, five college students, with MacKinnon's advice and support, sued Yale University in the first sexual harassment lawsuit under the Civil Rights Act. Later that year Dolly Parton starred as a sexually harassed office secretary in *9 to 5*. In 1986, the U.S. Supreme Court ruled in *Meritor Savings Bank v. Vinson* that a hostile work environment constituted sexual discrimination. In 1991, Professor Anita Hill testified before Congress during the Clarence Thomas confirmation hearings and "sexual harassment" became a household phrase. That same year, the Civil Rights Act of 1991 created a right to a jury trial for discrimination claims and allowed additional types of damages.

Starting in the early '90s, therefore, many plaintiff attorneys turned away from representing car accident victims and started bringing sexual harassment cases. These attorneys were not traditional labor law attorneys, but they sparked an explosion in "employment law" litigation around the country. No significant knowledge of employment law was required. Any plaintiff attorney with a client who had been groped or harassed by her boss could work up a damages claim, similar to any negligence case. As the number of classically-trained labor law practitioners decreased, a flood of new "employment" law firms entered the market.

#Metoo

In late 2017, news broke of numerous women alleging sexual assault by Hollywood movie mogul Harvey Weinstein. A social media campaign using the hashtag #metoo prompted a flood of similar allegations in the entertainment industry, which then spilled over into politics, news media, and many other industries. Never before was so much attention paid to the issue of sexual harassment in the workplace.

Definition

"Sexual harassment" is defined by *Black's Law Dictionary* as "discrimination consisting in verbal or physical abuse of a sexual nature, including lewd remarks, salacious looks, and unwelcome touching."[222] Sexual harassment can also include a hostile work environment (for example, an employee is subjected to pornographic images shared by coworkers), or harassment occurring on a quid-pro-quo basis (for example, an employee receives threats of demotion or termination from a supervisor if they don't go on a date or perform a sexual act). Sexual harassment can include harassment by either individuals of the opposite sex or the same sex.

If You are the Victim of Sexual Harassment in the Workplace

Sexual harassment is not fair. If it happens to you, the most important thing is to preserve evidence and report it to a supervisor or HR. The United States Supreme Court has held that employers may assert a defense to some claims of sexual harassment if the company has a policy in place to deal with complaints, but the victim does not avail herself of the policy. This may result in the harasser being investigated, but not terminated. This can lead to resentment and subtle retaliation, but if you document everything and play by the rules, the law protects you as much as it possibly can. Inappropriate comments or emails should not be seen as a chance to file a lawsuit and win the lottery. Regardless of whether you are successful in obtaining a settlement, litigation will disrupt your career. Litigation takes months, if not years. It necessarily antagonizes your former employer and, depending on the industry, may become well-known. Litigation requires you to disclose your medical records and to have your deposition taken by an unpleasant defense attorney.

There are many exceptions to this rule. If the harassment does not stop, if the harasser is the owner of the company, or if you are fired for refusing to agree to a quid pro quo request for sex or in retaliation for making a complaint, you should consult an attorney and consider seeking damages.

If You are Accused of Sexual Harassment

Maxim: Don't do it! First of all, don't ever make comments or touch other people in the workplace in a way that would make them uncomfortable or that common sense says is inappropriate. Thousands of powerful men (and some women) have had careers and marriages destroyed by a momentary lack of judgment. Dominque Strauss-Kahn of France discovered how seriously the American legal system takes these matters. Even Bill Clinton got sued for sexual harassment. Here in Minnesota, the CEO of Best Buy, resigned in 2012 after it was alleged he was having an affair with a subordinate, and the Best Buy founder later resigned after it was suggested that he failed to follow up on a complaint about the relationship. Bill O'Reilly was forced out of Fox News because of allegations of sexual harassment and Harvey Weinstein lost control of his company because of his bad behavior. After the #metoo movement in 2017, scores of other powerful men were accused of inappropriate behavior including Kevin Spacey, Louis C.K., Jeffrey Tambor, Matt Lauer, public radio news chief Michael Oreskes, journalist Charlie Rose, Minnesota's own Garrison Keillor, and Minnesota Senator Al Franken, among many others.

If the claims are baseless, try to stay calm and work with the system. Cooperate in the investigation. If the allegation is completely false, you might consider a defamation action (See Chapter 11); but initially it is best to try to resolve it quietly through investigation and cooperation and seek indemnification if there is a lawsuit against you. If you have been engaged in a consensual relationship, but one which might be viewed as improper because of power disparity, you may want to disclose this immediately. If the allegations involve non-consensual touching, you should be engaged in damage control and may possibly need to consult with a criminal law attorney about invoking your rights under the 5th Amendment.

Whistleblowing and Other Forms of Retaliation

An executive who loses her job because she refused to follow an illegal directive, reported an illegal action by the company, or cooperated in a government investigation may have a whistleblower claim. Many states have laws or public policy provisions protecting employees in this situation, and a growing number of federal laws protect whistleblowers as well. In fact, executives considering making a report of wrongful activity now have more options, more protection, and more incentive than ever before. Congress seems almost irresistibly drawn to thumb-tacking a whistleblower provision on every complicated regulatory scheme that comes down the pike. These provisions do not directly cost the federal government any money, and federal representatives argue to their constituents that they will actually save the government money because they allow common citizens to report and expose fraud, waste and other wrongdoing. Whether or not that's true is hard to say.

Studies have suggested that whistleblowers often end up dissatisfied after their experience, even if their complaints were vindicated and even if they received significant monetary compensation. Human nature is such that co-workers tend to shun anyone perceived as a "snitch", "narc", or "rat", and the whistleblower inevitably feels like he has been ejected from the tribe as a pariah.

Perhaps the first major federal whistleblower law was the False Claims Act (FCA) which has its origins in a law signed by President Lincoln during the Civil War to prevent war profiteers from cheating the federal government. In modern times, the FCA has allowed citizens to report fraud against the U.S. government without risk of retaliation and even to receive a portion of funds recovered as a result of the report as part of a *qui tam* lawsuit filed by an individual on behalf of the government. As these cases often involve health care or defense contracts, the amounts can be quite large. This law has been largely successful as a means of discovering fraud at the federal level.

The Sarbanes-Oxley Act, which was enacted as a result of scandals at Enron and other publicly traded companies, launched the modern era of expanded whistleblowing. SOX created protections for any employee of a publicly-traded company from retaliation for reporting "fraud." In practice, this Act has exposed few scandals, but generated many lawsuits and administrative claims.

The American Recovery and Reinvestment Act prohibits employers who receive funds from the Troubled Asset Relief Program from retaliating against any employee who discloses information that the employee believes is evidence of waste or mismanagement of TARP funds, a substantial and specific danger to public health or safety related to the implementation or use of funds, an abuse of authority related to the implementation or use of covered funds, or a violation of a law, rule, or regulation related to an agency contract or grant relating to covered funds. There is no publicly-known example of anyone invoking this relatively narrow protection so far.

Not surprisingly, the whistleblower protection trend continued with the Patient Protection and Affordable Care Act, also known as "Obamacare." The ACA provides that employers cannot discriminate against any employee who provides information to the government or the employer regarding a violation of Title I of the ACA. In other words, employees of hospitals, clinics and physician's offices who complain of violations of the law's many requirements have statutory protection against termination of employment or other retaliation.

Finally, the Dodd-Frank Act Wall Street Reform and Consumer Protection Act (DFA) is perhaps the furthest expansion of federal whistleblower protection. The DFA added new whistleblower rights for direct reporting to the Securities and Exchange Commission and Commodities Futures Trading Commission (CFTC), added new whistleblower rights for financial services executives, and enhanced the existing provisions of both the Sarbanes Oxley Act and the False Claims Act mentioned above. This law allows individuals who provide original information to the SEC or CFTC which results in monetary sanctions in excess of $1 million in civil or criminal proceedings to receive a reward ranging from 10 percent to 30 percent of the amount recouped by the government. In contrast to *qui tam* actions under the FCA, the DFA does not provide a private cause of action to whistleblowers to prosecute securities fraud or other SEC violations. It does, however, create a private right of action for employees or other individuals who have suffered retaliation due to lawful whistleblower acts involving the SEC. The DFA also contains dedicated whistleblower protection for financial services employees who disclose information about fraudulent or unlawful conduct related to the offering or provision of a consumer financial product or service.

Minnesota's law on whistleblowing is very broad. It states in part, as follows:

181.932 DISCLOSURE OF INFORMATION BY EMPLOYEES.

Subdivision 1. Prohibited action. An employer shall not discharge, discipline, threaten, otherwise discriminate against, or penalize an employee regarding the employee's compensation, terms, conditions, location, or privileges of employment because:

(1) the employee, or a person acting on behalf of an employee, in good faith, reports a violation, suspected violation, or planned violation of any federal or state law or common law or rule adopted pursuant to law to an employer or to any governmental body or law enforcement official;

(2) the employee is requested by a public body or office to participate in an investigation, hearing, inquiry;

(3) the employee refuses an employer's order to perform an action that the employee has an objective basis in fact to believe violates any state or federal law or rule or regulation adopted pursuant to law, and the employee informs the employer that the order is being refused for that reason;

(4) the employee, in good faith, reports a situation in which the quality of health care services provided by a health care facility, organization, or health care provider violates a standard established by federal or state law or a professionally recognized national clinical or ethical standard and potentially places the public at risk of harm;

(5) a public employee communicates the findings of a scientific or technical study that the employee, in good faith, believes to be truthful and accurate, including reports to a governmental body or law enforcement official; or

(6) an employee in the classified service of state government communicates information that the employee, in good faith, believes to be truthful and accurate, and that relates to state services, including the financing of state services, to:

(i) a legislator or the legislative auditor; or

(ii) a constitutional officer.

The disclosures protected pursuant to this section do not authorize the disclosure of data otherwise protected by law.

Discrimination

Employment discrimination is a pernicious reality. From an executive-law perspective, however, a discrimination claim is the bluntest tool in the tool box. A sharply-defined contract is a stronger and less judgmental form of legal leverage. Proving discrimination requires the plaintiff to prove what was in the mind of the decision maker. Proof can be either direct, such as an e-mail with discriminatory comments; or indirect, such as statistical evidence. Most lawsuits involve indirect evidence which is evaluated based under a "burden-shifting" analysis developed by the courts, an analysis which nobody really likes, but with which we are stuck. One would think that a discriminatory motive would be a fact question that would preclude dismissal of such cases as a matter of law, but judges find a way to dismiss many of these claims.

Workplace discrimination covers a wide area of law. "Discrimination" in employement means that an employee has suffered an "adverse employment action" because of that person's status in a "protected class." Discrimination is illegal under both federal and Minnesota law, but Minnesota law includes many more types of "protected classes."

The Minnesota Human Rights Act includes the following protected classes: "race, color, creed, religion, national origin, sex, marital status, status with regard to public assistance, familial status, membership or activity in a local commission, disability, sexual orientation, [and] age."[223] Minnesota's protected classes include several classes which are not included under federal law, such as marital status and sexual orientation. In theory, everybody falls into at least some protected classes. For example, marital status includes the status of being married, single, or divorced.

A discrimination claim will result in the company and the decision-making executive becoming defensive. Nobody wants to be accused of discrimination. These disputes can therefore take on a hostile tone and, like many other types of legal claims, can have a detrimental impact on the plaintiff's career even if the plaintiff "wins" the case or obtains a significant settlement.

Unlike most other types of potential legal claims, discrimination allegations may be pursued initially through an intermediate administrative process before going to court. At the federal level, the U.S. Equal Employment Opportunity Commission (EEOC) will investigate a "charge" of discrimination. A charge can be filed without an attorney and is typically a one-page form. The process is free. The EEOC may take months, or even a year to investigate. Most claims, as many as 80%, are dismissed for lack of "probable cause." Even if the agency finds in your favor, it cannot award financial damages. At most, it can push for a conciliation or mediation. If the employer does not settle, the matter starts from scratch in district court. The Minnesota Department of Human Rights also investigates claims in a similar manner at the state level, including claims based on sexual orientation or familial status that are not governed by federal law. In federal court, an EEOC charge may be a required prerequisite to a lawsuit; in state court, filing an administrative charge is an option that can be skipped if the employee wishes to go directly to litigation.

Although the threat of a discrimination claim may be useful leverage in negotiating a severance agreement, actually filing a lawsuit is no panacea. Many individuals who have gone through the process of suing their former employer for discrimination regret it. According to the American Bar Association (ABA), "Many plaintiffs report experiencing depression, alcoholism and divorce flowing from the stress of litigation. Many plaintiffs begin litigation hoping to get their job back; that almost never happens."[224] A scientific survey of employment civil rights lawsuits cited by the same ABA article showed that 36% of plaintiffs had their case dismissed on summary judgment; 50% received an early settlement with an average value of $30,000; and 6% went to trial. Of the cases that went to trial, only one-third ended with a win for the plaintiff.[225]

CHAPTER 10

"WHAT COLOR IS MY PARACHUTE?"– NEGOTIATING SEVERANCE AND RELEASE AGREEMENTS

Receiving a termination notice, being fired, is an intensely emotional experience. Executives usually have a portion of their identity and pride wrapped up in their job, title, and position and relate to their company and colleagues in a way that is about more than collecting a paycheck. But lay-offs, reductions in force, and termination are a fact of life. Often, they can lead to bigger and better things. A severance package may not salve all wounds, but money helps in other ways. If the reality of your termination has been established, your next mission is to negotiate the best severance package you can.

Negotiating for More Severance

If you are offered severance, generally speaking you should ask for more. It is possible that the company will say "no." It is unlikely, however, that they will be so insulted by your counter-offer that they take their original offer off the table. **Maxim: You want severance negotiations to be like a ratchet.** A ratchet moves forward, or it may stop, but it does not move backward. Why are severance negations different than other negotiations in this regard? If the company is willing to pay "X" dollars for a release of claims and you respond and make a fuss, the company is usually going to be willing to pay the original amount, even if they do not offer more. The company's goal is to get closure. Once the decision to terminate has been made, that decision will not change. To be able to close the matter and put the file in a drawer, the company needs your signature on a release of legal claims. It is also rare for a company to yank the rug from under a severance offer because of a federal law called the Older Worker's Benefit Protection Act (OWBPA) which requires employers to allow employees over 40 years of age a certain amount of time to consider a severance offer, either 21 days in the case of a single layoff or 45 days in the event of a reduction in force. During this timeframe, you can make a demand for more severance without putting the original amount offered at significant risk. Theoretically, even if the company changes its mind, you can still sign and return the original offer within the 21 or 45 day time frame.

Severance is usually measured not in dollars, but rather in weeks, months, or years.[226] Many large companies in the 1990s offered departing executives one or two weeks of base pay per year of service as a severance. Back then it was also said that it takes a month per $10,000 of salary to find a new position. That rule of thumb does not necessarily apply these days. Another rule is that only CEOs with pre-existing contracts or employees with very obvious and strong legal claims ever receive more than one year of severance. Of course, there are exceptions that prove this rule, but one year is a strong psychological barrier which employers rarely cross.

Maxim: It is all about leverage. Negotiating for severance requires leverage. Leverage comes in several forms. The first and most obvious, is a potential legal claim. Leverage comes in other forms as well. If you know what other departing employees have received, use that information to form a floor for your negotiations. If you are leaving involuntarily on good terms and you have a long positive relationship with the company, instead of threatening legal claims, play to sympathy and kindness. Sometimes it works.

If possible, try to delay the actual date of termination. It is easier to find a job when you have a job. The best severance scenario (if there is such a thing) is one where you know you have to leave, but the company allows you to not only stay on the payroll but use the corporate office, telephone, email, etc. as you network to find a new position. This is rare, but it happens. Employers are reluctant to retain these types of zombie employees for at least two reasons: First, they cannot effectively obtain a release of legal claims until you have been separated from employment and second, they fear creating liability by allowing a possibly disgruntled employee open access to confidential information, trade secrets, and company email.

In negotiating a severance agreement, an effective technique is to ask for a list of items, bells and whistles such as severance (again, measured in months or some other unit of time, not dollars), reimbursement for health insurance (COBRA), accelerated vesting of stock options, a "bridge" to pension vesting, forgiveness of a company debt, your bonus or pro-rata bonus, a delayed effective date, a letter of reference, an agreed-upon press release, payment for professional memberships, waiver of a non-compete, a post-employment consulting agreement, the right to keep the company car or computer, payment of attorney's fees, or any number of other bells and whistles as described below. Providing a wish list of various items allows the other side to say "no" to some items and yes to others, especially ones that do not cost money. Once the company agrees to an item, it stays on the list and you can push back for more money. This also allows you to find out what issues they care about, and which issues they do not. **Maxim: Take the wish list approach.** The worst that can happen is the company says "no."

Hypothetical Scenario # 1 – Jane the SVP

Jane Smith is a 57-year old Senior Vice President for Acme Corporation which is traded on the New York Stock Exchange. She reports to Fred Jones, Executive Vice President, who reports to Wile E. Coyote, CEO. Smith has been with the company for 20 years. She has a B.S. in accounting. She earns $175,000 in salary and has 100 shares of restricted stock that vest in two months and another 100 shares that vest in 14 months, with a current valuation of $500 per share. She is openly gay. She has served on several committees with Jones and considers him a friend and a decent guy, although she knows he will support the company over her. Thirteen months earlier, Smith reported to the company's in-house counsel and compliance officer that she thought her peer (who also reports to Jones) was offering bribes in China in violation of the Foreign Corrupt Practices Act (FCPA). Nothing was ever proven, but the employee in question eventually resigned and stronger policies were put in place.

Jones tells her that he is re-organizing the department and bringing in a younger male executive from another company where Jones used to work to replace her. The younger male has an MBA, but otherwise has less experience than Smith. He presents her with a proposed severance agreement offering her one week of severance per year of service pursuant to an ERISA-governed company severance plan, which comes to 20 weeks or about $67,300, plus $5,000 for outplacement services. The company is six months through its fiscal year and doing very well. Smith was on track to receive a bonus equal to 50% of her salary at the end of the fiscal year.

Smith has several points of leverage for severance negotiations. First, she has good-will with Jones, who presumably wants to "bring in his own guy" without too much fuss. Second, she has a long tenure with the company. Third, she engaged in protected activity as a whistleblower when she reported her FCPA concerns, although that was over a year ago. Fourth, she may have potential claims for discrimination based on age, sex, and sexual orientation. Smith thinks it will be very difficult for her to obtain comparable employment as an executive, but she is financially secure and is considering starting her own small business. She has one adult daughter who is still on her health insurance. COBRA for the two of them will cost $1,000 per month.

The lowest-hanging fruit in terms of negotiating terms is the restricted stock that vests in two months, worth $50,000. The 20 weeks of severance are essentially guaranteed under the ERISA-governed severance plan, but in order to receive the severance she would have to sign a release of claims. An "opening bid", which might come in the form of a demand letter from her executive law attorney, might be 12 months of severance ($175,000), 18 months of COBRA reimbursement ($18,000), accelerated vesting in all 200 shares of restricted stock ($100,000); a pro-rated portion of her annual bonus ($43,750); cash in lieu of the outplacement services ($5,000), and attorneys' fees ($5,000), which comes to $346,750. Even if she ends up with half of that amount, $173,375, she is still $106,075 better off than the original offer. The risk is that the company takes a hard line, forces the matter into litigation, and Smith loses at trial, ending up with nothing after two years.

Hypothetical Scenario # 2 – Jim the CTO

Jim Rodriguez is 49 years old with a PhD from MIT. He joined ABC, Inc. four years ago as the Chief Technology Officer (CTO). ABC makes long-lasting batteries for electric cars and is owned by a private equity fund. Upon hire, Rodriguez received 10,000 shares of stock options at a strike price of $5 per share vesting 20 percent over five years and agreed to a two-year non-compete agreement covering the manufacture and development of "batteries, automobiles, and other automobile components." Rodriguez thinks the company will be purchased by a major automobile manufacturer in the next 12 to 18 months for $20 per share. Rodriguez has seven patent applications which he has been working on, but has not yet assigned to the company. Rodriguez did not sign a compliant assignment-of-inventions clause. He is listed as a witness in a major products liability case which is scheduled to go to trial in a year if it does not settle. The board of directors and CEO believe that Rodriguez, although a brilliant scientist, does not have the managerial skills to lead the growing team of 15 research employees in R&D and wants to bring in someone new in order to position the company for sale. Distrust and lack of confidence has increased since Rodriguez was anonymously accused of having an affair with a 33-year old engineer. The allegation is true, but the relationship is consensual. Rodriguez is fairly well-known in the electric car industry and president-elect of the American Car Battery Association. Rodriguez has an employment contract that states he is entitled to a severance of one year of base salary ($250,000) if he is terminated without cause. "Cause" is not defined. The contract contains a two-year non-compete and an arbitration clause.

Here, Rodriguez has several points of leverage: (1) He has a contract; (2) The company needs him to cooperate with assigning patents; (3) he is well-known in the industry; and (4) the Company will want him to abide by a non-compete. Rodriguez would need to show that his poor managerial skills and consensual affair with a subordinate do not constitute "cause," but the company would probably not challenge the one-year severance based on his leverage. Rodriguez would want to vest in his fifth tranche of options and, if possible, be allowed to hold them until the company is sold. He might also offer to consult for the company; but at 49, he will likely want to move forward with his career, so the non-compete will be an important point of discussion as well. Rodriguez should probably try to narrow the scope of the non-compete as much as possible (perhaps by referencing specific competitors) rather than try to get it removed altogether.

Common Provisions of a Severance Agreement

Separation agreements, containing general releases of employment claims to avoid future litigation, are a way of replacing the uncertainty for employers and executives of employment disputes with certainty of defined rights, compensation, benefits, and the settlement of all disputes. Common provisions contained in a separation agreement are as follows:

Resignation/Termination

Identify whether separation is a resignation or a termination. This may include recharacterizing a termination as a resignation, to improve the executive's job-searching opportunities, although this may preclude the executive from seeking unemployment insurance.

Transition and Timing

A phased final employment stage, together with outplacement and executive offices, may be very helpful in enhancing the executive's or professional's hiring opportunities. It is always easier to find a new job when you are still employed.

Unemployment Insurance

If the separation is structured as a resignation, an employer might suggest that it will agree not to contest an executive's claim for reemployment insurance benefits, since an executive who quits is not entitled to unemployment compensation. Minnesota law, however, prohibits such contractual promises.[227] For high-level executives, this is usually not a significant consideration.

Severance/Settlement Payment

Identify the payment to be made to the executive for releasing his/her potential claims against the employer. Common payment considerations include:

- A lump sum payment, or bi-weekly or monthly payments.
- Payment in succeeding calendar year may reduce tax liability.
- Section 409A issues.
- Automatic forfeiture clauses favor the employer by providing for automatic loss of future payments upon an alleged breach by the executive.

Bonus Eligibility

Eligibility for yearly bonus before the end of the year, or deferred or long-term incentive compensation before it is vested may be negotiated for the executive; either in full, or more likely, on a prorated basis.

Employee Benefits / COBRA Reimbursement

Executives may request that employers continue to provide various employee benefits, including, but not limited to, medical and dental benefits. While COBRA allows for 18 months of continued health care coverage following employment termination, the full cost of coverage is at the executive's expense. Thus, the executive may negotiate for shifting this cost to the employer.

Pension Plans

Although traditional defined-benefit pension plans have largely disappeared, some companies still maintain them, at least for grandfathered employees. In certain circumstances, executives participating in such a plan may attempt to negotiate a bridge to full vesting for retirement. Special attention should be given to the effective date of employment termination or continuing service credit during the severance period where this results in a bump up in the benefits provided under the executive's defined benefits retirement plan, e.g., reaching the "Rule of 90's" based on a combination of years of tenure and age.

Equity Compensation and Vesting Issues Upon Termination

As discussed, stock options, phantom stock, stock grants, stock appreciation rights, stock-funded deferred compensation plans, and ESOPs are all various forms of equity compensation. In the course of severance negotiations, qualified (incentive) or unqualified (non-statutory) stock options, which are unvested, may be vested, in whole or in part, by agreement; and exercise dates, which otherwise expire at termination or shortly thereafter, may be extended by agreement. Most employers allow executives

30 to 90 days post termination to exercise options, but some plans provide that unexercised options are lost immediately upon termination, providing an expensive trap for the unwary. Note that with regard to incentive stock options, such changes may require a "swap out" and replacement with unqualified options. Generally, stock option plans will allow the compensation committee some discretion to accelerate vesting, extend the exercise period, or even re-price or offer new stock grants as part of a settlement with the executive. The application of variable accounting rules and disclosures to shareholders of publicly-held companies, however, has made corporate leadership wary of such maneuvers. Claw-back provisions, taking back stock options, or gains upon violation of non-compete or other employee restrictions, may be demanded. An easier tactic for the executive in negotiations may be to request that the effective date of employment termination be extended in order to allow vesting in at least the near term installment of bonuses, restricted stock, or stock option grants.

401(K) or 403(B) Plans

401(k) accounts belong to and are controlled by the executive. Upon termination of employment, executives should transfer their funds to a qualified IRA rollover account or possibly a new employer qualified plan to avoid adverse tax consequences.

Letter of Reference/Press Release/Internal Communications/and Notice to Customers and Suppliers

Executives often request positive letters of reference and that, if the employer receives a request for a verbal reference, the employer provide information consistent with the reference letter. For a senior executive of a large company, an agreed-upon press release and internal announcement within the company may be necessary and appropriate.

Board Position

Any executive being severed from the company will usually agree in writing to resign from his or her board seat as well.

Cooperation

A contract may provide that the executive continue to cooperate with the employer post-termination for purposes of ongoing projects, litigation, audits, or investigations and allow for payment for his or her time spent in this regard, often on an hourly basis.

Patent Assignments

In some cases, executives may need to execute assignment of patents developed by them in the course of employment.

Non-Disparagement

Employers and executives often mutually agree not to disparage each other after the termination of the employment relationship. **NOTE:** Non-disparagement clauses are becoming more common in executive contracts and severance agreements. You should understand that "disparagement" is a broader concept than "defamation." Defamation is the act of making a provably false statement. Disparagement is the act of saying anything negative or pejorative, *even if true*. Because there is little legal guidance in Minnesota regarding non-disparagement clauses, companies often do not place an expiration date on these restrictions, unlike non-competes. Theoretically, then, if you sign a non-disparagement clause with your former employer, the one that fired you, in exchange for a few weeks of severance, you could be restricted from saying anything bad about the company for the rest of your life. I have seen executives sued for breach of a non-disparagement clause, so take these provisions seriously, even if you are the type of person who does not typically speak ill of others.[228]

Confidentiality

Employers and executives often mutually agree not to disclose their separation disputes or the terms of any separation/settlement agreement. Sometimes these clauses are tied to a "liquidated" penalty. Liquidated just means pre-determined. If you are found to have breached, you will pay a pre-determined penalty, sometimes $1,000, sometimes the total amount of the severance.

You should also take these clauses seriously. I have been involved in a case where a plaintiff agreed to a confidential settlement of legal claims including payments over time. When she blabbed about her settlement in the small town where she lived, our client, the owner of the business where she formerly worked, successfully went to court and was relieved of any future payments.

Release of Claims

All severance agreements include a release of claims, pursuant to which the executive agrees to waive and not pursue any employment-related claims arising up to the date of the separation agreement. This is the primary value that the company receives in a severance agreement – closure. The executive might request that the release be mutual such that the company releases any claims it may have against the executive. Some employers are resistant to such requests.

To ensure the validity of the release, mandatory state and federal law provisions must be included, such as the 21- or 45-day consideration period, advice to seek legal counsel, and the 7-day rescission period under the Older Worker's Benefits Protection Act.[229] In Minnesota, a release of claims under the Minnesota Human Rights Act (MHRA) is not effective unless it includes a statement allowing the employee 15 days after signing to rescind.

Understanding Consideration Periods, Rescission, and Revocation

Both Federal law and Minnesota law govern the release of employment-related legal claims. The concept is similar to lemon laws, which allow a consumer to change their mind after a cooling off period, after being pressured to sign a contract, or after seeing an attorney. "Rescission" and "Revocation" provisions can seem complicated to the un-initiated. (Ironically, the same federal law that requires a revocation period requires that release agreements be easy to understand.)

Here's the deal: Federal law only protects individuals 40 years of age and older. If you are over 40, you are entitled to have 21 days to consider a severance agreement that contains a release of claims under the federal Age Discrimination in Employment Act, and you have 7 days to change your mind after you sign and "revoke."

But, if you are part of a reduction in force in which two or more employees are let go at the same time, you are allowed 45 days to consider the severance agreement.

Under Minnesota law, a release of claims under the Minnesota Human Rights Act is not valid unless the employee is allowed 15 days after signing to rescind. Because the 15 days is longer than the 7 days, many agreements in Minnesota only reference the 15 days.

Typically, therefore, you have either 21 or 45 days to consider an offer and 15 days to change your mind.

Outplacement Assistance

Many companies pay for the cost of outplacement assistance or temporary executive offices at firms such as Lee Hecht Harrison or Right Management Consultants. My clients have found these services to be extremely valuable. If, however, you know what you want to do next and feel that you do not need this type of service, sometimes you can swap this out for additional monetary payments during severance negotiations.

Boilerplate Clauses

Separation Agreements also will include boilerplate clauses, such as those mentioned above in connection with Employment Agreements.

Who is "ERISA" and What Does She Have to do with my Severance?

The federal Employee Retirement Income Security Act of 1974 (ERISA) was originally passed to protect pension plans from abuse by private companies. It has broader implications to other types of employee benefit plans. Some larger companies have a severance "plan" that, for example, provides for a certain number of weeks of severance for laid off employees based on their years of service. If the plan is generally applicable to all employees and is based on a formula, the plan may be considered an ERISA plan, whether or not the employer designated it as such. An employee participating in such a plan may have a quasi-contractual right to this severance. It is permissible, however, for an employer to require a release of potential legal claims in exchange for payment of the severance. For an executive in transition, therefore, the ERISA severance plan may provide a floor of benefits, but the executive may try to negotiate for more.

CHAPTER 11

"YOU'VE DESTROYED MY CAREER" – DEFAMATION, TORTIOUS INTERFERENCE AND OTHER CLAIMS AGAINST THIRD-PARTIES

Social media is increasing the potential for defamation claims arising out of the workplace. Never before has it been so easy to have a career smeared so publicly and so quickly. The stakes are high when it comes to one's professional reputation. Many litigants decide to sue after they are unsuccessful finding a new job and feel they have no other choice. The majority of these cases are dismissed before trial at the "summary judgment" stage. Those that survive dismissal, however, can lead to unpredictable results, and two recent defamation verdicts in Minnesota were for $4 million and $1 million.[230] If an individual has destroyed your professional reputation, filing a defamation lawsuit sounds like a powerful way to fight back. But defamation claims are expensive and hard to win. A lawsuit may also cause the defamatory statements to become more public and more widely distributed than ever.

Defamation claims arising out of the workplace present special challenges. An employee might assert a defamation claim based on the stated reason for her termination, which she believes is false, whether the reason is communicated to another person within the company, to a potential new employer in the context of a reference, to the world at large, or even only to her (under a theory of compelled self-publication). Employees also sometimes sue coworkers for defamation. Professionals (like doctors and lawyers) also run the risk of being anonymously "rated" by clients or members of the public on online evaluation sites.

Workplace Defamation

What is "Defamation"?

To establish a claim for defamation, a plaintiff must demonstrate the following elements: (1) a defamatory statement; (2) published to a third person; (3) which is false; and (4) that tends to harm her reputation and to lower him in the estimation of the community.

Qualified Privilege

Qualified privilege is a recognized defense to defamation claims.[231] The most commonly litigated issue in workplace defamation cases is whether the defendant acted out of malice so as to defeat the conditional privilege that surrounds most employment matters. A "conditional privilege will virtually always attach, as an initial matter, to statements made about employees[.]"

Because defamation traditionally requires a communication to a third-party, the question may arise whether an internal corporate communication is sufficient to establish this element of a defamation claim. The Minnesota Supreme Court has held that "treating intra-corporate communications as publications that may be qualifiedly privileged, is the better view."[232] In other words, instead of deciding whether a communication between corporate executives about an employee of the corporation is a communication to a "third party," Minnesota law generally assumes it is, and focuses on the qualified privilege.

An allegedly defamatory statement is protected by a qualified privilege if the statement was made in good faith and upon a proper occasion, from a proper motive, and was based on reasonable or probable cause. The concept of qualified privilege is often applied to communications between former and prospective employers about employees. The concept is broader, however, and can be asserted in any context where the speaker had a legitimate purpose and good faith.

The Minnesota Supreme Court explained the rationale behind the qualified privilege in employment situations as follows:

> [A]n employer called upon to give information about a former employee should be protected so that he can give an accurate assessment of the employee's qualifications. It is certainly in the public interest that this kind of information be readily available to prospective employers, and we are concerned that, unless a significant privilege is recognized by the

courts, employers will decline to evaluate honestly their former employee's work records.[233]

Minnesota appellate courts have repeatedly and consistently recognized a qualified privilege with regard to communications by an employer about an employee relationship. A qualified privilege, however, can be defeated by a showing of "malice." Malice has been defined as "actual ill will, or a design causelessly and wantonly to injure a plaintiff."[234] Because a requirement of a qualified privilege is that the statement be made in good faith, this can be seen as the flip side of the same coin.

Workplace defamation litigation therefore follows a ping-pong-like pattern, starting with plaintiff's complaint of defamation, then defendant's assertion of a qualified privilege, next plaintiff's claim of malice, and finally defendant's motion arguing that there is no evidence of malice. There are various means of establishing facts to show "malice." Where there is an accusation of theft, misconduct, or a crime committed on the job, an employer may be barred from invoking the qualified privilege if it did not conduct an investigation. The second method to determine if a defendant acted out of malice or knew the statement was false is look for "extrinsic evidence of ill feeling, or intrinsic evidence such as exaggerated language or the extent of publication."[235]

Whether the defendant acted out of malice may be appropriate for summary judgment. Plaintiffs often argue that the question of malice should go to the jury. A court need not submit the question of whether malice exists to a jury, however, "in situations where the totality of the evidence does not support a finding of malice."[236] As the Minnesota Court of Appeals has noted: the "assertion that the issue of malice is always a jury question is without merit."[237]

Compelled Self-Publication

Minnesota is one of a minority of states that recognizes the doctrine of self-publication where the "plaintiff was compelled to publish a defamatory statement to a third person [and] it was foreseeable to the defendant that the plaintiff would be so compelled."[238] This holding seemingly opens the door for any terminated employee to file suit for a slanderous statement, even if it was communicated only to them. As a practical matter, however, few plaintiffs have successfully exploited this narrow doctrine and courts have construed it narrowly.

In recognizing the doctrine of compelled self-publication, the Minnesota Supreme Court stated:

> We acknowledge that recognition of this doctrine provides a significant new basis for maintaining a cause of action for defamation and, as such, it *should be cautiously applied*. However, when properly applied, it need not substantially broaden the scope of liability for defamation. The concept of compelled self-publication does no more than hold the originator of the defamatory statement liable for damages caused by the statement where the originator knows, or should know, of circumstances whereby the defamed person has *no reasonable means of avoiding publication of the statement or avoiding the resulting damages*; in other words, in cases where the defamed person was compelled to publish the statement. (*emphasis added*).[239]

Statutory and Other Defenses

The Minnesota legislature, recognizing that employers are wary of potential defamation claims by employees or former employees, has taken steps to provide protection from this type of litigation. This has created a number of statutory defenses to defamation claims by employees. These statutory limitations, all located in Chapter 181 of Minnesota Statutes, are sometimes overlooked, but are critical to any discussion of defamation in the workplace. These statutes may be underutilized, however, because they are either cumbersome or limited to narrow circumstances.

First, Minn. Stat. § 181.962, Subd. 2 limits defamation claims based on the content of an employee's personnel file. It provides, in part, that "No communication by an employer of information contained in an employee's personnel record after the employee has exercised the employee's right to review pursuant to section 181.961 may be made the subject of any common law civil action for libel, slander, or defamation" unless the employee has disputed information and the employer has either refused to remove or revise the information or refused to allow the employee to provide a position statement in the file.

Second, Minn. Stat. § 181.967, Subd. 2 limits an action against an employer by an employee or former employee based on an employee reference made to a prospective employer or employment agency, unless the employee or former employee demonstrates by clear and convincing evidence that: 1) the information was false and defamatory; and 2) the employer knew or should have known the information was false and acted with malicious intent to injure the current or former employee. The "references" must fall within the definition provided in 181.967, Subdivision 3 which is limited to:

1. Dates of employment;
2. Compensation and wage history;
3. Job description and duties;
4. Training and education provided by the employer; and
5. Acts of violence, theft, harassment, or illegal conduct documented in the personnel record that resulted in disciplinary action or resignation and the employee's written response, if any, contained in the employee's personnel record.

A disclosure under clause (5) must be in writing with a copy sent contemporaneously by regular mail to the employee's last address.

Finally, if an employee requests a letter stating the truthful reason for her termination pursuant to Minn. Stat. § 181.933, the letter furnished by the employer cannot be the subject for any action for libel, slander, or defamation by the employee against the employer.

Truth is always a defense. Defamatory statements are also considered privileged and therefore not actionable if the plaintiff consents to their publication. Depending on the alleged defamatory statement in question, a defendant may attempt to argue that the statement is one of "opinion", not "fact". According to commentary in the Minnesota Jury Instruction Guides, "[t]he cases [in this area] are difficult to reconcile and must be examined carefully."[240] Indeed, in one case, the Minnesota Court of Appeals stated that Minnesota law "makes no distinction between 'fact' and 'opinion.'"[241] Other appellate court decisions have held that only statements that "suggest verifiable false facts" are actionable.

Damages

Under the common law, there are four categories of slander *per se*: statements that falsely (1) accuse a person of a crime, (2) accuse a person of having a loathsome disease, (3) accuse a person of serious sexual misconduct or "unchastity," or (4) accuse a person of improper or incompetent conduct regarding a person's business, trade, or profession. In employment cases, category (4) regarding a person's business, trade or profession is most commonly relied upon, and attorneys sometimes misapprehend what "per se" defamation means. It does not mean, for example, that the claim automatically survives summary judgment, and it does not mean that the plaintiff automatically receives an award of damages or some pre-set amount of damages. Defamation "per se" simply means that the plaintiff need not show the existence of some harm or damage as an element of the claim. Under Minnesota law, libel of any kind is actionable "per se." Most defamation litigation these days probably involves libel of some kind, and therefore proving the existence of harm is rarely an issue.

So, what is the measure of damages in a defamation case? A plaintiff can potentially seek presumed damages, actual damages, and punitive damages, depending on the facts. Both plaintiff and defendant are likely to ask their counsel how much a potential verdict might be. The answer is generally that it is up to the jury and therefore there is little predictability. A few recent cases, however, suggest that large verdicts are on the increase.

Tortious Interference

Tortious interference has broad applications in civil disputes involving employment relationships and commercial transactions, yet it may be an unfamiliar concept to most non-lawyers and is little studied, even in law school. "Tortious" is an adjective describing conduct for which an actor is subject to civil liability under the law of torts. A tort is a wrongful act or injury creating a legal claim. (The word is derived from the Latin for "twisted" or wrong.) Torts are generally considered distinct from contract-based claims, but torts and contracts intersect in many ways. "Interference" can mean blocking, causing the breach of, or preventing the performance of a contract or business relationship. Tortious interference therefore requires three parties—two parties to a contract or other relationship and a third party interfering with that relationship. This triangular dynamic means a one-dimensional dispute solely between parties to a contract cannot give rise to a tortious interference claim.

There are several types of possible "tortious interference" claims under the law of various states including interference with contract, interference with business relations, interference with prospective economic advantage, negligent interference, and interference with inheritance, among others. Some commentators place them into two broad categories: contractual relationships, whether or not they involve business; and business relationships or activities, whether or not they involve a contract.

Requirements

Various states set forth different requirements for a claim of tortious interference. In Minnesota, the claim of tortious interference with contract requires:

- The existence of a contract;

- The alleged wrongdoer's knowledge of the contract;
- Intentional procurement of its breach;
- No justification; and
- Damages.[242]

According to the Restatement (Second) of Torts, § 766, a non-binding scholarly treatise relied often on by courts, tortious interference with a third-party contract laws means that:

- One who intentionally and improperly interferes with the performance of a contract (except a contract to marry);
- between another and a third person;
- by inducing or otherwise causing the third person not to perform the contract;
- is subject to liability to the other for the pecuniary loss resulting to the other from the failure of the third person to perform the contract.

The Restatement and some courts distinguish a sub-set of claims for intentional interference with another's performance of his own contract, as opposed to interfering with the performance of the third party. The restatement defines this situation as:

- The existence of a contract between the plaintiff and a third party;
- actual or constructive knowledge of the contract by the defendant;
- intentional and improper acts by the defendant inducing the plaintiff to breach the contract with the third party or causing performance of the contract to be more expensive or burdensome; and
- damages suffered by the plaintiff as a direct result of the defendant's actions.[243]

Tortious Interference with Prospective Business Advantage

Tortious interference may arise even when the parties have not yet entered into a binding contract. This is known as tortious interference with a prospective economic advantage. The Minnesota Supreme Court has held that to recover for tortious interference with prospective economic advantage, a plaintiff must prove the following five elements:

- The existence of a reasonable expectation of economic advantage;
- The defendant's knowledge of that expectation of economic advantage;

- That the defendant intentionally interfered with the plaintiff's reasonable expectation of economic advantage, and the intentional interference was either independently tortious or in violation of a state or federal statute or regulation;
- That in the absence of the wrongful act of the defendant it is reasonably probable that the plaintiff would have realized an economic advantage or benefit; and
- That the plaintiff sustained damages.[244]

What is "Improper"?

A viable tortious interference claim requires an improper act. The question of what is wrongful or improper is complicated and fact-specific. Originally, interference claims were limited to cases of violence, intimidation, fraud, or defamation, most of which were separately actionable as torts in and of themselves. For example, if Party C causes Party A to breach its contract with Party B by sabotaging Party A's delivery of goods or making untrue statements that the goods have been contaminated, a court would likely see that behavior as wrongful because it is outside the bounds of fair competition. Depending on the facts, Party A could also sue for defamation or trespass to chattel. A claim of tortious interference, however, captures both the consequence and the motive of the wrongful act in a more holistic way. For example, trespass to chattel might only allow recovery of the value of the goods, whereas a tortious interference claim might allow Party A to seek the lost value of the contract with Party B.

The Restatement uses the word "improper" and explains that that term includes, but is not limited to, "malice." Malice, also known as "ill will," is not required under the Restatement, but malice can be used as strong evidence of impropriety or intent. In response to a claim that an action is improper, a defendant can assert "justification." Justification includes but is not limited to, the legal concept of "privilege," but these distinctions are not always clear. What is improper or justified can be based on consideration of the "varying ethical standards of the community, and especially the standards of business ethics [in that community].[245]

Potential Damages

Plaintiffs asserting a tortious interference claim might claim economic losses including lost profits; equitable remedies (in the form of an injunction); attorney fees (as damages); and, sometimes, punitive damages, depending on the nature and severity of the improper act.

In Minnesota, damages can, in certain circumstances, be "limited to those that might have been recovered for a breach of the contract itself."[246] Damages must be proven to a reasonable certainty and recovery or "speculative, remote or conjectural damages is not allowed."[247] Double recovery of breach of contract damages is not allowed.[248]

In a case called *Kallok v. Medtronic, Inc.,*[249] the Minnesota Supreme Court expansively held that damages may be recovered for "all harm, past, present, and prospective, legally caused by the tort." It even held that attorney fees may be available if a new employer's tortious interference thrusts a former employer into litigation with a third party (the former employee). In that case, the attorneys' fees incurred in successfully enforcing the non-compete contract were considered damages in an exception to the "American Rule" that each side bears its own attorney's fees in the absence of a fee-shifting statute.

In theory, injunctive relief may be available against defendants in a tortious interference claim, so long as plaintiff otherwise meets the standard for injunctive relief.[250]

Because tortious interference claims almost always involve an allegation of intentional improper conduct, it is not uncommon for plaintiffs to seek punitive damages, but being allowed to claim punitive damages is by no means a given. "Even though liability and punitive damages contain the common elements of willfulness, a finding of liability for compensatory damages does not dictate an award of punitive damages."[251] In Florida, for example, the main criteria for punitive damages are "(1) whether the interference was justified, and (2) the nature, extent and enormity of the wrong."[252] That court held that, "to sustain a claim for punitive damages, the tort must be committed in an outrageous manner or with fraud, malice, wantonness or oppression."[253] In Minnesota, a plaintiff must present the court with "clear and convincing evidence that the acts of the defendant showed deliberate disregard for the rights or safety of others" in order to even ask for punitive damages at trial.[254]

Defenses to Tortious Interference Claims

Potential affirmative defenses to a tortious interference claim include fair competition, truth, justification, privilege, and advice of counsel. Other potential defenses include (1) the principle that you cannot interfere with your own contract (i.e. the lack of a triangle); (2) that the underlying contract was invalid, or there was no contract; (3) that no breach of the contract occurred (and its performance was not frustrated or hindered); (4) that the defendant lacked knowledge of the contract; (5) lack of causation between the act and the breach; (6) lack of a separate underlying wrongful act such as fraud or defamation; and (7) lack of damages. Truth is almost always a good defense, whether to a claim of defamation, fraud, or tortious interference.[255] The First Amendment protects spiteful, yet truthful, statements made by individuals.[256] "Fair competition" is also often raised as a defense.[257]

The advice of counsel that a contract is not enforceable can be a defense to the impropriety element of a tortious interference claim. The Minnesota Supreme Court held that the advice of an outside attorney opining that the non-compete agreement of a potential hire was not enforceable was considered a justification defense sufficient to defeat a claim for tortious interference against the new employer, even though the non-compete was found to be enforceable at trial.[258] This decision may have the practical effect of limiting interference claims in Minnesota under *Kallok v. Medtronic* (discussed above) against a company that knowingly hires a candidate with a non-compete, so long as the company can show that it received advice from a lawyer that the non-compete agreement was invalid. Similarly, lack of actual knowledge of a non-compete agreement can be a defense to a tortious interference claim against the hiring defendant.[259]

Tortious Interference in Employment Law

There are several ways a tortious interference claim arises in the employment context:

- An employee might sue a former employer or third-party for causing him to be fired, for example by defaming him.
- A former employee might attempt to sue his manager or supervisor for wrongful termination.
- A former employer might attempt to sue the new employer of a former employee for inducing the breach of a non-compete or other restrictive covenant, or possibly for interfering with an at-will employment relationship by raiding or inducing a breach of duty of loyalty even in the absence of a restrictive covenant.
- A former employer might sue a former employee for inducing the breach of a contract with its customers, vendors, or other employees.
- A former employee might attempt to sue a former employer for preventing him from being hired by wrongfully or falsely claiming that an enforceable restrictive covenant exists.

An Ohio court succinctly articulated the triangular requirement of interference claims as they intersect with employment law:

> "There are three players in a tortious interference claim: the plaintiff, the defendant, and a third-party employer. The employer being sued cannot be the third party in this type of claim."[260]

Because one cannot interfere with its own contract, an employer cannot be sued for tortious interference by its former employee. Sometimes, however, former employees attempt to sue their former boss individually, alleging that the former boss fired them out of personal animosity. As a practical matter, these claims are exceedingly difficult to win, but as a technical matter of pleading they may state a cognizable claim. In Minnesota, a company officer, agent, or employee is privileged to interfere with or cause a breach of another employee's employment contract with the company if that person acts in good faith, whether competently or not, believing that his actions are in furtherance of the company's business."[261] "This privilege may be lost, however, if the defendant's actions are predominately motivated by malice and bad faith; that is, by personal ill-will, spite, hostility or a deliberate intent to harm the plaintiff employee."[262]

Tortious interference claims can arise whenever there is a triangle involving two parties to a contact or other business relationship and a third-party attempting to interfere or hinder that relationship. The claim is elastic enough to be applied to a variety of fact patterns, but it is subject to many defenses as well.

CHAPTER 12

"I'LL SUE!"–LITIGATION AND HIRING A LAWYER

Attorneys find representing executives rewarding, but challenging, because the executives channel their formidable skills and energy, typically applied to their high-powered careers, toward their severance or contract negotiations. Executives demand 24-hour access and involve themselves in all aspects of strategy. Most executives are willing to pay for representation on an hourly basis and may have leverage that will enable them to drive a better deal. They may have egos, but they are prudent enough to seek and follow professional advice. These transactions are often not adversarial, but more like a complex business negotiation.

Finding an Executive-Law Attorney

Corporate executives often have an outside corporate counsel that they have worked with for years. When in need of personal legal advice, they may turn to this trusted advisor, only to be reminded that he represents the company, not the executive. These corporate lawyers may ethically refer you to a non-conflicted lawyer that they know and trust. If you are not comfortable seeking a referral from your former employer's counsel, look for someone with experience in the area and get referrals. There are thousands of lawyers in private practice. Your aunt who works in the area of wills and estate planning is probably not the best choice.

There are many plaintiff-side attorneys in the Twin Cities legal marketplace who practice employment law, but beware the plaintiff shops which file personal injury suits along with wrongful termination cases. These lawyers may not appreciate the subtlety of your situation and may be focused on threats and money more than your career. A good executive-law attorney is often someone who has former experience at a large corporate firm, where she was exposed to complex executive compensation issues and knows that these negations should be handled carefully, but left to found or join a smaller law firm to avoid conflicts.

Paying For an Attorney – Contingency or Hourly?

There are several ways to pay for an attorney. One is by the hour. Another is by "contingency", which in employment law is typically 33% to 40% of the amount recovered. If your attorney is willing to take your case on a contingency, that is a good thing. It shifts the risk almost entirely to the lawyer. Many plaintiff employment attorneys are extremely selective, however, as many employment law cases are dismissed on summary judgment.

Higher-level executives may not prefer a contingency. You may be able to negotiate a large severance without a lawsuit. It may require only a few demand letters and negotiation or confidential mediation. If you have contract claims which are likely to result in a $250,000 severance, it may make more sense to hire a lawyer on an hourly basis, at least at first. Forty percent of $250,000 is $100,000 whereas the cost on an hourly basis may end up only being $7,000 or $10,000, which most people would have difficulty paying, but executives may be in a position to fund.

Another form of retainer agreement is a "blended" or "hybrid" contingency. Under this type of arrangement, for example, the executive might agree to pay for the lawyer's time at half her normal hourly rate and agree to pay a reduced contingency of 20 percent of the recovery. The executive and the attorney may negotiate a different formula or different terms as well. These terms should be clear and understood by both sides.

Employment Practices Liability Insurance

If you bring a lawsuit against your former employer, the company may tender the defense to its insurance carrier under an Employment Practices Liability Insurance (EPLI) policy. EPLI carriers typically require that the defense is handled by an insurance defense law firm. An outside attorney and insurance adjuster can make negotiations with a former high-level executive like yourself more removed and less personal for the company, which can be a good thing. Insurance companies like to resolve disputes. For small companies, however, insurance means that they have the financial ability to defend without feeling the full sting of attorneys' fees.

The Demand Letter, the True Reasons Letter, and the Demand for Personnel File

The first step for attorneys representing terminated executives in Minnesota is often to request a copy of the individual's personnel file. The attorney may also request what is known as a "true reasons letter." Employers are legally required to respond to both requests.[263] There are several reasons for taking these initial steps. One is to obtain all relevant documents, including employment agreements, compensation records, non-competes, and performance reviews in order to evaluate potential legal claims under both contract and common law. Another is to lock in the employer as to one theory of the case or reason for termination so that it cannot make up another excuse later without having to explain its shifting explanation. Yet another reason is to show the employer you have rights and to force them into action. This letter can also put the employer on notice that there may be a legal claim and may invite settlement discussions.

Sometimes an executive law attorney will prepare and send a detailed "demand letter" to the former employer before commencing a lawsuit. This is especially appropriate if the executive has already been offered a severance agreement and has come to the executive law attorney to review its terms. The demand letter will set forth the background facts of the executive's tenure, highlighting her achievements, and asserting potential legal claims for leverage. It will also address drafting concerns with the language of the severance agreement, especially any restrictive covenants. Sending a letter before litigation allows the executive and the employer an opportunity to work out differences without escalating the negotiations to a public lawsuit which could be embarrassing for both parties. Discussions at this stage are more like contract negotiations than a lawsuit, but they may lead to a lawsuit if unsuccessful.

Litigation

Litigation starts with a summons and complaint. The complaint sets forth allegations. The summons informs the defendant that he, she, or it has been sued. Litigation can be in either federal district court or state district court. In Minnesota state court, the action is considered "commenced" upon personal service of the summons and complaint on the defendant(s). The case can then be filed with the court and will be assigned a judge and court file number. In federal court, the action is filed first and then served on the defendant(s). In Minnesota state court, an answer is required within 20 days; in U.S. District Court an answer must be provided within 21 days. In some cases, a defendant will file a motion to dismiss in lieu of (instead of) an answer to the allegations.

After the complaint and answer are served, the litigation enters its longest phase: discovery. This entails the exchange of information and documents in written form as well as depositions of witnesses. Depositions take place outside of the courtroom, typically in an attorney's conference room, but are under oath and very important.

On average, lawsuits take about 12 to 18 months to get to trial. Few civil disputes actually get to trial, however. In federal court for the District of Minnesota, only about one percent of filed employment law disputes go to trial. Some cases are dismissed at "summary judgment" and almost all of the rest are settled, whether at mediation or a settlement conference with a judge or magistrate.

Arbitration

Arbitration is an alternative to litigation. Arbitration is a process by which a private neutral party (an arbitrator), or perhaps a panel of arbitrators, is endowed with the power to resolve a legal dispute, and their decision is binding and enforceable. Arbitration is not the same as mediation. "Mediation" is a voluntary process where parties meet to attempt to resolve their dispute based on a common agreement, facilitated by a mediator.

Some of the more common arbitration forums are the American Arbitration Association (AAA), Conflict Prevention & Resolution (CPR), and Judicial Arbitration & Mediation Services (JAMS). Financial sector executives are also subject to mandatory arbitration under rules established by FINRA. In Minnesota, AAA is the most commonly used arbitration provider. AAA has rules specifically applicable to employment disputes which are available online.

Arbitration clauses are quite common in executive contracts, and for this reason executive law attorneys find themselves in arbitration on a regular basis. The arguments for arbitration are that it is confidential, that it is faster, and that it can be less expensive. One might challenge the cost factor considering that the parties must pay not only for their attorneys but also part of the cost of the arbitrator, who is not a public employee like a judge. But arbitrator fees typically amount to a small fraction of a party's attorney's fees, and if the process is streamlined as compared to sprawling district court arbitration, and potentially appeals, the total cost is often less. Confidentiality is a significant plus for executive employees because court documents are public, and in an age when access to data is so easy, an executive might prefer to not have their name show up on a Google search so as not to be viewed as "litigious."

Arbitration can also take many months, especially if attorneys attempt to engage in the same types of discovery and motion practice available in district court. The process is, however, usually less protracted than litigation, and good arbitrators are charged with making the process more efficient. A typical district court lawsuit can last 12 to 18 months. The median time for an arbitration to be resolved is 280 days.[264]

The AAA has published data that its arbitrators do not usually "split the baby", as is commonly assumed. Its survey showed that arbitrators made decisions in favor of one party in over 90% of cases.[265] An "all or nothing" decision was defined as an award in which the arbitrator awarded less than 20% or greater than 80% of the amount claimed. Only 5.34% of decisions fell in the range of 41% to 60% of the amount claimed.

It is generally not possible to appeal an arbitration decision unless there is a basis to argue that the arbitrator was corrupt, evidently partial, engaged in misconduct regarding evidence or scheduling, or exceeded his or her powers, or possibly that the decision was "arbitrary and capricious."

One of the criticisms of arbitration in small commercial contracts like cell phone contracts is that the arbitrator knows he or she has a repeat customer in the form of a company, whereas the arbitrator will not likely have another arbitration with the customer. This dynamic does not necessarily apply with regard to disputes involving employment agreements. I am aware of many disputes where the individual executive obtained very favorable and confidential outcomes in arbitration.

Litigating Claims for Unpaid Wages and Commissions

Anyone who has seen *Glengarry Glen Ross* knows that sales can be stressful and that "coffee is for closers." It can be especially vexing when, despite your successful efforts, your employer refuses to pay your hard-earned commissions. The law in Minnesota provides special protections for employees seeking unpaid wages, however, including potential penalties and attorney's fees. In theory, this is because wages are sacred and an employee who has to sue to get paid is not whole if he has to pay to hire a lawyer. Executives often have sizeable claims for unpaid commissions and wages, sometimes based on written contracts. These claims, if large enough, are attractive to attorneys representing such individuals because of the penalties and fee-shifting provisions in the law.

Minnesota statutes on unpaid wages and commissions are found in Chapter 181. The starting point is Minn. Stat. Section 181.13:

181.13 PENALTY FOR FAILURE TO PAY WAGES PROMPTLY.

(a) When any employer employing labor within this state discharges an employee, the wages or commissions actually earned and unpaid at the time of the discharge are immediately due and payable upon demand of the employee. Wages are actually earned and unpaid if the employee was not paid for all time worked at the employee's regular rate of pay or at the rate required by law, including any applicable statute, regulation, rule, ordinance, government resolution or policy, contract, or other legal authority, whichever rate of pay is greater. If the employee's earned wages and commissions are not paid within 24 hours after demand, whether the employment was by the day, hour, week, month, or piece or by commissions, the employer is in default. In addition to recovering the wages and commissions actually earned and unpaid, the discharged employee may charge and collect a penalty equal to the amount of the employee's average daily earnings at the employee's regular rate of pay or the rate required by law, whichever rate is greater, for each day up to 15 days, that the employer is in default, until full payment or other settlement, satisfactory to the discharged employee, is made. In the case of a public employer where approval of expenditures by a governing board is required, the 24-hour period for payment does not commence until the date of the first regular or special meeting of the governing board following discharge of the employee. An employee's demand for payment under this section must be in writing but need not state the precise amount of unpaid wages or commissions. An employee may directly seek and recover payment from an employer under this section even if the employee is not a party to a contract that requires the employer to pay the employee at the rate of pay demanded by the employee, so long as the contract or any applicable statute, regulation, rule, ordinance, government resolution or policy, or other legal authority requires payment to the employee at the particular rate of pay. The employee shall be able to directly seek payment at the highest rate of pay provided in the contract or applicable law, and any other related remedies as provided in this section.

To trigger the penalty of up to 15 days of pay, the employee, or her attorney on her behalf, must send a written demand for wages or commissions. If the employer does not pay after 15 days, the employee may sue for wages, the 15-day penalty, and attorney's fees.[266] Another provision of Minnesota law allows for double damages ("twice the amount in dispute) if an employer alters the "method of payment, timing of payment, or procedures for payment of commissions earned through the last day of employment after the employee has resigned or been terminated if the result is to delay or reduce the amount of payment."[267] Commissioned salespeople who act as independent contractors and not employees, can also sue for double damages in the case of commissions which are not paid within 15 days of demand. It is not always clear, however, whether commissions have actually been "earned," depending on the timing, whether the transaction was completed at the time of termination, and whether the employee was the procuring cause of the sale. Much depends on the terms of the written commission plan or employment agreement, if any. Disputes can also arise as to the application of safe harbor provisions in the law.[268] Finally, there is a separate statute in Minnesota governing manufacturer sales representatives, defined as individuals or companies that sell products on a commission basis to non-end users (in other words to retailers) and are independent contractors, not employees.[269]

Litigating Non-Compete Disputes

As noted earlier in this book, litigation involving non-competes can be very different than most lawsuits. In order to enforce a non-compete agreement, the former employer must first start a lawsuit. An employer may believe that the former employee may cause irreparable damage to the former employer by diverting customers or revealing confidential business information to the new employer. For these reasons, many employers seek to "enjoin" the former employee from violating terms of the non-compete agreement in the meantime by asking a judge for "injunctive relief." There are several types of injunctive relief that can be requested and granted during a non-compete lawsuit: a temporary restraining order, a temporary injunction, and a permanent injunction. These remedies are considered "equitable relief" and can be granted in the court's discretion after applying legal standards developed over many years by the Minnesota courts.

In Minnesota, courts have developed specific legal standards that parties must establish in non-compete related litigation. Under Minnesota law, the party seeking the injunction must establish that his "legal remedy is not adequate, and that the injunction is necessary to prevent great and irreparable injury."[270] The injury must be of such a nature that money damages alone would not provide adequate relief.[271] Additionally, under Minnesota law, "the burden is on the moving party to establish the material allegations."[272]

A temporary restraining order is the most extreme type of relief because it can be granted even without the other side (the defendant employee in a non-compete case) or her attorney being present. It is an extraordinary equitable remedy that may be granted only if "it clearly appears from specific facts shown by affidavit or by the verified complaint that immediate and irreparable injury, loss, or damage will result to the applicant before the adverse party or that party's attorney can be heard in opposition."[273]

A party seeking injunctive relief "must establish that his legal remedy is not adequate, and that the injunction is necessary to prevent great and irreparable injury."[274] In other words, the party seeking injunctive relief "must show that the particular relief requested will prevent the certain occurrence of an event that will cause significant injury—harm that cannot be redressed by a legal remedy."[275] Minnesota courts have held that, "[g]enerally, the failure to show irreparable harm is, by itself, a sufficient ground for denying a temporary injunction."[276]

Where the party seeking relief meets "the threshold showing irreparable harm," it must "make an adequate showing on the factors a court is to consider in granting injunctive relief."[277] These factors are:

(1) The nature and background of the relationship between the parties preexisting the dispute giving rise to the request for relief.
(2) The harm to be suffered by plaintiff if the temporary restraint is denied as compared to that inflicted on defendant if the injunction issues pending trial.
(3) The likelihood that one party or the other will prevail on the merits when the fact situation is viewed in light of established precedents fixing the limits of equitable relief.
(4) The aspects of the fact situation, if any, which permit or require consideration of public policy expressed in the statutes, State and Federal; and
(5) The administrative burdens involved in judicial supervision and enforcement of the temporary decree.[278]

Of these factors, "the most important is a party's likelihood of prevailing on the merits at trial."[279] "The burden of proof rests upon the complainant to establish the material allegations entitling him to relief."[280] "The trial court's ruling on a motion for a temporary injunction is largely an exercise of judicial discretion."[281] In federal court, the judge must consider four factors in deciding whether to grant a temporary restraining order or a preliminary injunction: (1) the movant's likelihood of success on the merits; (2) the threat of irreparable harm to the movant; (3) the balance between this harm and the injury that granting the injunction will inflict on the other litigants; and (4) the public interest.[282]

In some cases, irreparable harm may be inferred from the breach of a non-compete agreement. Minnesota Courts repeatedly have stated that "irreparable harm can be inferred from the breach of a restrictive covenant if the former employee came into contact with the employer's customers in a way which obtains a personal hold on the good will of the business."[283] Moreover, the Minnesota Supreme Court also has held that systematic solicitation of a former employer's customers further supports inference of irreparable harm.[284]

The Preemptive Strike: Declaratory Judgment

Rather than waiting to be sued, an employee or former employee under a non-compete can start their own lawsuit to ask a judge to declare the non-compete or other contractual agreement invalid through a request for "declaratory judgment." Minnesota's Uniform Declaratory Judgments Act empowers courts "to declare rights, status, and other legal relations whether or not further relief is or could be claimed."[285] The Act further provides:

> [n]o action or proceeding shall be open to objection on the ground that a declaratory judgment or decree is prayed for. The declaration may be either affirmative or negative in form and effect; and such declarations shall have the force and effect of a final judgment or decree.[286]

Parties to a written contract "may have determined any question of construction or validity" arising under the contract.[287] The court has no jurisdiction over a declaratory judgment proceeding unless there is a justiciable controversy.[288] "A justiciable controversy exists if the claim (1) involves definite and concrete assertions of right that emanate from a legal source, (2) involves a genuine conflict in tangible interests between parties with adverse interests, and (3) is capable of specific resolution by judgment rather than presenting hypothetical facts that would form an advisory opinion."[289] Since the construction and effect of a contract are questions of law for a court, where parties to a lawsuit are clearly contesting the enforceability of a non-compete agreement, the case may be properly amenable to declaratory judgment.[290]

Litigation as Metaphor[291]

Litigation is not Like Poker

In Abraham Lincoln's day, lawyers would wait until trial to reveal their evidence, which likely made for good drama and unprepared witnesses. Since the 1940's, however, the American legal system has required pre-trial disclosure of evidence in the discovery system, ending the days of "gotcha" trials. In poker, no player knows the strength of the cards in the other player's hands. Often you will hear litigants and attorneys in a settlement negotiation say that they are reluctant to "show their hand," meaning what they would ultimately accept. In this context, the comparison may be apt, as each side metaphorically lays down a card with each offer or counter-offer. At the end of the process, however, it usually makes sense for both parties to show all their cards so that a rational settlement can be achieved. Sometimes you can even split the pot. Leaving mediation without getting the other side's best number is not an effective use of the tool.

Litigation is Sjort of Like Football

Football is a game of inches. Litigation sometimes feels like this too, as lawyers review document after document trying to scratch out a first down. A lawsuit kicks off with a complaint and the opposing team returns an answer. The two sides then slog it out to an ultimate conclusion. Litigation, like football, involves offense and defense. I tell clients that when they are being deposed it is pure defense. You don't "win" your own deposition. In football, however, you can score on the defense.

In civil litigation, the client is the team owner. He doesn't have to be good at football, he doesn't even have to know the rules or anything about the game. He will demand a win and may switch coaches if he doesn't like how things are going. (If a team switches coaches in the middle of the season, or in the middle of a game, that is usually a sign of weakness.) Wealthy owners may be more likely to win, but the Green Bay Packers win lots of games too. Larger cases definitely require a team approach with a good quarterback. And, like football, the contest is played out in a large building paid for by the public. The way litigation is most like professional sports is that it has a referee in the form of a judge. Just as a football game can be lost with penalties and bad calls, a lawsuit can hinge on a motion for partial summary judgment or a motion to compel evidence.

Litigation is like War

Not to be hyperbolic, but litigation is really most like war. War is to be avoided if possible. War is bad for all participants. War is unpredictable and new parties can enter the conflict on either side. Most importantly, war requires resources. It can be expensive and drawn out. It tends to escalate out of proportion to the initial dispute. But, sometimes war is necessary. World War II was the equivalent of a bet-the-company litigation. Like war, litigation can be resolved at any time under any terms agreed to by all parties. And these days, litigation is like trying to wage war with a very robust United Nations insisting on multiple peace conferences.

Jury Trials are Like Elections

A party or her lawyer may state with confidence that they will let a jury decide the case. Former UK Prime Minister David Cameron was confident when he sent Brexit to a referendum, yet it did not turn out as he expected. Jurors decide on emotion, spin, personal experience, and a hundred other unpredictable intangibles. Many people were surprised by Donald Trump's 2016 presidential election after numerous polls projected Hillary Clinton would win. Trusting polls and trusting a jury are equally dangerous.

Litigation is like Life

Life's not fair. Stuff happens. It is better to look to the future than to dwell on the past. Don't hold grudges. The best revenge is a life well lived. Do your best and move on. Time heals all wounds.

CHAPTER 13

SPECIAL CIRCUMSTANCES – SCIENTISTS, FINANCIAL SECTOR EMPLOYEES, DOCTORS, LAWYERS, INTERNATIONAL EXECUTIVES, PUBLIC SECTOR EMPLOYEES, AND NON-PROFIT EXECUTIVES

Certain types of professionals and industries have unique considerations when it comes to executive law.

Scientists

A scenario I have observed more than once involves a brilliant engineer who invents a new widget that becomes the foundation for a successful business. For a period of time, the scientist runs the company. He then sells a portion of the stock in the company to obtain capital in order to grow. Then the new owners bring in a professional CEO to manage and grow the company, so the scientist can concentrate on what he is good at, tinkering and inventing, and not be bogged down with managing. Sometimes the founder or scientist stays on as Chairman of the Board or carries the title of Chief Technology Officer.

Scientists may need special legal protection if they are not politically-attuned or otherwise fail to look out for their own interests. It is important for an inventor to seek counsel and to protect her own intellectual property and her own ownership stake in any enterprise that results. (See discussion of assignment of inventions in Chapter 5 and shareholder rights in Chapter 8.) On the other hand, scientists need to know when to hand off the reins so that an MBA can run the company, not a PhD.

In larger companies, including many of the technical and medical device companies in Minnesota, employees with technical degrees may resent being passed over for promotion or being subject to the direction of non-technical managers without technical degrees. This frustration manifested itself as a putative class action lawsuit in the case of *Martens v. Minnesota Mining and Manufacturing Company*,[292] in which technical employees of 3M sought compensation for promises made under 3M's dual ladder program, designed in the 1950s to recruit and retain technical employees by providing opportunities for advancement for those who choose to pursue their career in a purely technical environment rather than in the corporation's administrative structure. Brochures distributed by 3M to its employees and prospective employees describe the dual ladder as "a worldwide organizational framework within which members of the 3M technical community may realize career development in either management or in the continued pursuit of their technical interests." The Minnesota Supreme Court upheld dismissal of the plaintiff's claims of fraud and promissory estoppel based on representations made under the program.

Financial, Banking, and Securities Executives

Executives in the financial sector often have especially complicated compensation packages. Brokers, wealth managers, and other executives working with clients also have an interest in being able to protect and move their book of business. Finance is highly-regulated, and many brokers are subject to mandatory arbitration under the Financial Industry Regulatory Authority (FINRA). For all of these reasons, financial executives face special challenges.

The Broker Protocol

In the early 2000s, contentious and expensive litigation between brokerage firms over non-competes had reached an all-time high. In 2004, in an attempt to minimize costly litigation, three major firms—Smith Barney (now Morgan Stanley), Merrill Lynch, and UBS—created the 'Broker Protocol' which eventually grew to include over 1,500 signatories. Effectively a sort of peace treaty, the Broker Protocol allows broker-dealers to move between signatory firms with certain, limited types of confidential client information without facing enforcement of a non-compete. At the time of publication of this book, the future of the Protocol had come into question following the withdrawal of Morgan Stanley, which claimed the Protocol was unsustainable and susceptible to legal tricks.[293]

FINRA and the U5

Each time a financial firm governed FINRA by hires an employee to work in investment and securities operations it must file a Form U4 for that individual, which lists him or her on the FINRA Central Registration Depository (CRD). Over 640,000 U.S. employees are currently listed in the CRD. When an employee governed by FINRA is subsequently terminated, the former employer must file a Form U5—Uniform Termination Notice for Securities Industry Regulation—within 30 days that sets forth the reasons for termination. Other FINRA firms can then access this information through the CRD before making a final decision to hire that person. FINRA rules require that the information on the U5 be truthful and sufficiently detailed to allow a reasonable person to understand the circumstances that triggered the termination. A negative U5 may make it impossible for an individual to work again in the financial services industry.

A public radio piece about fallout from the Wells Fargo scandal involving unauthorized bank accounts is a telling lesson for any executive in the securities or banking industry.[294] Jeremy worked in a Wells Fargo branch in Los Angeles. He told his District Manager at an L.A. Lakers basketball game that co-workers were falsifying accounts, that he did not approve, and that he would not participate. About a year later, he was told the bank was going to open an investigation as to whether *he* opened accounts of customers without their consent, or it would give him the option to resign. Frustrated, Jeremy resigned, but soon found it difficult to get hired at another bank. Finally, a hiring manager at another financial institution told him, "I really liked you, [but] there's this thing on your U5. I can't hire you." Jeremy eventually determined that Wells Fargo wrote on his U5 that he admitted to opening accounts for customers without their permission.

As noted, any individual who signs a U4 agrees that any employment disputes will be resolved through FINRA arbitration. An executive who thinks his or her U5 is inaccurate must therefore seek relief through this confidential arbitration process. The arbitration demand should be filed within 6 years of the entry on the U5 and should specifically request expungement. The individual may also seek compensatory damages for defamation or wrongful termination.

FINRA Arbitration can be costly and can take up to a year to complete. A more pro-active approach is to address the U5 in the context of severance negotiations. Although financial firms must tell the truth in a U5, sometimes a discussion with the executive's attorney may assist the company in understanding the facts and negotiating the characterization of events. (U5s may be amended if new information comes to light.) Financial executives and executive law attorneys should therefore remember to consider the U5 in the context of a termination.

Doctors

Almost half of all doctors, 49%, believe they are underpaid.[295] The same survey said that average income ranges from $315,000 for orthopedic surgeons to $156,000 for pediatricians, but typical debt is $141,000 and doctors do not start earning doctor-level salaries until they are in their 30's. Add to that the consolidation of medical practices as fewer doctors practice in small physician-owned practices and health care reform, and you can start to see where the frustration originates.

With a multi-trillion-dollar health care industry, however, there have never been more interesting and lucrative ways to earn money with an M.D. degree. A number of Minnesota doctors have successfully invented medical devices and gone on to establish their own multi-million dollar companies. Many move into management of hospitals, HMOs, and other health care-related companies where salaries run in the seven figures.

Stark Laws

Doctors may encounter special legal restrictions. The so-called "Stark Laws"or The Stark legislation as expanded by the 1993 Omnibus Budget Reconciliation Act[296] sought to address the practice of "self-referrals" by physicians. This occurs where a physician refers a patient to an independent clinical laboratory in which to undergo testing and the physician has a compensation agreement with the lab or has an ownership interest in the lab. I first encountered this in the early '90s with an oncologist who was also an owner of a chain of radiation treatment centers. The Stark legislation attempts to address the perceived overutilization of health care services resulting from such referrals by making such referrals illegal. In addition to specifying the illegality of such referrals, the law prohibits physicians from billing for specific "designated health services" paid for by Medicaid or Medicare when such services were provided pursuant to an illegal referral.

Stark Laws do not prohibit all physician referrals. The law specifically prohibits physicians, or their immediate family members, who have a financial relationship with an organization providing a designated health service from making a referral. In addition, the law provides a number of exceptions to the seemingly bright line rule, and legitimizes a number of specific arrangements between physicians and the entity to which the referral is made.

For example, the law provides for certain exceptions relating to physician compensation agreements so that payments provided by a hospital to a physician in an effort to induce the physician to relocate to the geographical area served by the hospital in order to become a member of the medical staff of the hospital is considered an exception to the Stark Laws. However, this exception is only applicable if 1) The physician is not required to refer patients to the hospital; 2) The amount of the payment made to the physician under the agreement is not determined, either directly or indirectly, based on the volume or value of any referrals made by the physician; and 3) The agreement meets other requirements imposed by the Secretary of Health and Human Services.

Termination and Discipline Issues for Doctors

Doctors faced with termination often face licensing issues as well. In Minnesota, an employer must notify the Minnesota Board of Medical Practice when a licensed doctor is terminated from employment. A physician involved in a dispute in the workplace may therefore find herself fighting on two fronts: a wrongful termination suit against her employer and a disciplinary action before the licensing Board. Common causes of physician complaints and "career sickness" are (1) drug and alcohol abuse, (2) boundary issues with patients, and (3) "disruptive physician" behavior which is typical of high-powered surgeons who intimidate or even alienate their staff and over time lose support of the institution.[297] There are a multitude of resources to help physicians address all of these issues if you acknowledge that you have a problem and you are sincere in trying to fix it.

Non-Competes for Doctors

Doctors often would like to know whether they must sign a non-compete agreement or whether a non-compete agreement they have signed is enforceable. In many cases, doctors with established practices use non-compete agreements to prevent their doctor employees from competing with them after their employment has terminated. When a doctor leaves the practice, the covenant not to compete places limitations on practice options, such as the scope of the employee doctor's future activities, the locations where the employee may not open a practice, and the duration for how long these restrictions will last.

Unlike some courts in other parts of the country, Minnesota courts have not, in a published opinion, squarely addressed a "public policy" argument in determining the enforceability of non-compete agreements for physicians.[298] Minnesota has recognized and upheld the validity of physician non-compete agreements since the Minnesota Supreme Court first weighed in on the issue in 1924.[299]

In 1983, however, the Minnesota Supreme Court declined to address the issue of public policy for physician non-competes, because it found the underlying contract unenforceable, but hinted that a public policy exception might be appropriate:

Dr. Freeman also argues that the covenant not to compete, even if valid, is unenforceable by way of injunctive relief because it is against public policy. We do not reach this issue, having already found the covenant unenforceable for lack of consideration. We note, however, that the Judicial Council of the American Medical Association discourages restrictive covenants as not being in the public interest and that three states have refused to grant injunctive relief in noncompetition cases involving certain medical specialists.[300]

In determining the enforceability of non-compete agreements against physicians, Minnesota courts have relied on the common law rules of analyzing non-compete agreements.[301]

The American Medical Association (AMA) has adopted a Code of Medical Ethics which dictates the professional conduct for practicing doctors. In an ethics opinion, the AMA has discouraged restrictive agreements, stating that "covenants-not-to-compete restrict competition, can disrupt continuity of care, and may limit access to care."[302] The AMA takes the position that "physicians should not enter into covenants that: (a) unreasonably restrict the right of a physician to practice medicine for a specified period of time or in a specific geographic area on termination of a contractual relationship; and (b) do not make reasonable accommodation for patients' choice of physician."[303]

In 2017, the Minnesota Senate introduced a bill, S.F. No. 1309, which would have prohibited non-competes for primary-care physicians. The bill was not taken up by the House of Representatives and was not passed into law. In some jurisdictions outside of Minnesota, legislatures have limited or prohibited restrictive covenant agreements applied to doctors.[304] In Massachusetts, the legislature adopted a statute that expressly prohibits non-compete agreements with doctors. Tennessee passed a law that permits non-compete agreements for doctors, establishes guidelines for the enforceability of those agreements, but states that the statute shall not apply to doctors who specialize in emergency medicine.[305] Colorado's law prohibits non-compete agreements for physicians, but makes an exception for the recovery of damages reasonably related to the injury suffered.[306]

In some jurisdictions outside of Minnesota, courts have limited or refused to enforce restrictive covenants entered into with physicians even in the absence of legislation prohibiting such agreements. For example, the Arizona Supreme Court refused to enforce a non-compete agreement with a doctor on the grounds that it would interfere with the doctor-patient relationship.[307] This logic has been adopted by courts in other states.[308]

In contrast, other jurisdictions outside of Minnesota have expressed a willingness to enforce restrictive covenants entered into with physicians, provided that the agreements are otherwise enforceable. For example, the Michigan Court of Appeals upheld a doctor's non-compete agreement because it was enforceable under common-law rules governing non-compete agreements.[309] The court addressed the principles of medical ethics issued by the AMA, concluding that "this standard merely reflects the common-law rule of reasonableness and states that restrictive covenants are unethical only if they are excessive in geographical scope or duration. Moreover, patient's choice of physician is protected by the modest geographical scope of the covenant and the liquidated damages clauses."[310] The Supreme Court of Illinois enforced non-compete agreements against multiple physicians, because it protected the employer's interests.[311] The Superior Court of Pennsylvania enjoined a doctor, because the court found there was irreparable injury.[312] The Missouri Court of Appeals enforced a doctor's non-compete agreement from the time of the injunction rather than the time of employment[313].

The professional code of the dental profession, adopted by the American Dental Association (ADA), provides "freedom of choice" for patients to pick the dentist of their choice "without any type of coercion." While this is not equivalent to a bar on non-competes, it does suggest that the ADA disfavors any agreements that might widely interfere with the ability of patients to see the dentist of their own choosing. Minnesota has enforced non-competes in the dental profession.[314] Minnesota courts have also analyzed non-competes for chiropractors and veterinarians under the same principles that apply for any other profession or industry.[315]

Nurses

Nurses in Minnesota who work for staffing companies, known as supplemental nursing services agencies, have special protection under the law. Specifically, the nursing agency "must not restrict in any manner the employment opportunities" of their employees and may not require a health care facility to pay a penalty if it hires the nurse directly.[316]

Lawyers

Many lawyers have successfully transitioned from corporate counsel to Vice President and eventually CEO. The more they act like an executive and the less they are providing legal advice, the less likely they are to be governed by attorney rules and the more they are fair game like any other executive employee.

In Minnesota, it is generally understood that lawyers cannot be bound to non-competes. This understanding is based on Rule 5.6 of the Minnesota Rules of Professional Conduct, which states:

Rule 5.6

Restrictions on Right to Practice

A lawyer shall not participate in offering or making:

(a) a partnership, shareholder, operating, employment, or other similar type of agreement that restricts the right of a lawyer to practice after termination of the relationship, except an agreement concerning benefits upon retirement; or

(b) an agreement in which a restriction on the lawyer's right to practice is part of the settlement of a client controversy.

A non-compete for an in-house attorney *might* be enforceable, however, depending on what other duties the attorney was performing, what information they were exposed to, and the scope of competition presented by the new potential employer. Professional ethical rules will likely be more constraining than any contract.

The lack of enforceability of non-compete clauses against lawyers is not universal. For example, in Michigan, the courts have not ruled definitely, but appear receptive to the possibility that "reasonable" non-competes on attorneys might pass muster. Both California, which generally bars non-competes, and Arizona, which does not, take the approach that forfeiture clauses may be upheld as to those lawyers who leave law firms and then compete with their former firms. At the same time, the American Bar Association has numerous protocols and rules addressing attorneys' conduct and professionalism. Although not binding upon states, they provide guidance that non-competes should not be entered into between lawyers.

In private practice, compensation is almost always based on client origination and collections as well as hours billed. Few viable alternatives exist. The Wall Street law firm of Dewey & LeBoeuf disintegrated in 2012 in part because it offered high-flying lateral partners contracts with guaranteed compensation.

International Executives

The Twin Cities region is highly connected to the global economy and thousands of foreign citizens come to Minnesota to work every year. Executives from large, European companies sometimes spend decades in the United States working for a U.S. subsidiary pursuant to a "delegation agreement" with their European-based parent company. American citizens posted abroad can advance their career but sometimes feel isolated from events back at headquarters. Americans moving to take a position in another country are usually provided with additional benefits to cover moving, lodging, and education for their spouse and family, and often have a staff including a driver and housekeeper as well if stationed in a country with lower labor costs.

Whether you are a non-U.S. citizen working here or a U.S. executive about to be posted overseas, you may have unique concerns regarding immigration questions, visas, payment for return visits to the home country, education for your children, relocation, housing and moving expenses, paid tax planning and immigration services, "delegation agreements" from foreign corporations, international taxation, coordination of dual countries' pension and "social security" programs, and related issues depending on the exact circumstances.

Getting Terminated in the U.S. for Non-Residents

Foreign executives sometimes get laid off right alongside their American counterparts. Often, these employees are high-ranking executives who would otherwise receive a sizable severance package. Whereas, a typical fired executive might negotiate a severance package and simply move on to new employment, self-employment, or retirement, however, executives who are in the United States by virtue of an employer-based visa face special challenges.

If the executive obtained his or her visa through the employer, the employer will have employed counsel to file the paperwork. In such instances, most attorneys consider themselves to have a dual representation of both the employer and the executive and should explain the risks and benefits of such an arrangement to the employee. Following a termination of employment, the immigration attorney who arranged the visa will likely counsel the client to notify U.S. Citizenship and Immigration Services. The employer may advise the employee to consult with an independent immigration attorney. If the individual seeks out the advice of an employment law attorney, that attorney should, at a minimum, have an immigration law practitioner available for consultation on the immigration consequences of the termination. In many situations, the employee will need to retain the new immigration lawyer directly to work on an adjustment of status or otherwise sort out the mess created by the untimely termination.

Technically, if you are here on an employer-sponsored visa and the company terminates your employment, you may go "out of status" immediately upon being fired. This reality has led to allegations of abuse or "indentured servitude" as employers require long hours, withhold pay, or worse from foreign workers, knowing that these employees will be reluctant to protest. Regulatory changes made in 2017 aimed to alleviate this concern by creating a 60-day grace period, under which holders of non-immigrant visas such as an H-1B could see a new qualifying employer, petition for a change of status, or, at a minimum, make arrangements to leave the country.[317] (H1-B visas are portable, but L-1 visas are not.) Regardless, individuals wishing to remain in this country after a lay-off will need to look for ways to change their status or find a new employer-sponsor. Even individuals who might be willing to return to their country of origin should be careful not to do, or fail to do, anything that might jeopardize their ability to return to the United States in the future. You should have a solid understanding of your immigration status, including what type of visa you have, when it would otherwise expire, and what other restrictions are placed on your ability to live and work in the United States.

Certain non-U.S. citizens present in the United States, including those whose immigration is family-member sponsored or based on the lottery system, are considered permanent residents and should have a permanent resident card ("green card") which allows them to work anywhere. Permanent residents are essentially like U.S. citizens when they get fired, because they have the right to look for any other job they can find.

It is not necessary to be a U. S. citizen to avail oneself of protections under state and federal law, and anyone who is otherwise lawfully working has the right to be free from employment discrimination or retaliation, to enforce contracts, and generally sue or be sued.[318]

An executive from Western Europe may be surprised to learn that the United States, unlike most other countries, has what is known as "at-will" employment. That means that an employer can fire an employee for any reason, or no reason at all, so long as it is not an illegal reason. A major exception to the rule is if the employee has an employment contract.

Because the application process for an H-1B visa requires employers to make certain representations, more than one terminated visa holder has tried to argue that the application alone constitutes an employment contract for a three-year period, which is the typical approval period of an H-1B. None have been successful. **Maxim: An offer to sponsor an employee's visa, by itself, is probably not an employment contract.**

In one case, the plaintiff, a French citizen residing in Venezuela and working in Puerto Rico, claimed that an H-1B visa application and renewal constituted an enforceable employment contract.[319] The Court disagreed, holding that "neither the filing of a petition for an employment visa nor the Permanent Resident Agreement signed by the parties can, in and of itself, constitute a contract, or even promissory estoppel." Similarly, another court held that documents relating to the defendant employer's petition to obtain a work visa for the plaintiff did not constitute a "memorandum or note" sufficient to satisfy the statute of frauds.[320]

According to a current interpretation, even if an individual is receiving a regular paycheck, including benefits, as part of a severance, the individual cannot properly be considered to be maintaining proper status for the purposes of an employment-based visa. The federal government has noted that "reduction in force (RIF) programs have become common in the workplace, including among employers of H-1B and L-1 immigrants ... but once the nonimmigrant's services are terminated, the alien is no longer in valid nonimmigrant status."

A nonimmigrant alien who is laid off from his or her position as an executive does have some options. For one thing, if there is a valid employment-law claim, it can still be pursued if the alien returns to his or her country of origin, although there are obvious practical limitations. In any case, a nonimmigrant alien who is laid off is best served by consulting an immigration lawyer.

Assuming the alien wishes to remain in the United States, however, he or she will need to seek some form of immediate solution, such as obtaining a new employment offer and nonimmigrant work visa or applying for permanent residence based on a bona-fide marriage to a U.S. citizen. Based on the government's interpretation as noted above, efforts to bridge the foreign national's employment status with severance pay in order to avoid immediate immigration consequences, especially if an employee who has been given notice of termination, is allowed to continue working long enough to work out an appropriate solution. Such a solution may be as simple as allowing the employee to continue employment until he has received a new employment offer. Generally, a person transferring his H-1B status to a new employer may commence employment as soon as the new employer's petition is filed with the U.S. Citizenship and Immigration Service (USCIS). An employee whose adjustment of status (permanent residence) application has been pending with the UCSIS for at least 180 days may leave the petitioning employer and change jobs—provided the new position is in the "same or similar occupational classification."

Public-Sector Executives

There are many non-elected and non-appointed high-level positions in state government which are well-paying and not significantly different from private sector executive jobs. Examples include county executives, city managers, and school district superintendents. It is common for many of these positions to have contracts. A significant difference from the private sector is that the terms of the contract, and even contract negotiations, cannot be kept confidential due to the Minnesota Government Data Practices Act.[321] Another difference is that you may be negotiating with a body of elected officials, such as a county board or a city council. Minnesota's Governor's Salary Cap Law limits pay so that no state employee, such as a school district superintendent, receives more than 110% of the governor's salary.[322] Payments excluded from the definition of compensation under this law include vacation and sick leave, health and dental insurance, disability and term life insurance, pension benefits, dues for professional organizations, reimbursement for actual expenses, and relocation expenses paid during the initial year of employment.

The executive branch in Minnesota is legally authorized to, and has on occasion, authorized severance payments for departing leaders of state agencies[323]. Legislators have criticized these severance payments as wasteful of tax dollars.

Non-Profit Executives

Non-profit corporations are different from for-profit corporations in many ways, but executives in both sectors are increasingly demanding, and receiving, employment law contracts. Although CEOs, or as they are often referred to in the non-profit sector, Executive Directors, may earn less than their for-profit peers, six- and seven-figure salaries are not uncommon, especially for leaders in higher education and health systems, according to annual surveys by the Minneapolis Star Tribune.

Nearly all non-profits, when they reach a certain size, recognize the importance of having a paid professional manager with experience in management, leadership, organization and fund-raising to keep the ship running smoothly. The Board of Directors may be composed of volunteers, and many of the staff may be volunteers, but having a paid, even well-compensated CEO is usually a wise decision and best for the organization. CEOs with non-profit acumen not only help further the organization's goals but can also prevent costly liabilities and problems in the long run, such as 501(C)(3) compliance that can bedevil even the most well-intentioned volunteer. The CEO of Community Action of Minneapolis pled guilty to theft and fraud in 2015 after being accused of violating several laws governing non-profits.

Attracting the best person for the job can be challenging, however, because of limited resources, and job security in the form of an employment contract may help. It is also appropriate in a non-profit context to protect against the whims of directors, who are not, after all, owners or elected by shareholders. Some of the unique aspects of non-profit executive contracts include the following:

Different Constituencies

Private sector CEOs report to a Board of Directors, but ultimately serve the shareholders. All share the same goal: to maximize profit. In smaller businesses, the CEO is often a significant shareholder in his or her own right. Non-profits, on the other hand, have goals as varied as the mission statements in their by-laws. The prospective CEO should be able to share the values of the organization while tending to its financial stability and interacting with the Board. While success can be determined in part by fund-raising, profit is obviously not the standard of measurement. Bonuses for non-profit executives are doable, however, and becoming more common.

Unpredictable Boards of Directors

The Board may be comprised of volunteers with little business experience and differing opinions on what the priorities of the organization should be. In some cases, the lack of business experience may lead to sloppy contracts overly favorable to the Executive Director, political infighting, nepotism, or mixed messages.

Government Oversight

Non-profits, especially charities, are subject to oversight both at the state level, usually by the Attorney General's office, as well as the Internal Revenue Service at the federal level. Excessive compensation or perquisites for executives and directors can lead to revocation of tax-free status, legal action, or other investigation. Along with limited resources, this increases pressure not to over-compensate the Executive Director. For example, the New York Attorney General sued Richard A. Grasso to recover part of the $187 million that Grasso received as compensation for serving as CEO of the New York Stock Exchange, a not-for-profit organization.

Lack of Equity Compensation

For obvious reasons, non-profits cannot offer stock options, stock, or other equity compensation to executives, and this serves as a handicap in recruiting. 401(k) plans are not available, although the non-profit equivalent, the 403(b), achieves the same purpose. In fact, one of the few legitimate benefits a non-profit can offer a potential executive director is job security in the form of an employment contract.

GLOSSARY OF EXECUTIVE LAW TERMS

The drafting and negotiation of employment agreements for CEOs and other high-level executives involves unique and sometimes colorful terminology, such as, "golden handcuffs," "blue-pencil", "red-line," "evergreen," "yellow dog" and even "brown M&Ms." Understanding this terminology and its application can assist executives, employers, and their advocates to negotiate the best deal possible. The following is a list of key terms for executive contracts, and their definitions:

1. **Arbitration:** An arbitration clause requires parties to the contract to resolve disputes regarding the contract with a private arbitrator instead of the court system. These proceedings are more confidential than a public lawsuit, but there is generally no right of appeal.

2. **Backdated Stock Options:** Stock options retroactively granted at a strike price equal to the lowest price of that stock in a particular year. Backdating is improper in most circumstances. *See, e.g., In re UnitedHealth Group Inc. Shareholder Derivative Litigation*, 591 F.Supp.2d 1023 (D. Minn. 2008).

3. **Blue-Pencil:** In some jurisdictions, a judge may have discretion to modify restrictions such as a non-compete provision by taking out a mythical "blue pencil" and crossing out some terms, while allowing other restrictions to remain, or possibly editing and revising the scope in terms of time, geography or otherwise. Some states allow blue-penciling, and others do not.

4. **Brown M&Ms:** The hard rock band Van Halen included a provision in its standard performance contract that required a bowl of M&M candy backstage, with all of the brown M&Ms removed. The provision was meant as a test to see if the performance venue had read the contract, which also contained many technical and substantively important requirements for the band's equipment. A brown M&M clause might refer to a trivial but specific term which is included to see if the other party is reading or complying with the agreement, or it might be set up as a basis

for a party to claim breach. It can also refer to prima donna-type demands of both celebrities and executives (such as former Tyco CEO Dennis Kozlowski who was accused of purchasing a $6,000 shower curtain with corporate funds).

5. **C-Suite:** A metonym representing all of the top executive officers at a company.

6. **Change-in-Control:** A clause triggered by a change in ownership or controlling ownership of the employer corporation, whether by acquisition, merger, sale of stock or assets, public offering, change in the composition of the board of directors, or otherwise, often resulting in certain benefits or protections for the executive. Sometimes referred to as a "Change of Control."

7. **Clawback:** A provision requiring the executive to surrender or pay back gains from the exercise of stock options if he or she competes or engages in other detrimental behavior after leaving the employer. Sometimes the company itself will initiate the clawback, but the Sarbanes-Oxley Act also authorizes the SEC to claw back compensation. *E.g. Securities and Exchange Commission v. Jenkins*, 718 F.Supp.2d 1070 (D. Az. 2010).

8. **Closely-held:** Generally, a corporation or business entity is considered closely-held if it has 35 or fewer shareholders or owners. Employees who are also shareholders in a closely-held corporation may have certain rights to continued employment.

9. **COBRA:** Consolidated Omnibus Budget Reconciliation Act. A federal law requiring 18 months of continued medical insurance, at employee expense, following termination.

10. **CxO:** Chief [something] Officer, describing the highest or "C"-level executives.

11. **Defend Trade Secrets Act of 2016 (DTSA):** The DTSA is a federal law which, among other things, requires any agreement regarding trade secrets or confidential information to include notice of certain immunity provisions for whistleblowers.

12. **Delegation Agreement:** Used by some European-based companies to govern the terms of employment for an executive sent overseas, i.e. to the United States.

13. **Double Trigger/Single Trigger:** Used in conjunction with a change-in-control clause (q.v.), a double trigger requires both (A) a change in control and (B) the termination of employment. A single trigger provision could allow an executive to quit and be entitled to a golden parachute (q.v.) in the event of a change in control.

14. **ERISA:** Employee Retirement Income Security Act. A 1974 law regulating private company pension and benefit plans.

15. **EU Banker Bonus Cap:** European Union regulations capping bonuses for banking industry executives at 100% of salary, unless 65% of the bank's shareholders

approve an increase to 200% of salary. An example of regulation meant to curb perceived "abuses" in executive compensation.

16. **ESPP:** Employee Stock Purchase Plan. A regulated stock purchase plan with specific tax benefits.

17. **Evergreen:** A contract that automatically renews.

18. **FINRA:** Financial Industry Regulatory Authority, successor to the NASD.

19. **Garden Leave:** Developed in the United Kingdom, a paid leave which does not allow the executive to perform any actual work, but prevents him or her from competing. A law proposed in Massachusetts in 2016 would have required garden leave pay for non-competes.

20. **Golden Handcuffs:** Any terms or restrictions that make it prohibitively expensive for the executive to leave, usually because he or she would be forfeiting significant stock options or other types of bonus or equity.

21. **Golden Hello:** A make-whole payment (q.v).

22. **Golden Parachute:** Any benefit, often a substantial severance package and/or the acceleration of stock options, that is given to a departing executive on his or her departure, sometimes as a result of a change in control.

23. **Good Reasons Clause:** A provision stating the conditions under which the employee can quit for good reason and receive some type of severance payment

24. **Hurdle Options:** A type of premium stock option commonly used in the United Kingdom, Australia, and New Zealand.

25. **Incentive Stock Options:** Stock options (q.v.) issued pursuant to a plan that is in compliance with and subject to provisions of Section 422 of the Tax Code. Taxable to the executive as capital gains when the stock is ultimately sold (not at grant, vesting or exercise.)

26. **Inclusion Rider:** A contract term required by certain A-list Hollywood actors mandating certain diversity goals in casting and possibly the crew working on a particular movie. Frances McDorman raised awareness of this type of provision at the 2018 Academy Awards.

27. **Katie Couric Clause:** A proposed SEC rule on Executive Compensation and Related Party Disclosure that would have required publicly-traded companies to disclose not only the salaries of their top five executives, but also those of top-earning non-executives, even celebrities like Katie Couric. The SEC did not finalize the rule.

28. **KERP:** Key Employee Retention Plan. Incentives offered to management and key employees of a company in Chapter 11 bankruptcy. Limited by changes to

the bankruptcy code in 2005. Often replaced with a Key Employee Incentive Program (KEIP).

29. **KESPA:** Key Employee Severance Protection Agreement.

30. **Key-Man:** A key-man provision may refer to any contractual provision that depends on the status of another individual who is not a party to the contract. Key-man insurance is a policy on another person, typically a key employee. Musicians use key-man provisions to ensure that they can leave a management agency if their agent is no longer with the agency. Newscaster Greta Van Susteren had a key-man clause in her agreement with Fox News which allowed her to leave on certain terms because former Fox News CEO Roger Ailes was no longer with the company.

31. **Loaned Executive Program:** A program whereby a corporation "lends" an executive to a charitable organization such as the United Way by paying his or her salary, as a way of giving back to the community, while at the same time providing the executive with a unique opportunity to work outside the corporate structure; sometimes but not necessarily as an alternative to severance or termination.

32. **Make-whole Payment:** A signing bonus designed to compensate for whatever the executive is leaving behind or forfeiting at his or her former position.

33. **Mega-grant:** Generally describing any stock option grant in excess of three to eight times the executive's salary and bonus.

34. **Morality Clause:** Also known as a Morals Clause, Bad-Boy Clause, or Bad-Girl Clause. A clause in a contract requiring a party to adhere to certain "moral standards" (i.e. by not being convicted of a crime or using illegal drugs) the breach of which can lead to cancellation of the contact. Often used with athletes like Tiger Woods in sponsorship and endorsement agreements. (Olympic swimmer Ryan Lochte, baseball legend Babe Ruth, and NBC anchor Brian Williams also had Morality Clauses.) In executive contracts, this is sometimes referred to as "moral turpitude" and serves as the basis for "cause" termination of employment. "Reverse morals clauses" allow the individual the same rights if a company is involved in wrongdoing.

35. **Non-Circumvention:** Agreement not to circumvent another party to take advantage of a contact, idea, or other opportunity.

36. **Non-Compete:** A restriction on future activity in competition with the former employer, whether as an employee, contractor, or business owner.

37. **Non-Disclosure:** A form of confidentiality clause, an agreement not to disclose information.

38. **Non-Disparagement:** An agreement not to make negative comments about the other party. "Disparagement" is generally considered broader than defamation, which requires an element of untruth.

39. **Non-Qualified Stock Options:** Options which are not subject to the restrictions of Incentive Stock Options. Taxable on the amount of gain at date of exercise.

40. **Non-Recruitment:** An agreement not to attempt to recruit away other employees from the old employer, generally for a limited period of time.

41. **Non-Solicitation:** An agreement not to contact or seek business from certain persons or entities, generally customers or clients, or potential customers, of the old employer. May also be a restriction on soliciting employees.

42. **Phantom Stock:** Phantom stock plans use units that are equivalent to, but are not actual, shares of stock, providing the employee with the value of an increased stock price without the corresponding ownership rights.

43. **Premium Stock Options:** Options priced above market so that the price must go up for the executive to cash in.

44. **Red-line:** A draft of a contract showing changes and edits, typically using the "track changes" feature on Microsoft Word.

45. **Reloaded Stock Options:** An enhancement allowing an employee to exercise a valuable stock option before the end of its term, using already-owned mature shares, without giving up the benefit of future price appreciation on the full number of shares covered by the option. When the option is exercised using a stock-for-stock exchange, a new option is granted covering the same number of shares as those tendered to exercise the original option. The new option, or reload option, has an option price equal to the trading price on the day it is granted and expires on the same date as the original option.

46. **Restricted Stock:** Stock that is issued to an employee, sometimes with voting and other ancillary rights, but which cannot be sold for a restricted period of time and is subject to forfeiture if the employee leaves before the vesting date.

47. **Sarbanes-Oxley Act:** Law passed in 2002 to combat corporate fraud.

48. **SEC:** Securities and Exchange Commission.

49. **Section 409A:** 26 U.S. Code Section 409A is an Internal Revenue Code provision applying to deferred compensation.

50. **SERP:** Supplemental Executive Retirement Plan, a non-qualified retirement plan for key company employees, such as executives, that provides benefits above and beyond those covered in other retirement plans such as an IRA, a 401(k), or

Non-Qualified Deferred Compensation (NQDC) plans. There are many different kinds of SERPs available to companies wishing to ensure their key employees are able to maintain their current standards of living in retirement. Sometimes also known as "top hat plans."

51. **Shadow Stock:** Another term for phantom stock.

52. **Silver Parachute:** A less generous golden parachute awarded to lower-level executives.

53. **Stock Appreciation Rights:** The right to be paid an amount equal to the increase in value or spread between the value of a share of stock on the date of the grant and the date the grant is exercised.

54. **Stock Option:** The right, usually given to an employee, to purchase stock at a certain price ("strike price"). If the actual or trading price is higher, the employee benefits from the difference.

55. **Stock Option Mandate:** A requirement that certain executives purchase and hold a certain amount of stock in the company in which they work.

56. **TARP:** Troubled Asset Relief Program.

57. **Term of Years Agreement:** A contract pursuant to which an employee promises to work for a time period, such as three years. If the executive leaves before the end of the term, the employer may not stop the executive from leaving, but may seek consequential damages and lost profits that result. *See, e.g., St. Jude Medical, S.C., Inc. v. Biosense Webster, Inc.*, 818 F.3d 785 (8th Cir. 2016).

58. **Tin Parachute:** Benefits or awards granted to all employees below the executive level, usually upon a change in control.

59. **Top Hat Plan:** An unfunded, non-ERISA plan maintained for providing deferred compensation to a select group of management or highly-compensated employees.

60. **Yellow Dog Contract:** Historically, an agreement whereby an employee promises as a condition of employment that he or she will not join a union. Such agreements are now prohibited by federal law. Rarely, the term is used in a different sense to refer to an employment contract with other restrictions, such as a non-compete.

TEMPLATE EXECUTIVE EMPLOYMENT AGREEMENT

This EXECUTIVE EMPLOYMENT AGREEMENT (the "Agreement"), is entered into and made effective _____, ____ (the "Effective Date"), by and between _____, a _____ corporation (the "Company"), and _____ (the "Executive"). Company and Executive may be referred to individually as a "Party" or collectively as the "Parties".

RECITALS:

A. Company wishes to employ Executive pursuant to the terms, and subject to the conditions, of this Agreement;
B. Executive wishes to be employed by Company pursuant to the terms, and subject to the conditions, of this Agreement; and
C. Executive acknowledges that Executive is receiving contractual benefits under this Agreement to which Executive would not otherwise be entitled.

AGREEMENT:

NOW THEREFORE, in consideration of the promises and mutual covenants contained in this Agreement, Company and Executive agree as follows:

ARTICLE I.

Employment and Duties

1.1   Term of Employment. Subject to the provisions for termination set forth in Article III of this Agreement, the term of this Agreement shall commence on the Effective Date and shall continue until terminated by Company or Executive as provided in Article III of this Agreement (the "Term"). Upon the effective date of such termination, all of Company's and Executive's obligations and rights under this Agreement (except those covenants, restrictions, and obligations which expressly survive the termination of this Agreement) shall terminate.

1.2   Employment and Duties. Company hereby employs Executive to fulfill the duties of_____, reporting to Company's Board of Directors. Executive shall have such powers, duties, and authority as may from time to time be prescribed by Company's Board of Directors, and Executive hereby accepts such employment. Executive shall perform such duties as are reasonably assigned to Executive by Company's Board of Directors. Executive, at all times during employment with Company, shall comply with Company's rules, regulations, policies and directives as may be in effect from time to time. Executive specifically agrees to sign, from time to time, and to comply with, any and all standard written policies of Company concerning sexual harassment, discrimination, use of alcohol or controlled substances, protection of confidential information and trade secrets, or related matters.

1.3   Full and Faithful Service.

   (a)   During Executive's employment with Company, Executive shall devote substantially all of Executive's business time and attention and best efforts to the business and affairs of Company, and will ensure that Executive is not at any time engaged in conduct that would constitute a conflict with the interests of Company without the express prior written consent of Company's Board of Directors.

   (b)   During Executive's employment with Company, Executive shall not engage in any other employment or gainful occupation, or be a director, officer, or agent of any corporation or other person or entity, with or without compensation, without the express prior written consent of Company's Board of Directors.

   (c)   Nothing contained in this Agreement shall prohibit Executive: (i) from being a passive owner of not more than five percent (5%) of the outstanding stock of any class of a corporation or other entity which is publicly traded, so long as Executive has no active participation in the business of such corporation or entity; or (ii) from managing Executive's personal investments and affairs; attending industry conferences, trade shows, and participating in professional or trade associations or engaging in other professional development activities; or engaging in charitable activities, provided that such activities do not constitute a conflict with the interests of Company or interfere with Executive's duties.

1.4   Principal Place of Employment. Executive's principal place of employment shall be _____, Minnesota. Executive shall travel from time to time to such other locations as may be necessary or desirable in connection with Executive's duties under this Agreement. Executive acknowledges that Executive's employment may require a significant amount of travel to _____ and _____.

1.5   Appointment to Board of Directors. Executive shall serve as a director of Company's Board of Directors unless or until: (a) Executive is removed as a director by the shareholders of Company; or (b) Executive's employment with Company is terminated as provided in Article III of this Agreement. Further, Executive shall serve as a director of any subsidiary or affiliate of Company upon Company's request. Executive shall not receive additional compensation for his service as a director of Company or its affiliates.

ARTICLE II.

Compensation and Fringe Benefits

2.1   Compensation and Fringe Benefits. The compensation and fringe benefits set forth in this Article II shall represent all of the compensation to which Executive is entitled for all the services rendered by Executive to Company and its affiliates in any capacity, including service as a director, officer, employee, or in any other capacity.

2.2   Salary. During the Term of this Agreement, Company shall pay Executive an annual salary of _____ Dollars ($_____), less withholdings required by federal, state and local laws or with the consent of Executive ("Salary"). The Salary shall be paid in accordance with Company's current payroll practices, shall be reviewed annually, and shall be prorated to reflect employment from the Effective Date. Company's Board of Directors may adjust Executive's Salary from time to time. [OPTIONAL: In no event shall the Salary be reduced unless such reduction is approved by Executive or implemented as part of a general reduction in the base salary for all executive officers of Company as a result of financial difficulties experienced by Company.]

2.3   Bonuses.

2.3.1 Signing Bonus. Company shall pay to Executive a signing bonus of $_____, less customary and legally required withholdings and deductions, within thirty (30) days following Executive's execution of this Agreement and provided that Executive actually commences employment on the start date specified by Company.

2.3.2 Discretionary Bonus. Executive shall be entitled to an annual discretionary bonus at Company's sole and absolute discretion. Such bonus, if any, will be determined by Company's Board of Directors.

2.3.3 Executive Bonus Plan. By December 31st of each calendar year, Company shall draft and provide to Executive an executive bonus plan, developed and approved by Company's Board of Directors, after consultation with its Compensation Committee, under which Executive will have the potential of earning objectively defined bonus amounts by achieving company-wide and individual performance goals (the "Executive Bonus Plan"). Company shall pay any amounts owed to Executive under the Executive Bonus Plan on or before March 15th of the following calendar year. Executive must be employed by Company on December 31st in order to earn or receive any amounts under the Executive Bonus Plan.

2.4   Stock Options. Executive shall be eligible to participate in Company's stock option plan. Upon execution of this Agreement, Executive shall receive a grant of ___ stock options in the form of a stock option agreement approved by the Board of Directors. Executive may receive additional grants of stock options annually, at the discretion of Company's Board of Directors. All stock options received by Executive are subject to the terms and conditions of Company's stock option plan, as amended from time to time.

2.5   Customary Benefits. Executive shall be entitled to participate in any life, disability, accident and health insurance, pension, profit sharing, retirement, or other employee benefit plan or programs in effect from time to time, generally provided by Company to employees holding similar positions and with similar tenure, if and to the extent that Executive is eligible to participate in such plans or benefits under the terms of the governing plan documents. Company reserves the right to alter, modify, amend, replace, discontinue, terminate, and/or supplement all of its employee benefits, in its sole and absolute discretion.

2.6 Reimbursement of Authorized Expenses. In connection with the business of Company, Executive may incur legitimate business-related travel, entertainment and other business expenses, all in accordance with Company's policy in effect from time to time with respect to the reimbursement of business expenses. Company will reimburse Executive for all such expenditures, subject to receipt of appropriate expense documentation from Executive; provided that Executive shall not incur any single expense in excess of \$_____ or expenses, in the aggregate, in excess of \$_____ for any calendar year without the express written approval of Company' Board of Directors or Chief Financial Officer. Executive agrees to repay or reimburse Company, on demand, for any expenses that are not reasonable or necessary for the conduct of Company's business.

2.7 Paid Time Off. Executive shall be entitled to _____ (__) weeks of paid time off ("PTO") each calendar year in accordance with the paid leave policies of Company then in effect. Executive shall schedule vacations so as not to unduly disrupt the business operations of Company. The Board of Directors may permit Executive to take additional paid vacation in its sole discretion. Unused PTO or vacation time will not carry over from year to year unless authorized by Company's Board of Directors. Executive shall not be entitled to payment of unused or accrued PTO or vacation pay upon termination of employment for any reason.

2.8 Paid Holidays. Executive shall receive paid holiday leave each calendar year in accordance with Company's policies and practices regarding holidays as in effect from time to time. Notwithstanding the foregoing, Company may require Executive to work on holidays as directed by Company or necessitated by operating requirements.

2.9 Taxes. Executive authorizes Company to make customary and legally required withholdings and deductions from Executive's compensation under this Agreement, including but not limited to, federal, state, and local income tax, FICA, Medicare tax, and other amounts Company may be required to withhold or deduct pursuant to applicable law. Executive shall report to the IRS and other appropriate taxing authorities all income received from Company under this Agreement as required by law, and shall be responsible for paying all federal, state, and local income taxes, payroll taxes, and other taxes and assessments with respect to all payments received from Company as required by law.

ARTICLE III.

Termination of Employment

3.1 Termination Upon Death. Executive's employment under this Agreement shall automatically terminate if Executive dies during the Term of this Agreement.

3.2 Termination Upon Disability. Executive's employment under this Agreement shall automatically terminate if Executive becomes totally disabled. Total disability means a physical or mental condition that prevents Executive, with or without reasonable accommodations required by law, from performing substantially all of the essential functions of Executive's position, which will, in all probability, continue for a period of more than six (6) months. Any Director may assert the existence of such a permanent total disability by giving notice to Executive and all other Directors. In the event of a dispute as to the existence of such a total disability, the matter shall be submitted to the decision of a physician licensed to practice medicine in the State of Minnesota, agreeable to both the Directors and to Executive. If the Directors and Executive are unable to agree upon a physician, then each Party shall select a physician and those two (2) physicians shall select the physician who will make the determination as to the existence of total disability. If Executive refuses to submit to such examination, Executive shall be presumed to be totally disabled for purposes of this Agreement. The date of total disability for purposes of this Agreement shall be the date upon which written notice of total disability is given or upon the written decision by the examining physician that Executive is totally disabled as defined in this Section.

3.3 Termination by Company Without Cause. Executive's employment with Company is "at will." Accordingly, Company may terminate Executive's employment with Company and this Agreement at any time, for any reason or no reason, in its sole discretion, upon thirty (30) days' advance written notice of such termination to Executive.

3.4 Termination by Company for Cause. Company may terminate Executive's employment with Company and this Agreement for Cause immediately upon written notice of such termination to Executive and the grounds therefor. For purposes of this Agreement, Company shall have "Cause" to terminate Executive's employment for any of the following reasons:

    (a) Executive's repeated failure or refusal to perform or observe Executive's duties, responsibilities or obligations as an employee of Company (for any reason other than Executive's total disability);

(b)   Executive's failure to follow or comply with the reasonable and lawful directives of Company's Board of Directors or Executive's supervisors (for any reason other than Executive's total disability);

(c)   Executive's material breach of any provision of this Agreement that is not cured by Executive within thirty (30) days of receiving written notice of such breach;

(d)   Executive's dishonesty or other breach of the duty of loyalty of Executive which materially impacts Company or any customer, vendor, or employee of Company;

(e)   Executive's malfeasance in the conduct of Executive's duties involving the misuse or diversion of Company funds or property, embezzlement, self-dealing, usurping corporate opportunities, accepting bribes or kick-backs, or material misrepresentations or concealments on any written reports submitted to Company;

(f)   Executive's use of alcohol or controlled substances in a manner which has a material detrimental impact on the performance of Executive's duties, responsibilities, or obligations to Company or otherwise violates Company's written policies regarding drugs and alcohol;

(g)   Executive's conviction of, or plea of nolo contendere to, any felony or to any crime or offense causing substantial harm to Company or involving acts of theft, fraud, embezzlement, fraud, moral turpitude, or similar conduct;

(h)   Executive's commission of any other willful or intentional act which has a detrimental impact on the reputation, business, or business relationships of Company and/or Executive;

(i)   The existence of any court order, judgment, or settlement agreement prohibiting Executive's continued employment with Company; or

(j)   Any other reason or act of material misconduct by Executive which would permit discharge of an employee of Company under written disciplinary guidelines applicable to Executive that continues for a period of thirty (30) days following Executive's receipt of written notice describing such misconduct and the corrective steps required to cure the same.

3.5   Resignation by Executive Without Good Reason. Executive's employment with Company is "at will." Accordingly, Executive may terminate Executive's employment with Company and this Agreement at any time, for any reason or no reason, in Executive's sole discretion, upon thirty (30) days' advance written notice of such termination to Company.

3.6   Resignation by Executive for Good Reason. Executive may terminate Executive's employment with Company and this Agreement for Good Reason upon thirty (30) days' advance written notice of such termination to Company and the grounds therefor. For purposes of this Agreement, Executive shall have "Good Reason" to terminate Executive's employment upon the occurrence, without Executive's consent, of any one or more of the following events, unless Company cures such event within thirty (30) days following delivery of such written notice:

(a)   Company has, without Cause, removed Executive as the _____ of Company;

(b)   Company has, without Cause, materially reduced Executive's duties and responsibilities, compensation, employee benefits, or title;

(c)   Company has materially breached any of the provisions of this Agreement;

(d)   Company requires Executive to relocate outside of the Minneapolis/St. Paul, Minnesota metropolitan area;

(e)   Company's bankruptcy or insolvency; or

(f)   Company's assignment for the benefit of creditors or similar disposition of the assets of Company's business.

3.7   Resignation From Other Positions. Executive agrees that following notice of termination of this Agreement by either Party, for any reason, Executive will resign, in writing, from all other positions with Company and its affiliates, including those as an officer, manager, director, governor, or committee member, effective on the date this Agreement terminates.

3.8   Notification of Subsequent Employer. Executive agrees that Company may provide a copy of this Agreement to and notify any of Executive's subsequent employers of Executive's obligations under this Agreement.

ARTICLE IV.

Payment in the Event of Termination of Employment

4.1   Termination Upon Death or Disability. In the event Executive's employment terminates as a result of Executive's death or total disability: (a) Company shall pay Executive or Executive's estate any unpaid Salary earned through the date of termination; (b) Company shall reimburse Executive or Executive's estate for all unpaid expenses incurred prior to the date of termination in accordance with Company policy; (c) Company shall pay Executive or Executive's estate any bonus payments earned prior to Executive's death or disability (and such payment will be made on the date any such bonus payments are made to other officers of Company); and (d) Executive shall not be entitled to any other salary, compensation, or benefits following the date of termination, except as expressly required by applicable law.

4.2   Termination by Company With Cause or by Executive Without Good Reason. If Company terminates Executive's employment with Cause, or Executive terminates this Agreement without Good Reason: (a) Company shall pay Executive any unpaid Salary earned through the date of termination; (b) Company shall reimburse Executive for all unpaid expenses incurred prior to the date of termination in accordance with Company policy; (c) Company shall pay Executive any bonus payments earned prior to termination (and such payment will be made on the date any such bonus payments are made to other officers of Company); and (d) Executive shall not be entitled to any other salary, compensation, or benefits following the date of termination, except as expressly required by applicable law.

4.3   Termination by Company Without Cause or by Executive for Good Reason. If Company terminates Executive's employment without Cause, or Executive terminates this Agreement for Good Reason: (a) Company shall pay Executive any unpaid Salary earned through the date of termination; (b) Company shall reimburse Executive for all unpaid expenses incurred prior to the date of termination in accordance with Company policy; (c) Company shall pay Executive any bonus payments earned prior to termination (and such payment will be made on the date any such bonus payments are made to other officers of Company); (d) Company shall pay severance to Executive in an amount equal to twelve (12) months of Executive's base Salary last in effect on the date of termination (the "Severance Pay"), provided that Executive executes, returns to Company within twenty-one (21) calendar days after the date this Agreement terminates, and does not rescind or revoke, a release of claims in favor of Company in the form attached hereto as Exhibit A (the "Release of Claims"); and (e) Executive shall not be entitled to any other salary, compensation, or benefits following the date of termination, except as expressly required by applicable law.

4.4   Termination Following a Change in Control. The Board of Directors of Company has determined that it is in the best interests of Company and its stockholders to assure that Company will have Executive's continued dedication, notwithstanding the possibility, threat, or occurrence of a Change in Control (as defined in Section 4.4.1 below). In light of the foregoing, Company believes it is imperative to diminish the inevitable distraction to the Executive by virtue of the personal uncertainties and risks created by a pending or threatened Change in Control and to encourage

Executive's full attention and dedication to Company currently and in the event of any threatened or pending Change in Control, and to provide Executive with compensation and benefits arrangements upon a Change in Control that are satisfactory to Executive and are competitive with those of other similarly-situated companies. Therefore, in order to accomplish these objectives, Company and Executive agree as follows:

4.4.1   Definition of Change in Control. "Change in Control" shall mean, and shall be deemed to have occurred if, on or after the Effective Date of this Agreement: (i) any "person" (as such term is used in Sections 13(d) and 14(d) of the Securities Exchange Act of 1934, as amended) or group acting in concert, other than a trustee or other fiduciary holding securities under an employee benefit plan of Company acting in such capacity or a corporation owned directly or indirectly by the stockholders of Company in substantially the same proportions as their ownership of stock of Company, becomes the "beneficial owner" (as defined in Rule 13d-3 under said Act), directly or indirectly, of securities of the Company representing more than fifty percent (50%) of the total voting power represented by Company's then outstanding voting securities; (ii) during any 12-month period, individuals who at the beginning of such period constitute the Board of Directors of Company and any new director whose election by the Board of Directors or nomination for election by Company's stockholders was approved by a vote of at least two thirds (2/3) of the directors then still in office who either were directors at the beginning of the period or whose election or nomination for election was previously so approved, cease for any reason to constitute a majority thereof; (iii) the consummation of a merger or consolidation of Company with any other corporation other than a merger or consolidation which would result in the voting securities of the Company outstanding immediately prior thereto continuing to represent (either by remaining outstanding or by being converted into voting securities of the surviving entity) at least fifty percent (50%) of the total voting power represented by the voting securities of the Company or such surviving entity outstanding immediately after such merger or consolidation; or (iv) the sale or disposition by Company of (in one transaction or a series of related transactions) all or substantially all of Company's assets.

4.4.2   Payment Upon Change in Control. In addition to any Severance Pay provided under Section 4.3, if (i) within twelve (12) months after a Change in Control, Company (or a successor) terminates Executive without Cause or Executive terminates for Good Reason; or (ii) within four (4) months after Company terminates Executive without Cause or Executive terminates for Good Reason, a Change in Control occurs, then Company shall pay additional severance to Executive in an amount equal to six (6) months of Executive's base Salary last in effect on the date of termination (the "Change in Control Severance Pay"). The combined Severance Pay and Change in Control Severance Pay shall equal eighteen (18) months of Executive's base Salary last in effect on the date of termination.

4.4.3   Acceleration of Vesting of Equity Awards. If (i) within twelve (12) months after a Change in Control, Company (or a successor) terminates Executive without Cause or Executive terminates for Good Reason; (ii) within four (4) months after Company terminates Executive without Cause or Executive terminates for Good Reason, a Change in Control occurs; or (iii) Executive remains employed by Company (or any successor) at least six (6) months following a Change in Control, then one hundred percent (100%) of the then unvested equity awards granted to Executive, whether stock options, restricted stock, restricted stock units or stock purchase rights under Company's equity compensation plan, or other equity awards, shall immediately become fully vested and exercisable, notwithstanding anything contained herein or in any of Executive's equity grant agreements to the contrary (including any provision that would otherwise result in a termination of such award). Subject to this Section , Executive will be entitled to exercise such vested equity awards in accordance with the applicable grant agreements.

4.4.4.   Conditions Precedent. Company's obligations to Executive described in Sections 4.4.2 and 4.4.3 are contingent on Executive's delivery to Company or its successor of a signed Release of Claims in the form attached hereto as Exhibit A and Executive not revoking such Release of Claims. Moreover, Executive's rights to receive ongoing payments and benefits pursuant to Sections 4.4.2 and 4.4.3 (including, without limitation, the right to ongoing payments under Company's equity plans) are conditioned on the Executive's ongoing compliance with the obligations described in Articles V, VI, and VII of this Agreement. Any cessation by Company of any such payments and benefits shall be in addition to, and not in lieu of, any and all other remedies available to Company for Executive's breach of the obligations described in Articles V, VI, and VII of this Agreement.

4.5   Taxation, Gross-Up and Excess Parachute Payments.

4.5.1 Excess Parachute Payment. If the post-Change in Control payment(s) set forth in Section 4.4 of this Agreement would be subject to the excise tax imposed by Section 4999 of the Internal Revenue Code of 1986, as amended (the "Code"), on "excess parachute payments" within the meaning of Section 280G(b)(1) of the Code, Company will pay to Executive, with respect to the payments (or events treated as payments under such Section 4999) that give rise to such Excise Tax (an "Excise Taxable Payment"), an additional amount (the "Gross Up Payment") that is equal to the lesser of: (a) an amount such that the net amount retained by Executive from all such Excise Taxable Payments, after deduction of any Excise Tax on all Excise Taxable Payments and any federal, state and local income taxes and employment taxes (together with penalties and interest) as well as the Excise Tax upon the payment or payments provided for by this clause (a) of this Section 4.5.1, will be equal to the aggregate amount of all such Excise Taxable Payments (excluding all amounts payable pursuant to this clause (a)); or (b) an amount equal to 1.25 multiplied by Executive's annual base Salary in effect immediately prior to the date of the Change in Control. Company's independent outside executive compensation consultant has reviewed this provision and determined that it is reasonable based upon a comparison of comparable executive compensation retirement benefits provided to similarly situated executives like Executive in comparable corporations.

4.5.2 Applicable Rates. For purposes of determining the amount of the Gross Up Payment, Executive will be deemed to pay federal income taxes at the highest marginal rate of federal income taxation in the calendar year in which the Gross Up Payment is to be made and state and local income taxes at the highest marginal rates of taxation in the state and locality of Executive's primary residence for the calendar year in which the Gross Up Payment is to be made, net of the maximum reduction in federal income taxes that could be obtained from deduction of such state and local taxes.

4.5.3 Time for Payment. Company will pay the estimated amount of the Gross Up Payment in cash to Executive at such time or times when the Excise Tax is due. Executive and Company and their respective tax advisors agree to confer and reasonably cooperate in the determination of the actual amount of the Gross Up Payment. Without limiting the foregoing, Executive shall, if requested by Company, cooperate in a determination of Executive's obligations under this Section 4.5 by a valuation firm selected and paid for by Company. Furthermore, Executive and Company agree to make such adjustments to the estimated amount of the Gross Up Payment as may be necessary to equal the actual amount of the Gross Up Payment, which in the case of Executive will refer to refunds of prior overpayments and in the case of Company will refer to makeup of prior underpayments.

4.6   Section 409A.

    4.6.1   Compliance with Code Section 409A. To the extent applicable, it is intended that the compensation arrangements under this Agreement be in full compliance with Section 409A of the Code and the Treasury Regulations and guidance issued thereunder ("Code Section 409A"). This Agreement shall be construed in a manner to give effect to such intention. In no event, however, shall the Company or any of its affiliates be liable for any tax, interest, or penalties that may be imposed on Executive under Code Section 409A. Neither Company nor any of its affiliates have any obligation to indemnify or otherwise hold Executive harmless from any or all such taxes, interest or penalties, or liability for any damages related thereto.

    4.6.2   Application to Severance Compensation. This Section 4.6 shall apply to all or any portion of any payment or benefit payable under this Agreement as a result of termination of Executive's employment that is not exempted from Code Section 409A ("409A Severance Compensation").

    4.6.3   Separation from Service. A termination of employment shall not be deemed to have occurred for purposes of any provision of this Agreement providing for the payment of any amounts or benefits upon or following a termination of employment unless such termination is also a "Separation from Service" within the meaning of Code Section 409A and, for purposes of any such provision of this Agreement, references to a "termination," "termination of employment" or like terms shall mean Separation from Service.

    4.6.4   Specified Employee. If Executive is deemed on the date of termination of employment to be a "specified employee", within the meaning of that term under Code Section 409A(a)(2)(B) and using the identification methodology selected by Company from time to time, or if none, the default methodology, then with regard to any payment or the providing of any benefit required to be delayed in compliance with Code Section 409A(a)(2)(B), and any other payment or the provision of any other benefit that is required to be delayed in compliance with Code Section 409A(a)(2)(B), such payment or benefit shall not be made or provided prior to the earlier of: (a) the expiration of the six-month period measured from the date of Executive's Separation from Service; or (b) the date of Executive's death.

4.6.5 Change in Control. Notwithstanding any provision in this Agreement to the contrary, solely to the extent necessary to comply with Code Section 409A, a Change in Control as defined above shall not be deemed to have occurred unless the transaction (or series of related transactions) in question also constitutes a change in the ownership or effective control of Company or the ownership of a substantial portion of Company's assets within the meaning of Code Section 409A.

4.6.6 Separate Payment. For the purposes of this Agreement, each payment that is part of a series of installment payments shall be treated as a separate payment for purposes of Code Section 409A.

4.6.7 Acceleration of Payments. Neither Company nor Executive, individually or in combination, may accelerate any payment or benefit that is subject to Code Section 409A, except in compliance with Code Section 409A and the provisions of this Agreement, and no amount that is subject to Code Section 409A shall be paid prior to the earliest date on which it may be paid without violating Code Section 409A. The exercise date of any stock right shall not be extended to a date that would cause the stock right to be subject to Code Section 409A as a result of the extension.

ARTICLE V.

Non-Disclosure of Confidential Information

5.1 Non-Disclosure of Confidential Information. Executive shall not in any manner or form disclose, provide, or otherwise make available, in whole or in part, any Confidential Information to any person or entity, or use any Confidential Information for Executive's own benefit or for the benefit of any person or entity other than Company, without the prior written consent of Company. Executive shall not in any manner or form use or permit others within Executive's control to use any Confidential Information for Executive's own benefit or for the benefit of any person or entity other than Company, without the prior written consent of Company. Executive may disclose Confidential Information to other employees of Company so long as such disclosure is in confidence and for purposes specifically related to Executive's work for Company and so long as such persons are subject to Executive's security and control. Executive shall take all necessary or advisable action, whether by instruction, agreement or otherwise, to ensure the protection, confidentiality and security of, and to satisfy Executive's obligations under this Agreement with respect to the protection, confidentiality and security of, all Confidential Information. These obligations do not apply to any Confidential Information that is now, or becomes generally available to the public through no fault of Executive or to Executive's disclosure of any Confidential Information required by law or judicial or administrative process.

5.2   Definition of Confidential Information. For purposes of this Agreement, "Confidential Information" shall mean any information, compilation of information, knowledge and know-how that Executive receives from Company, becomes aware of, learns of, or develops during the course of Executive's employment which is not generally known or readily ascertainable by proper means by persons who are not employees of Company. It includes, but is not limited to, information relating to any of the business affairs of Company, trade secrets, pricing information, marketing information, strategic planning, selling information, leasing information, servicing and financing information, compensation information, customer and client information, customer lists, manuals, training material, correspondence, research and development, engineering and other manufacturing processes, and any other non-public material relating to the business of Company.

5.3   Documents and Tangible Items. All documents and tangible items, including, but not limited to, manuals, written descriptions and other documentary evidence or manifestations of Confidential Information, provided to Executive by Company or created by Executive for use in connection with Executive's employment with Company, are the sole property of Company. Upon Company's request and immediately upon termination of Executive's employment with Company, Executive shall promptly return all such documents and tangible items together with all copies, recordings, abstracts, notes, computer diskettes, computer or computer assisted data storage or reproductions of any kind made from or about the documents and tangible items or the information they contain.

5.4   Trade Secrets Act. Executive acknowledges that Executive been requested by Company, and has had an opportunity, to review Chapter 325C of Minnesota Statutes, known as the Minnesota Uniform Trade Secrets Act (the "UTSA"), and acknowledges that violation of the UTSA or of Executive's agreements, covenants, and representations contained in this Agreement may give rise to a cause of action in favor of Company against Executive for general and special damages, exemplary damages, injunctive relief, and attorney's fees. Executive acknowledges that the restrictions contained in this Agreement are in addition to Company's rights and remedies under the UTSA and other applicable law.

5.5   Survival. The obligations of this Article V are continuing and will survive the termination or expiration of this Agreement and the termination of Executive's employment with Company for any reason, whether voluntary or involuntary.

ARTICLE VI.

Assignment of Innovations

6.1   Assignment of Innovations. Executive hereby assigns to Company all of Executive's right, title, and interest in and to the Innovations made, authored, conceived, or reduced to practice by Executive either individually or jointly with others, during the period of Executive's employment with Company (whether such period of employment occurs before, during, or after the Term of this Agreement).

6.2   Works Made for Hire. Executive acknowledges that all original works of authorship which have been made or are made by Executive (solely or jointly with others) within the scope of Executive's employment and which are protectable by copyright have been created or are being created at the instance of Company and are "works made for hire," as that term is defined in the United States Copyright Act (17 U.S.C. § 101). If such laws are inapplicable or in the event that such works, or any part thereof, are determined by the Copyright Office or a court of competent jurisdiction not to be works made for hire under the United States copyright laws, Section 6.1 of this Agreement shall operate as Executive's irrevocable and unconditional assignment to Company of all of Executive's right, title, and interest (including, without limitation, all rights in and to the copyrights throughout the world, including the right to prepare derivative works and the right to all renewals and extensions) in the works for the copyright term(s).

6.3   Definition of Innovations. For purposes of this Agreement, "Innovations" shall mean any invention, improvement, discovery or idea, whether or not shown or described in writing or reduced to practice, and works of authorship, whether or not patentable or copyrightable, including "works made for hire" as that term is defined in the United States Copyright Act (17 U.S.C. § 101), which: (a) relate directly to the business of Company; (b) relate to Company's actual or demonstrably anticipated research and development; (c) result from any work performed by Company's employees, agents, independent contractors, shareholders or officers; (d) are developed or conceived through the use of Confidential Information or equipment, supplies or facilities of Company; or (e) were in the past, or are in the future, generated, conceived of, or reduced to practice by Executive, either alone or with others, during or after working hours, while Executive is employed by Company.

6.4   Disclosure and Cooperation. Executive shall promptly and fully disclose and describe the Innovations to Company, and shall acknowledge and deliver to Company such written instruments and do such other acts as may be necessary in the opinion of Company to preserve Company's property rights to the Innovations against forfeiture, abandonment or loss, and to obtain and maintain letters patents and copyrights to the Innovations, if applicable, and to vest the entire right, title, and interest thereto in Company.

6.5   Exclusions: NOTICE REQUIRED BY MINNESOTA LAW. Pursuant to Minnesota Statutes Section 181.78, Subdivision 3, Executive is hereby notified that Article VI of this Agreement does not apply to any Innovation for which no equipment, supplies, facility or trade secret information of Company was used, and which was developed entirely on Executive's own time, and (a) which does not relate (i) directly to the business of Company or (ii) to Company's actual or demonstrably anticipated research or development, or (b) which does not result from any work performed by Executive for Company.

6.6   Survival. The obligations of this Article VI are continuing and will survive the termination or expiration of this Agreement and the termination of Executive's employment with Company for any reason, whether voluntary or involuntary.

ARTICLE VII.

Restrictive Covenants and Non-Competition

7.1   Restrictive Covenants. Except with the prior written consent of Company, Executive shall not, during the Restricted Period (as defined below), within the geographic areas in which Company or any affiliate or subsidiary of Company, as of the date of Executive's termination of employment with Company, conducts business, in any manner, directly or indirectly, either personally, as a shareholder, member, partner, affiliate, part of a joint venture, independent contractor, agent, servant, employee, representative, or through an employer, firm, organization, or any other entity:

(a)   engage in any commercial activity in competition with any part of the Business of Company as of the date of termination as conducted during the time that Executive was an officer, director, and/or employee of Company, or with any part of Company's contemplated business with respect to which Executive has had access to Confidential Information;

(b) solicit, accept solicitation from, contact, or initiate communications with customers or prospective customers of Company or any affiliate or subsidiary of Company as of the date of termination, whose identities became known to Executive during Executive's employment by Company, in connection with the marketing, distribution, promotion, leasing, selling, merchandising, or servicing of a product or service which competes with the business, products, or services of Company or any affiliate or subsidiary of Company;

(c) request, advise, or entice any suppliers or vendors of Company or any affiliate or subsidiary of Company as of the date of termination, whose identities became known to Executive during Executive's employment by Company, to cease doing business or change the manner in which they do business with Company or any affiliate or subsidiary of Company, or to provide services or products to Executive or a third party which will limit or restrict the ability of such suppliers or vendors to provide such services or products to Company or any affiliate or subsidiary of Company; or

(d) employ, retain the services of, or offer to employ or retain the services of any individual who provided services to Company or any affiliate or subsidiary of Company as of the date of termination (whether as an employee, independent contractor, consultant or otherwise) or within the one (1) year period preceding the termination of Executive's employment, or request, advise, or entice any such individual to leave the employment of or association with Company or any affiliate or subsidiary of Company.

7.2 Definition of Business of Company. For purposes of this Section, the "Business of Company" shall mean _____ as well as all new ventures, commercial activities, products, and services offered by Company or any affiliate or subsidiary of Company, or under development or consideration by Company or any affiliate or subsidiary of Company, at the time of the termination of Executive's employment.

7.3 Definition of Restricted Period. For purposes of this Section, the "Restricted Period" shall commence on the Effective Date of this Agreement and shall continue for a period of one (1) year following the termination or expiration of this Agreement, for any reason, voluntarily or involuntarily, whether initiated by Company or Executive.

7.4 Reasonableness. Executive acknowledges that the time period and the described scope of this Section are the reasonable and necessary time and scope needed to protect the legitimate business interests of Company and its affiliates.

7.5   Survival. The obligations of this Article VII are continuing and will survive the termi-
        nation or expiration of this Agreement and the termination of Executive's employ-
        ment with Company for any reason, whether voluntary or involuntary.

ARTICLE VIII.

Remedies

8.1   Remedies. Executive agrees that all of the provisions contained in Articles V, VI, and
        VII of this Agreement are necessary to protect the legitimate business interests of
        Company, and to prevent the unauthorized dissemination and use of Confidential
        Information and Innovations to and by competitors of Company. Executive also
        agrees that Company will be irreparably harmed, and that damages alone cannot
        adequately compensate Company, if Executive breaches or threatens to breach
        this Agreement, and that injunctive relief is essential for the protection of Company.
        Executive therefore agrees that Company shall have the right, in addition to any
        other rights and remedies existing in its favor, to enforce its rights and the obliga-
        tions under Articles V, VI, and VII of this Agreement not only by an action or actions
        for damages, but also by an action or actions for specific performance, injunction
        and/or other equitable relief without posting any bond or security to enforce or
        prevent any violations, whether anticipatory, continuing or future.

8.2   Public Policy. It is the desire and intent of Company and Executive that the provi-
        sions contained in Articles V, VI, and VII of this Agreement be enforced to the fullest
        extent permissible under the laws and public policy applied in each jurisdiction in
        which enforcement is sought. Accordingly, if, at the time of enforcement of this
        Agreement, a court shall hold that the duration, scope, or area restrictions stated
        in Articles V, VI, and VII of this Agreement are unreasonable under circumstances
        then existing, the Parties agree that the maximum duration, scope, or area rea-
        sonable under such circumstances shall be substituted.

8.3   Independent Covenants. The covenants on the part of Executive contained in
        Articles V, VI, and VII of this Agreement shall be construed as an agreement inde-
        pendent of any other provisions of this Agreement, and the Parties agree that relief
        for any claim or cause of action of Executive against Company, whether predicated
        on this Agreement or otherwise, shall be measured in damages, and shall not con-
        stitute a defense to Company's enforcement of those covenants against Executive.

8.4   Non-Waiver. Failure by Company to declare any breach or exercise any right under
        Articles V, VI, or VII of this Agreement shall not waive the breach, and Company

will have the right at any time to declare that breach and take any action permitted by law. Company's waiver of or failure to exercise its rights under this Agreement with respect to Executive's violation of any provision of Articles V, VI, or VII of this Agreement shall not operate or be construed as a waiver of any other violation of such provision or any other provision in this Agreement.

8.5 Survival. The obligations of Articles V, VI, and VII of this Agreement are continuing and will survive the termination or expiration of this Agreement and the termination of Executive's employment with Company for any reason, whether voluntary or involuntary, and shall be binding upon Executive's assigns, executors, personal administrators, heirs, estates, and other legal representatives.

Article IX.

Representations and Warranties

9.1 Representations. Executive represents and warrants to Company that:

(a) The restrictive covenants and other provisions contained in Articles V, VI, and VII of this Agreement have been fully negotiated between Company and Executive;

(b) Executive has had the opportunity to be represented by Executive's own legal counsel in connection with drafting the scope and duration of the restrictive covenants contained in Articles V, VI, and VII of this Agreement;

(c) The compensation, benefits, and other consideration to be received by Executive under this Agreement represent fair and adequate consideration for Executive's agreement to be bound by the restrictive covenants contained in Articles V, VI, and VII of this Agreement;

(d) Executive possesses adequate skill, ability, and experience to obtain other gainful employment upon termination of Executive's employment with Company without violating the restrictive covenants contained in Articles V, VI, and VII of this Agreement; and

(e) The execution and performance of this Agreement by Executive will not result in or constitute a default, breach, or violation, of any understanding, agreement or commitment, written or oral, express or implied, or any court or administrative judgment or order, to which Executive is a party or by which Executive is bound.

9.2 Indemnification. Executive shall defend, indemnify and hold Company and its subsidiaries and affiliates harmless from and against any demand, liability, expense, claim, or loss (including reasonable attorney's fees and costs of litigation) in any way arising out of, relating to, or in connection with any incorrectness or breach of the representations and warranties in this Section.

Article X.

Indemnification of Executive

10.1 Indemnification. Excluding the fraudulent or intentional or knowing criminal activity of Executive, in the event that Executive receives a legal action, claim or demand, or is named as a witness, defendant, respondent, or party in litigation or other legal proceedings related to Executive's employment with Company or its affiliates, or which alleges liability related to or arising from any act, error, or omission of Executive in Executive's capacity as an employee, officer, or director of Company or its affiliates, Company shall indemnify, hold harmless, and defend Executive (at Company's sole expense):

(a) to the full extent required by Company's articles of incorporation, bylaws, corporate governance documents, and applicable law;

(b) to the extent that Executive is afforded coverage under any policy of insurance in effect for Company and its affiliates; and

(c) from and against all damages, awards, judgments, penalties, or fines claimed or levied against Executive, provided that Executive: (i) was acting in the performance of the duties of Executive's position; and (ii) was not guilty of intentional misconduct or bad faith.

10.2 Advances. Company's obligation to indemnify, hold harmless, and defend Executive under this Section shall include the obligation to pay and advance Executive's reasonable attorney's fees, costs, and disbursements (including the costs of investigators, experts, and witnesses) incurred by independent legal counsel selected by Executive as such fees and costs are incurred by Executive or Executive's legal counsel.

ARTICLE XI.

Miscellaneous

11.1   Notices. All notices given under this Agreement shall be in writing and shall be personally served or sent by registered or certified mail, postage prepaid, return receipt requested. Notices to Company shall be given to Company at its corporate headquarters, which as of the date of this Agreement is: _____, _____, _____, Minnesota _____, Attn: _____. Notices to Executive shall be addressed to Executive at Executive's residential address as the same appears on the records of Company. Notices to Company or Executive shall be sent to such other addresses as Company or Executive shall specify in writing to the other. A copy of any notice to Company also shall be sent to Company's legal counsel, _____, by registered or certified mail, postage prepaid, return receipt requested, and also by e-mail to _____.

11.2   Entire Agreement. This Agreement is intended by the Parties as a single, final, complete, and integrated expression of their agreement and understanding with respect to its subject matter and supersedes all prior oral and written agreements, promises, negotiations, commitments, representations, inducements, statements and communications. No oral representation and no prior or contemporaneous oral or written matters extrinsic to this Agreement shall have any force or effect as to the provisions of this Agreement. All prior and contemporaneous discussions concerning the subject matter of this Agreement have been merged and integrated into, and are superseded by, this Agreement. Company and Executive hereby acknowledge that there are no other agreements or understandings of any nature, oral or written, regarding Executive's employment, apart from this Agreement.

11.3   Modification by Writing Only. The terms of this Agreement are contractual and may not be amended, changed, modified, altered, or supplemented, nor may any covenant, representation, warranty, or other provision be waived, except by agreement in writing signed by the Party against whom enforcement of the amendment, change, modification, alteration, supplementation, or waiver is sought.

11.4   Non-Waiver. No course of dealing between the Parties will change, waive, modify, vary, or terminate any provision of this Agreement or any rights or obligations of any Party under this Agreement. No delay on the part of any Party in exercising any right under this Agreement shall operate as a waiver of such right. No waiver, express or implied, by any Party of any right or any breach by any other Party shall constitute a waiver of any other right or breach by the breaching Party or any other Party to this Agreement.

11.5 Severability. Whenever possible, each provision of this Agreement shall be interpreted in such a manner as to be effective and valid under applicable law, but if any provision contained in this Agreement, or the application thereof, shall be held illegal, invalid, or unenforceable, this Agreement will be interpreted and enforced as if the illegal, invalid, or unenforceable provision had never been a part of this Agreement and there will be added, as part of this Agreement, a provision as similar in terms to the illegal, invalid, or unenforceable provision as may be possible and still be legal, valid, and enforceable under applicable law. In such event, the remaining provisions of this Agreement will remain in full force and effect.

11.6 Rules of Construction. Each Party has participated in the drafting of this Agreement and any uncertainty or ambiguity shall not be interpreted against any one Party.

11.7 Independent Legal Counsel. Executive acknowledges that Executive has had an adequate opportunity to consult with independent legal counsel of Executive's own choosing with regard to the terms of this Agreement and has been advised by Company of Executive's right to seek such consultation before signing this Agreement. Executive has entered into this Agreement knowingly and voluntarily after receiving such independent legal consultation or notwithstanding the decision not to seek such consultation, as the case may be.

11.8 Survival; Continuing Obligation. The Parties agree that, notwithstanding the termination of Executive's employment or the termination or expiration of this Agreement, the terms of this Agreement which relate to periods, activities, obligations, rights, or remedies of the Parties upon or subsequent to such termination or expiration shall survive such termination or expiration and shall govern all rights, disputes, claims or causes of action arising out of or in any way related to this Agreement.

11.9 Additional Undertakings. The Parties agree to execute such other documents and perform such other acts as may be reasonably required by the other Party to this Agreement to effectuate the purpose and intent of this Agreement. The Parties do hereby covenant and agree that they, their heirs, executors, administrators, and permitted successors, and assigns will execute any and all instruments, releases, assignments and consents which may reasonably be required of them in order to carry out the provisions of this Agreement.

11.10 Third Parties. Nothing herein expressed or implied is intended or shall be construed to confer upon or give to any person or entity, other than the Parties to this Agreement, any right or remedies, under or by reason of this Agreement.

11.11 Mediation. All controversies, claims, disputes and matters in question arising out of or relating to this Agreement, its exhibits and attachments, or the breach thereof, shall be submitted to mediation in accordance with this Section; provided, however, that this Section does not apply to any dispute related to Competition Claims (as defined below). The Party who seeks resolution of a controversy, claim, dispute, or other matter in question other than Competition Claims shall notify the other Party in writing of the existence and subject matter of such dispute, and shall designate in such notice the names of three prospective mediators, each of whom shall be certified in Alternative Dispute Resolution pursuant to the Minnesota Rules of Civil Procedure and the Minnesota General Rules of Practice then in effect and none of whom shall have a conflict of interest that would prevent them from serving in a neutral capacity. The recipient Party shall select from such list one individual to act as a mediator in the dispute set forth by the notifying Party. The Parties may, by agreement, select any other mediator to resolve the dispute. The Parties agree to meet with said mediator in the City of Minneapolis, State of Minnesota, within two (2) weeks after the recipient Party has received notice of the dispute and shall attempt in good faith to resolve the matters in dispute. The mediation shall not continue longer than one (1) day without the written approval of both Parties. Neither Party shall be bound by any recommendation of the mediator. For purposes of this Agreement, "Competition Claims" shall mean any claim(s) by Company against Executive to enforce Articles V, VI, or VII of this Agreement and/or any claims by Company against Executive for unfair competition, deceptive trade practices, disparagement, defamation, tortious interference with contractual relations, tortious interference with prospective business advantage, conversion or theft of property, misappropriation of Confidential Information or trade secrets, or claims related to any injunctive relief sought by Company against Executive.

11.12 Governing Law; Exclusive Venue. This Agreement shall be construed and enforced in accordance with the laws of the State of Minnesota, without regard to its choice of law principles. By executing this Agreement, the Parties agree and submit to personal jurisdiction in the State of Minnesota for the purposes of any suit or proceeding arising out of or related to this Agreement or its validity, interpretation, construction, performance, breach, enforcement, or remedies, and the Parties agree that any such suit or proceeding shall be venued only in the state or federal courts located in Hennepin County, Minnesota.

11.13 Attorney's Fees and Costs. In the event of any legal proceeding arising out of this Agreement or its validity, interpretation, construction, performance, breach, enforcement, or remedies, the prevailing Party shall be entitled to recover from the non-prevailing Party the prevailing Party's reasonable attorney's fees and costs (include those on appeal and in connection with enforcing any order or judgment related to this Agreement) and the non-prevailing Party shall pay such attorney's fees and costs to the prevailing Party.

11.14 **Successors and Assigns.** This Agreement shall inure to the benefit of and shall be enforceable by Company and its successors and assigns. In this regard, Executive agrees that Company may assign its rights and obligations under this Agreement in its sole discretion, including but not limited to: (a) assignment to a parent, subsidiary, operating division, joint venture, or other affiliate of Company; (b) assignment in connection with the sale or transfer of Company's stock, business or assets (whether direct or indirect, by purchase, assignment, exchange, merger, reorganization, consolidation, acquisition of stock, stock exchange plan, or otherwise); and (c) any other assignment elected by Company. In the event of such assignment, all covenants and agreements under this Agreement shall inure to the benefit of, and be enforceable by, such successors and assigns. This Agreement is personal to Executive and Executive may not assign any of the rights or obligations under this Agreement, whether in whole or in part, voluntarily, involuntarily, or by operation of law, without the prior written consent of Company. This Agreement shall be binding upon and enforceable against Executive and Executive's personal and legal representatives, heirs, executors, and estates.

11.15 **Counterpart Signatures.** This Agreement may be executed in two or more counterparts, each of which will be deemed an original. A facsimile or electronic/digital copy of this Agreement, including its signature pages, will be binding and deemed to be an original.

IN WITNESS WHEREOF, the Parties have caused this Agreement to be executed and made effective as of the Effective Date, intending to be legally bound by its provisions.

"COMPANY" [NAME OF COMPANY]

By: _____
      [Name of Company Officer]

Its: _____

"EXECUTIVE"

_____
[Name of Executive]

EXHIBIT A TO EXECUTIVE EMPLOYMENT AGREEMENT

RELEASE OF CLAIMS

1.   Definitions. Specific terms used in this Release have the following meanings:

(a)   "I, me, my, mine" mean _____ and anyone who has or obtains any legal rights or claims through said named person.

(b)   "Company" means _____, a Minnesota corporation, and any and all of its parent corporations, subsidiaries, affiliates, successors and assigns, partners, insurers, and the present and former officers, directors, shareholders, partners, employees, attorneys, and agents of any of them, any persons acting by, through, under or in concert with them, the current and former trustees or administrators of any pension, welfare, employee stock option plan or other employee benefit plan of Company, and the predecessors, successors, and assigns of all of the foregoing, all in their official and individual capacities.

(c)   "My Claims" mean any and all claims, liens, demands, causes of action, controversy, losses, damages, costs, expenses, and liabilities that I, my heirs, executors, administrators, successors, and assigns now have, ever had, or may hereafter have against Company, whether known or unknown, suspected or unsuspected, contingent or noncontingent, whether concealed or hidden, by reason of any fact, matter, event, act, omission, transaction, occurrence, cause or thing whatsoever occurring at any time up to and including the date of this Release, without regard to the subsequent discovery or existence of such different or additional facts, including, but not limited to, claims for: breach of contract; breach of express or implied promise; breach of the covenant of good faith and fair dealing; equitable estoppel; promissory estoppel; unjust enrichment; quantum meruit; constructive trust; quasi-contract; payment of wages, commissions, bonus, reimbursements, sick pay, vacation pay, holiday pay, paid time off, employee leave, employee benefits, insurance, pension, or other compensation; fraud or misrepresentation; violation of any federal, state, and/or local law, regulation or rule, including but not limited to, the state and federal Constitutions, the Minnesota Human Rights Act, Minnesota Statute § 181.81 (which prohibits age discrimination), the Minnesota Personnel Records Act, the Minnesota Government Data Practices Act, the Minnesota Whistleblower Statute, the Minnesota Drug and Alcohol Testing in the Workplace Act, the Minnesota Minority Shareholder Rights Act; the Minnesota Fair Labor Standards Act; the Minnesota Labor Relations Act, the Minnesota Public Employee Labor Relations Act, the Minnesota Termination of Sales Representatives Act, the Minnesota Veterans Preference Act, the Women's Economic Security Act, state and federal prevailing wage laws, state and federal employee polygraph laws, state and federal OSHA laws, state and federal equal pay laws, Title VII of the Civil Rights Act of 1964, the Civil Rights Act of 1866, the Civil Rights Act of 1871, the Americans with Disabilities Act, the Rehabilitation Act, the Age Discrimination in Employment Act, the Family and Medical Leave Act, the Judiciary and Judicial Procedure Act, the Civil False Claims Act, the National Labor Relations Act, the Vietnam Era Veterans Readjustment Act, the Uniformed Services Employment and Re-employment Rights Act, the Employee Retirement Income Security Act, the Consolidated Omnibus Budget Reconciliation Act, the Family and Medical Leave Act, the state and federal Fair Labor Standards Act, the Worker Adjustment and Retraining Notification Act, the Fair Credit Reporting Act, the Consumer Credit Protection Act, and all other federal, state, and/or local civil rights laws prohibiting discrimination, reprisal, retaliation, or other unlawful activity on the basis of race, color, creed, marital status, sex, age, religion, national origin, disability, pregnancy, sexual orientation, political affiliation, status with respect to public assistance, membership in local commission, or any other protected class status; sexual harassment; defamation, slander, and libel (including compelled self-publication); intentional or negligent infliction of emotional distress; negligence; breach of fiduciary duty; wrongful termination of employment; constructive discharge; conversion; invasion of privacy; fraudulent inducement; negligent hiring, retention, training, and/or supervision; tortious interference with contractual relations or prospective business advantage; assault; battery; false imprisonment; all other claims for unlawful employment practices; all claims for attorney's fees, costs, disbursements, fees, interest, or other payments; and all other common law, legal, equitable or statutory claims (whether on a contract, tort, or other theory), whether they could be brought directly by me on my own behalf or by any other person, agency, or organization on my behalf.

2.   Agreement to Release My Claims.

(a)   On behalf of myself, my attorneys, heirs, executors, administrators, successors and assigns, I agree to release, discharge, and give up all My Claims against Company through the date I sign this Release of Claims in exchange for the Severance Pay Company has agreed to pay me for signing this Release pursuant to Article IV of the Employment Agreement between me and Company effective _____, _____ (the "Employment Agreement"). I agree to release and discharge Company not only from any and all of My Claims that I could make on my own behalf, but also from those claims that may or could be brought by any other person or organization on my behalf.

(b)   I have not caused or permitted to be served, filed, or commenced any lawsuits, charges, complaints, actions, notices, or other demands against Company with any federal, state, or local judicial or administrative agency or body based on My Claims.

(c)   In the event that any such charges, complaints, actions, notices, or other demands against Company have been or are asserted, I agree that this Release of Claims shall act as a total and complete bar to my re-employment or to recovery of any relief or sum or amount from Company, resulting directly or indirectly from any lawsuit, remedy, charge, or complaint, whether brought privately by me or by anyone else, including any federal, state, or local judicial or administrative agency or body, whether or not on my behalf or at my request.

(d)   This release shall not affect: (i) the payment of any undisputed earned but unpaid compensation, benefits, or expense reimbursements under the Employment Agreement through my date of termination; (ii) my vested balance in any deferred compensation, retirement, or pension plan of Company; (iii) my right to exercise vested options under any stock option plan or agreement with Company; (iv) my ownership of any stock or other securities of Company owned by me as of the date of this Release of Claims; (v) my rights under written plan documents governing Company's employee welfare benefits, pension plans, or retirement plans; (vi) my conversion or continuation of coverage rights under any employee welfare benefit plan of Company pursuant to applicable plan documents, COBRA, or other applicable law; (vii) my right to seek or receive workers' compensation benefits under applicable law; (viii) my right to seek or receive unemployment compensation benefits under applicable law; or (ix) any claims that arise after the date I sign this Release of Claims.

(e)   Notwithstanding anything to the contrary in this Release of Claims, nothing contained herein shall be construed as a waiver of any right that, as a matter of public policy or under applicable law, cannot be waived or released. Nothing in this Release of Claims shall prevent me from challenging the validity of my release of claims under the federal Age Discrimination in Employment Act (ADEA) and/or the Older Workers Benefit Protection Act, or any right which I may have to file a charge under the ADEA or other federal, state, or local civil rights statutes, regulations, or ordinances, or to participate in an investigation or proceeding conducted by the Equal Employment Opportunity Commission, the Minnesota Department of Human Rights, or other investigatory agency; provided, however, that this Release of Claims does waive and release my right to recover damages, reinstatement, back pay, front pay, compensatory damages, exemplary or punitive damages, attorney's fees or costs, or other individual remedies.

3. Non-Admission. Even though Company is paying me to release My Claims, Company does not admit that it is responsible or legally obligated to me. In fact, Company denies that it is responsible or legally obligated to me or that it has engaged in any wrongdoing.

4. Consideration Period and Rescission of Release of Claims.

(a)   I understand that I may take up to twenty-one (21) calendar days after receiving this Release of Claims to consider whether I wish to sign this Release of Claims. I understand that I shall be deemed to have received this Release of Claims on the date my Employment Agreement terminates. In addition, I understand that I may rescind (i.e., revoke and cancel) my release of claims arising under the federal Age Discrimination in Employment Act, 29 U.S.C. § 621 et seq., within seven (7) calendar days of signing this Release of Claims. I understand that I also may rescind (i.e., revoke and cancel) my release of claims arising under the Minnesota Human Rights Act, Minn. Stat. § 363A.01 et seq., within fifteen (15) calendar days of signing this Release of Claims.

(b)   I understand that to be effective, the rescission/revocation must be in writing and delivered to Company, in care of:

[NAME OF COMPANY]

Attn: _____

[address]

either by hand or by mail within the respective rescission/revocation periods. If sent by mail, the rescission must be (i) postmarked within the respective rescission/revocation periods as stated above; (ii) properly addressed, as stated above; and (iii) sent by certified mail, return receipt requested.

(c)   In the event I exercise any right of rescission or revocation, neither Company nor I will have any rights or obligations whatsoever under this Release of Claims, nor shall I be entitled to any Severance Pay or Change in Control Severance Pay pursuant to Article IV of the Employment Agreement.

(d)   This Release of Claims does not become effective until the sixteenth (16th) day after I sign it, and then only if it has not been rescinded by me in accordance with this Section.

5.   **Acceptance Period.** I have been informed that the terms of this Release of Claims shall be open for acceptance by me for a period of twenty-one (21) calendar days after receiving it, during which time I may consider whether or not to accept this Release of Claims and seek legal counsel to advise me regarding the same. Company has advised me to seek the advice of an attorney before signing this Release of Claims. I agree that changes to this Release of Claims, whether material or immaterial, will not restart this acceptance period.

6.   **Voluntary and Knowing Action.** I have read this Release of Claims carefully and understand and agree to all of its terms. I have been advised to consult with my own attorney regarding this Release of Claims and have had an opportunity to discuss this Release of Claims with my own attorney. I have had an adequate amount of time to consider whether to sign this Release of Claims. In agreeing to sign this Release of Claims, I have not relied on any statements or explanations made by Company or its attorneys. I am voluntarily entering into this Release of Claims to effectuate my separation of employment from Company and I intend this Release of Claims to be legally binding.

7.   **Reaffirmation of Restrictive Covenants.** By executing this Release of Claims and accepting the consideration being paid to me for signing this Release of Claims, I hereby reaffirm and agree to comply with all post-employment restrictive covenants contained in any non-disclosure, non-solicitation, non-competition, or other similar agreements with Company.

8.   **Continuation Rights.** I understand that my participation in all employee benefits plans will cease on the effective date of my employment termination, except in accordance with the terms of the governing benefit plan documents or applicable law.

9.   **Non-Disparagement.** I agree that I will not criticize, disparage or put in disrepute Company, or those associated with Company in any way, whether orally, in writing, or otherwise, directly or by implication, in communication with any person, including, but not limited to, customers or agents of Company, or in any media outlet or social media.

10.   Cooperation and Future Assurances. I will cooperate and provide information within my knowledge in response to Company's reasonable requests concerning any investigation, litigation, or any other matter that relates to any fact or circumstance known to me during my employment with Company. I agree to respond to Company's request for cooperation or assistance within two (2) business days of each such request. I acknowledge that I am not entitled to further compensation or consideration from Company for my cooperation or assistance, except to the extent any witness fees are mandated under federal or state law. I will inform Company of all subpoenas, correspondence, telephone calls, requests for information, inquiries or other contacts I may receive from third parties, including governmental agencies, concerning any fact or circumstances known to me arising from my employment at Company within two (2) business days of each such contact.

11.   Governing Law; Exclusive Venue. This Release of Claims shall be construed and enforced in accordance with the laws of the State of Minnesota, without regard to its choice of law principles. By executing this Release of Claims, I agree and submit to personal jurisdiction in the State of Minnesota for the purposes of any suit or proceeding arising out of or related to this Release of Claims or its validity, interpretation, construction, performance, breach, enforcement, or remedies, and I agree that any such suit or proceeding shall be venued only in the state or federal courts located in Hennepin County, Minnesota.

IN WITNESS WHEREOF, I have executed this Release of Claims by my signature below.

_____

[Name of Executive]

SUBSCRIBED AND SWORN to before me

this _____ day of _____, _____.

_____

Notary Public

BIBLIOGRAPHY

Crystal, Graef S. *In Search of Excess—The Overcompensation of American Executives*. Ecco, 1991.

Galso, Jodie-Beth, and McIntosh, Sandy. *Firing Back: Power Strategies for Cutting the Best Deal When You're About to Lose Your Job*. Wiley, 1997.

Kahnke, Randall E., and Bundy, Kerry L. *The Secrets to Winning Trade Secrets Cases*, Thompson Reuters, 2016.

Kutten, L.J., and Bernard D. Reams. *Executive and Professional Employment Contracts: The Major Legal Issues and Forms*. Butterworth Legal Publishers, 1992.

Lucht, John. *Rites of Passage: Your Insider's Lifetime Guide to Executive Job Changes and Faster Career Progress*. Viceroy, 2012.

Mackay, Harvey. *We Got Fired! (And It's the Best Thing That Ever Happened to Us)*. Ballantine, 2004.

Ross, Arnold S., et al. *Executive Employment & Compensation*. Hirshfield, Stem, Moyer & Ross, 1993.

Simon, Alan R. *Stock Options for Dummies*. Hungry Minds, 2001.

Sirkin, Michael S., and Lawrence K. Cagney. *Executive Compensation*. Law Journal Seminars, 2003.

Sklover, Alan S. *Fired, Downsized or Laid Off—What Your Employer Doesn't Want You to Know About How to Fight Back*. Holt, 2000.

Stein, Jotham S. *Executive Employment Law—Protecting Executives, Entrepreneurs and Employees*. Oxford UP, 2011.

Tarrant, John. *Perks and Parachutes—Negotiating Your Best Possible Employment Deal, From Salary and Bonus to Benefits and Protection*. Stonesong, 1997.

Tauber, Yale D., and Donald R. Levy. *Executive Compensation*. Bureau of National Affairs, 2002.

Woodard, Arthur F. *Executive Employment Agreements Line by Line*. Thomson Reuters, 2010.

ABOUT THE AUTHOR

V. John Ella practices in all aspects of employment law, business law, and commercial litigation. He advises businesses, employers, individual executives, and professionals in the areas of employment contracts, handbooks, non-compete and trade secret litigation, drug testing law, privacy law, commission claims, defamation, fraud, sexual harassment claims, employment and housing discrimination, ERISA benefits litigation, public accommodations under Title III of the Americans with Disabilities Act, wage and hour compliance, whistleblower and Sarbanes-Oxley claims, professional licensing issues, appeals, manufacturer sales representative contracts, and closely-held corporation and partnership disputes.

John has obtained successful verdicts in jury trials and court trials in federal and state district courts in Minnesota and Iowa, and has appeared before the Minnesota Court of Appeals, the Minnesota Supreme Court, the 8th Circuit Court of Appeals, and the Federal Circuit Court of Appeals. He has litigated non-compete disputes in Iowa, Florida, Minnesota, North Dakota, and Wisconsin.

John is the author of over one hundred articles or book chapters for various legal publications. He frequently lectures on the topic of workplace privacy and employee monitoring. He also speaks on common law fraud and was co-author of the Summary Guide to Fraud, Misrepresentation and Deceptive Trade Practices.

John is a recognized commentator on the topic of "Executive Law" and has been quoted in dozens of newspaper and magazine articles regarding stock options, executive compensation, non-competes, restrictive covenants, and executive severance agreements and has lectured at several CLEs on the topic of Executive Law.

John is certified by the Minnesota State Bar Association as a Labor and Employment Law Specialist. He is also certified as an Information Privacy Professional (CIPP/US) by the International Association of Privacy Professionals (IAPP). He served on the Minnesota Board of Medical Practice from 2010 to 2018 and currently serves on the Minnesota State Board of Legal Certification. He is also an arbitrator for the American Arbitration Association.

John was a Law Clerk for Judge Carol B. Amon, Eastern District of New York from 1996–1997 and for Judge William E. Kalar, Ninth Judicial District of Minnesota from 1994–1995. After ten years as an attorney at a local general practice firm he spent almost ten years at the nation's second-largest labor and employment defense firm as a partner where he represented many *Fortune* 500 and large global corporations in all aspects of employment law. He joined Trepanier MacGillis Battina P.A. in 2016. John and his wife Natasha have three boys: Alan, Charlie, and Douglas, and an Anatolian Shepherd named Codger.

Trepanier MacGillis Battina P.A. is a business law firm located in Minneapolis, Minnesota. www.trepanierlaw.com.

ENDNOTES

1 Michael M. Bowden, "Lawyer Specializes in Helping Displaced Executives – Underserved Market is Ripe for Small Firms," *Lawyers Weekly*, Sept. 18, 2000, p. B3.

2 Shannon Prather, "Twin Cities Businesses Ask Why Professionals of Color Leave," *Minneapolis Star Tribune*. Sept. 26, 2016.

3 See also, Chris Clayton, "The Diversity Drop Off," *Twin Cities Business*, Feb. 2018, p. 33.

4 V. John Ella, "Minnesota Med-Tech Companies Held Shaped the State's Non-Compete Law," *Minnesota Lawyer*, Aug. 1, 2016.

5 Theo Francis, "Why You Probably Work for a Giant Company," *Wall Street Journal*, Apr. 7, 2017, p. A10.

6 Greenstone Miller, Jody, and Matt Miller. "The Rise of the Executive Supertemp," *Harvard Business Review*, May 2012.

7 V. John Ella, "Let the Air Out of Title Inflation," *Minneapolis Star Tribune*, Aug. 10, 2003, p. D4.

8 For criticism of a non-disparagement clause involving a former Minneapolis police chief, *see* Adam Belz, "No Criticism Clause Gets Criticized," *Minneapolis Star Tribune*, Sept. 6, 2017, p. B1.

9 *See, e.g.*, California (West's Ann. Cal. Labor Code § 432.3).

10 Ben Fritz and Joann S. Lublin, "Disney Rebuffed Over Pay for CEO," *Wall Street Journal*, Mar. 9, 2018.

11 "The Rise of the Superstars," *The Economist*, Sept. 17, 2016, p. 4 of Special Report.

12 Nanette Burns, "Sarbanes-Oxley Lifts Some Director Pay Higher than $1 Million," *Business Week*, Feb. 12, 2010.

13 "TARP Programs: Executive Compensation," https://www.treasury.gov/initiatives/financial-stability/TARP-Programs/executive-comp/Pages/overview.aspx.

14 The Supreme Court of Virginia overturned a $655,000 breach of contract award to Scott Harvard, the former CEO of Hampton Roads Bankshares, Inc. Harvard resigned his employment following the acquisition of Gateway Bank in 2009 and requested a golden parachute payment equal to 2.99 times his base salary. The bank refused to pay due to federal restrictions on executive parachutes imposed on financial institutions as part of the EERA and TARP. Although the trial court ruled in his favor, the Virginia Supreme Court reversed, holding that federal law barred the payment on the basis of impossibility of performance. Hampton Roads Bankshares v. Harvard, 781 S.E.2d 172 (Va. 2016).

15 Internal Revenue Code, Section 162(m)(6).

16 Dalton Conley, "Rich Man's Burden," *New York Times*, Sept. 2, 2008.

17 *See* 29 C.F.R. § 541 as a starting point. A full discussion of wage and hour is beyond the scope of this book.

18 Joe Cheung et al., "Hurdle Rate: Executive Stock Options," *Australian Journal of Management*, July 2006.

19 *E.g.,* Lane v. Amoco Corp., 133 F.3d 676 (8th Cir. 1998) (applying Iowa law); Swift v. Speedway Superamerica LLC, 861 N.E.2d 1212 (Ind. Ct. App. 2007); Messina v. Lowe's Home Centers, Inc., No. 07-1214, 2007 U.S. Dist. LEXIS 47006 (D. La. 2007).

20 *E.g.,* Jensen v. International Business Machines Corp., 454 F.3d 382 (4th Cir. 2006); Rotter v. Cambex Corp., No. 93 C 4137, 1995 WL 374275 (N.D. Ill. June 21, 1995).

21 *See, e.g.*, Bley v. ClickShip Direct, Inc., No. 01-661 (MJD/SRN) 2001 U.S. Dist. LEXIS 21147 (D. Minn. 2001). See also, Gunderson v. N. Am. Life & Cas. Co., 78 N.W.2d 328, 332 (Minn. 1956) (holding that when "a commissioned sales person has been the procuring cause of a sale, the employer cannot avoid paying a commission that was earned by opportunistically terminating the employee or preventing the employee from doing whatever else might be required to perfect his or her right to the commission") (cited in *Galbraith v. U.S. Premise Networking Services, Inc.*, No. A03-1154, 2004 Minn. App. LEXIS 497, (Minn. Ct. App. 2004)) and V. John Ella, "Commission Impossible? Bonus and Commission Claims Get Boost From Court Decisions," *Hennepin Lawyer*, July/Aug. 2005, at p. 20.

22 Minn. Stat. § 181.950-957; see also V. John Ella, "What Do They Have in Mind? Minnesota's Drug-Testing Law Turns 20," *Bench & Bar of Minnesota*, Sept. 2007; V. John Ella & Craig W. Trepanier, "Three Decades of DATWA," *Bench & Bar of Minnesota*, Sept. 2017.

23 https://mn.gov/boards/hpsp/.

24 Evan P. Starr et al., "Noncompetes in the U.S. Labor Force," https://papers.ssrn.com/sol3/Papers.cfm?abstract_id=2625714.

25 Conor Dougherty, "How Noncompete Clauses Keep Workers Locked In," *N.Y. Times*, May 13, 2017.

26 Eutectic Welding Alloys Corp. v. West, 281 Minn. 13, 20, 160 N.W.2d 566, 571 (1968).

27 See, e.g., AutoUpLink v. Janson, Case No. A17-0485 (Minn. Ct. App., Dec. 4, 2017) (holding that non-compete signed on the second day of training was not enforceable for lack of consideration).

28 BDO Seidman v. Hirshberg, 93 N.Y.2d 382 (1999).

29 *See* V. John Ella, "Enforceability of Non-Solicitaiton of Employee Restrictions—The Grass is Not Always Greener," Trepanier MacGillis Battina, https://trepanierlaw.com/enforceability-of-non-solicitation-of-employee-restrictions-the-grass-is-not-always-greener/.

30 *See* Frank B. Hall & Co. v. Alexander & Alexander, Inc., 974 F.2d 1020, 1024, n. 5 (8th Cir. 1992) (assuming that the anti-raiding agreement was enforceable and observing that the non-solicitation clause "did not prohibit the parties from merely hiring an employee of the other without solicitation"); *Restatement (Second) of Agency* § 393 cmt. e (1958) (an employee is liable if, before or after leaving the employment, he causes fellow employees to break their contracts with his employer).

31 Jostens, Inc. v. National Computer Systems, 318 N.W.2d 691 (Minn. 1982).

32 Commercial Assoc., Inc. v. Work Connection, Inc., 712 N.W.2d 772, 782 (Minn. Ct. App. 2006) (citing *Pine R. State Bank v. Mettille*, 333 N.W.2d 622, 626-27 (Minn. 1983)).

33 Bennett v. Storz Broad. Co., 134 N.W.2d 892, 898 (Minn. 1965) (holding that non-compete agreements are "looked upon with disfavor, cautiously considered, and carefully scrutinized."); Jim W. Miller Construction, Inc. v. Schaefer, 298 N.W.2d 455, 459 (Minn. 1980) (holding that non-compete agreements are "looked upon with disfavor because their enforcement decreases competition in the marketplace and restricts the [employee's] right to work and his ability to earn a livelihood."); cf. Guidant Sales Corp. v. Niebur, No. 01–1772, 2001 WL 1636502, at *7 (D. Minn. Oct. 18, 2001) ("the public interest favors the enforcement of valid agreements and the protection of legitimate business interests in an industry propelled by vigorous but fair competition."); Boston Scientific v. Duberg, 10–CV–4525, 2010 WL 4970022, *6 (D. Minn. Nov. 24, 2010) ("Courts have repeatedly recognized that non-compete agreements in the medical device industry serve employers' important and legitimate interests in long-term customer relationships and preserving goodwill").

34 Bennett, 134 N.W.2d at 899 (citing 35 Am. Jur., *Master and Servant*, § 99; 36 Am. Jur., *Monopolies, Combinations, and Restraint of Trade*, § 78 and 79). See also Combined Ins. Co. of Am. v. Bode, 77 N.W.2d 533, 536 (Minn. 1956).

35 Schwandt Sanitation of Paynesville v. City of Paynesville, 423 N.W.2d 59, 67 (Minn. Ct. App. 1988).

36 Welsh v. Barnes-Duluth Shipbuilding Co., 21 N.W.2d 43, 46–47 (Minn. 1945) ("[w]here a signature is not required by some positive rule of law, as, for example, in certain cases by the statute of frauds, assent or mutuality may be shown by the fact that the parties accepted the writing as a binding contract and acted on it as such, even though it was not signed").

37 Asbestos Products, Inc. v. Healy Mechanical Contractors, Inc., 235 N.W.2d 807, 810 (Minn. 1975).

38 AutoMed Technologies, Inc. v. Eller, 160 F. Supp.2d 915 (N.D. Ill. 2001).

39 Computer Sales Int'l v. Collins, 723 S.W.2d 450 (Mo. Ct. App. 1986).

40 Workers Comp. Recovery, Inc. v. Marvin, No. A03-1549, 2004 WL 1244404, at *6 (Minn. Ct. App. June 8, 2004).

41 *See* Ecolab, Inc. v. Gartland, 537 N.W.2d 291, 294 (Minn. Ct. App. 1995) (holding that "[i]n order to be enforceable, [non-compete] agreements must be reasonable and supported by consideration").

42 Overholt Crop Ins. Service Co., Inc. v. Bredeson, 437 N.W.2d 698, 702 (Minn. Ct. App. 1989) (holding that where a non-compete agreement is entered into "at the inception of the employment relationship, no independent consideration is necessary to support the agreement").

43 Nat'l Recruiters v. Cashman, 323 N.W.2d 736, 740 (Minn. 1982) (holding that "where [a non-compete agreement] is not ancillary to the initial oral employment contract, it can be sustained only if supported by independent consideration.") (citing *Modern Controls, Inc. v. Andreadakis*, 578 F.2d 1264, 1267 (8th Cir. 1978)).

44 R.L. Youngdahl & Assoc., Inc. v. Peterson, No. C0-87-2418, 1988 WL 35346 *1 (Minn. Ct. App. Apr. 19, 1988) (holding that a $12,000 raise was adequate consideration); Webb Publ'g Co. v. Fosshage, 426 N.W.2d 445, 450 (Minn. Ct. App. 1987) (holding that a $40,000 raise adequate consideration).

45 Tenant Const., Inc. v. Mason, No. A07-0413, 2008 WL 314515, at *2 (Minn. Ct. App. Feb 5, 2008) (holding that additional consideration for a non-compete agreement was sufficient, because $500 was not an insignificant sum).

46 Guidant Sales Corp. v. Baer, No. 09-CV-0358, 2009 WL 490052, at *2 (D. Minn. Feb. 26, 2009) (stating that an employee received something substantial in exchange for signing a non-compete agreement when the employee received a promotion that increased his authority and responsibility).

47 *See* Universal Hosp. Servs., Inc. v. Joseph Hennessy, No. Civ. 01-2072, 2002 WL 192564, at *3 (D. Minn. Jan. 2, 2002) (stating that given that the stock options could potentially be received only if the agreement was signed, that eligibility, by itself, constituted adequate consideration, and that even when the value of stock options decline to a point where they are "underwater," the options are still sufficient consideration because the employee "was made eligible for a benefit he could not have received without signing the Agreement."); Medtronic, Inc. v. Hedemark, 2009 WL 511760, at *5 (Minn. Ct. App. Mar. 3, 2009) (stating that a stock option agreement supported the non-compete agreement, where it gave the employee the opportunity to purchase company stock but required forfeiture of any exercised stock options if he left employer less than six months after exercise and engaged in competition, and that unlike many non-compete agreements, the stock option agreement afforded the employee almost complete control over how it impacted him).

48 Millard v. Elec. Cable Specialists, 790 F. Supp. 857, 862 (D. Minn. 1992) (finding consideration where the employee received valuable training, gained economic and professional benefits); Witzke v. Mesabi Rehabilitation Servs., Inc., No. A07-0421, 2008 WL 314535, at *3 (Minn. Ct. App. Feb. 5, 2008) (finding that there was adequate consideration where the employee received training and support in licensing applications).

49 TestQuest, Inc. v. LaFrance, No. C0-02-783, 2002 WL 1969287, at *4 (Minn. Ct. App. Aug. 27, 2002) (stating that access to the employer's confidential information as a result of signing the non-compete agreement was adequate consideration).

50 *See* Freeman v. Duluth Clinic, Inc., 334 N.W.2d 626, 630 (Minn. 1983) (finding that an employee's status was unaffected in comparison to the employees who did not sign the non-compete agreement, and holding that the employee gained no advantage by signing the non-compete agreement, and consideration was therefore inadequate).

51 *See* Peoples Cleaning & Dyeing Co., Inc. v. Share, 210 N.W. 397, 398 (Minn. 1926) (holding that where a restrictive covenant was given contemporaneously with an employee's resignation from employ-ment and sale of his stock in the employer, the employer being under no obligation to buy stock otherwise, there was adequate consideration for the restrictive covenant).

52 Roth v. Gamble-Skogmo, Inc., 532 F. Supp. 1029, 1031 (D. Minn. 1982); Minn. Mining & Mfg. Co. v. Kirkevold, 87 F.R.D. 324 (D. Minn. 1980); Millard v. Elec. Cable Specialists, 790 F.Supp. 857 (D. Minn. 1992).

53 *See* Menter Co. v. Brock, 180 N.W. 553, 554 (Minn. 1920) (holding that a non-compete agreement would be enforced where it was shown the employee "has obtained knowledge of secrets in [the employer's] business the disclosure of which would result in irreparable damage to the employer, it appearing that the subsequent employment was the benefit of the secrets or there was danger that such secrets would be disclosed in the subsequent employment").

54 Modern Controls, Inc. v. Andreadakis, 578 F.2d 1264, 1268 (8th Cir. 1978) (holding that any "confidential information that does not rise to the level of a trade secret can be protected by a properly drawn covenant not to compete").

55 Menter, 180 N.W. at 554–55.

56 Softchoice, Inc. v. Schmidt, 763 N.W.2d 660, 670 (Minn. Ct. App. 2009).

57 *See* Medtronic v. Gibbons, 527 F. Supp. 1085 (D. Minn. 1981).

58 Bennett, 134 N.W.2d at 898 (Minn. 1965); Minnesota Mining and Manufacturing Company v. Kirkevold, 87 F.R.D. 324, 332-33 (D. Minn. 1980) (holding that the reasonableness of the covenant not to compete must be evaluated in the context of the employee's responsibilities and functions, as an employer cannot "unreasonably" extract from its employees commitments which are "far broader" than the employee's "actual functions and status") (citing *Eutectic Welding Alloys Corp. v. West*, 160 N.W.2d 566, 570 (Minn. 1968)).

59 *See* Snyder's Drug Stores, Inc. v. Sheehy Properties, Inc., 266 N.W.2d 882, 885 (Minn. 1978) (Stating that "while covenants against competition should be construed so as to give effect to the intention of the parties, such covenants should not be extended beyond their true intent").

60 Overholt, 437 N.W.2d at 703 (finding that in light of its purpose, the restriction was not overbroad since the scope of the covenant was limited to areas in which the employee actually worked for the employer).

61 Salon 2000, Inc. v. Dauwalter, No. A06-1227, 2007 WL 1599223, at *2 (Minn. Ct. App. June 5, 2007).

62 Cook Sign Co. v. Combs, No. A07-1907, 2008 WL 3898267, at *7 (Minn. Ct. App. Aug. 26, 2008) (enforcing a non-compete agreement restricting a custom salesman from competing in three states in which the employer does business and has customers).

63 Thermorama, Inc. v. Buckwold, 125 N.W.2d 844 (Minn. 1964).

64 *See* Eutectic Welding Alloys Corp. v. West, 160 N.W.2d 566, 568 n.3, 571 (Minn. 1968) (stating that a restrictive covenant applied to a technical representative in any territory in which the representative worked in his last two years of employment and within a radius of fifty miles from any such territory or territories was unreasonable because it prohibited the representative from working in a large industrial complex outside of his territory).

65 Manpower, Inc. v. Best Temporaries, Inc., 196 N.W.2d 288, 289 (Minn. 1972) (stating that a restriction against a job placement agent on working within a 200-mile radius of Minneapolis or within a 25-mile radius of any other city where the employer had an "affiliated company" was unreasonable); Klick v. Crosstown State Bank, Inc., 372 N.W.2d 85, 86 (Minn. Ct. App. 1985) (stating that a geographic restriction was unreasonable where a former bank vice president was prohibited from working for a bank within the employer's trade area as well as for any branch office for any institution that had a branch office in the trade area of the employer bank).

66 *See* Dynamic Air, Inc. v. Bloch, 502 N.W.2d 796 (Minn. Ct. App. 1993) (stating that while the policy considerations for a per se rule prohibiting enforcement of restrictive covenants unlimited as to geography are strong, there may be instances in which an unlimited restrictive covenant is reasonably necessary to protect the employer's interests, such as in employment with multi-national corporations); Medtronic v. Hedemark, No. A08-0987, 2009 WL 511760 (Minn. Ct. App. Mar. 3, 2009) (stating that a worldwide scope was reasonable in that it was limited to certain cardiology products,

and that the confidential information employee obtained while working with former employer would be potentially relevant to his sales of products at the new employer in any market).

67 *See* Johnson v. Menth, No. A06-1324, 2007 WL 2034365 (Minn. Ct. App. July 17, 2007).

68 Triple B & G, Inc. v. City of Fairmont, 494 N.W.2d 49, 53 (Minn. Ct. App. 1992).

69 Vital Images, Inc. v. Martel, Civ. No. 07-4195, 2007 WL 3095378, at *4 (D. Minn. Oct. 19, 2007).

70 Tom Schmidt Associates, Inc. v. Williams, No. CX-00-1547, 2001 WL 138519, at *2-3 (Minn. Ct. App. Feb. 20, 2001).

71 *Id.* at *2.

72 *See* Hart Forms & Sys. v. Goettsch, 1990 WL 195473, at *3 (Minn. Ct. App. 1990).

73 Bennett, 134 N.W.2d at 899 (Minn. 1965).

74 *See* Klick v. Crosstown State Bank, Inc., 372 N.W.2d 85, 88 (Minn. Ct. App. 1985).

75 Davies & Davies Agency, Inc. v. Davies, 298 N.W.2d 127, 131 (Minn. 1980).

76 *See, e.g.,* Thermorama, Inc. v. Buckwold, 125 N.W.2d 844 (Minn. 1964) (holding that a former employer was entitled to temporary injunction against solicitation of its customers by former employee who had agreed to refrain from competition for one year after termination of employment and who allegedly systematically solicited former employer's customers and actively participated in competitive business enterprise).

77 Benfield, Inc. v. Moline, 351 F. Supp. 2d 911, 918 (D. Minn. 2004).

78 *See, e.g.,* Overholt, 437 N.W.2d at 704 (upholding a two-year restrictive covenant prohibiting employee from soliciting any business from customers he personally serviced while employed with the former employer as reasonable); BFI-Portable Services, Inc. v. Kemple, No. C5-89-1172, 1989 WL 138978, at *2-3 (Minn. Ct. App. Nov. 21, 1989) (holding that a restrictive covenant which prohibited an employee for a portable toilet service company from soliciting its customers on behalf of competing businesses for a period of two years after termination of employment was enforceable because it reasonably protected the employer's interests and it was not overbroad).

79 *See, e.g.,* Medtronic, Inc. v. Sun, No. C7-97-1185, 1997 WL 729168, at *5 (Minn. Ct. App. Nov. 25, 1997) (upholding a reduction of restriction from two years to one year because two years was unreasonable for a research scientist employed only three years and unreasonable for an engineer with less exposure to confidential information than the research scientist); Ecolab, Inc. v. Ford, No. C0-94-1207, 1994 WL 510121, at *2 (Minn. Ct. App. Sept. 20, 1994) (enforcing a one-year non-compete agreement for a senior sales manager instead of a two year non-compete based on findings that (1) employee's break with the company was well publicized and known to customers; (2) employee's replacement was not new; (3) employee had had a one year non-compete for 23 years which had only recently been increased to two years, and that employer's motivation was not to protect legitimate interest but to protect its investment in the employee by forcing him to remain with the company).

80 *See, e.g.,* Klick v. Crosstown State Bank, 372 N.W.2d 85, 88 (Minn. Ct. App. 1985).

81 Head v. Morris Veterinary Ctr, Inc., No. A04-2334, 2005 WL 1620328, at *3-4 (Minn. Ct. App. July 12, 2005).

82 *See* B & Y Metal Painting, Inc. v. Ball, 279 N.W.2d 813, 815 (Minn. 1979) (holding that where a covenant not to compete arose out of both the sale of an individual's metal-painting business and his employment contract with purchaser of business, that seller's attorney drafted both the covenant not to compete and the employment agreement, and seller had signed covenant not to compete as part of sale, the covenant not to compete with buyer for a period of three years from termination of seller's employment with buyer was reasonable and seller's opening of new competing business year following termination of his employment was direct violation of contract).

83 *See, e.g.,* Young v. Meyer, No. C6-88-1543, 1989 WL 29594, at *2 (Minn. Ct. App. Apr. 4, 1989) (affirming the trial court's reduction of a non-compete agreement prohibiting the seller of interest in a partnership from working for any competitor within a fifty-mile radius of St. Cloud for a period of time extending until the contract was paid in full or three years from the date of termination of employment with Granite City from a three-year restraint to eighteen months).

84 Ikon Office Solutions, Inc. v. Dale, Nos. 01-2055, 01-2667, 2001 WL 1269994, at *1 (8th Cir. Oct. 24, 2001) (holding that the modification of a non-compete term for the sale of computer equipment sales and service business, which reduced the non-compete term from five to three years under Minnesota's "blue pencil doctrine," was not abuse of discretion).

85 Bennett, 134 N.W.2d at 892 (Minn. 1965) (holding that a non-compete agreement is enforceable where it is, among other factors, not unreasonably burdensome to the employee).

86 Menter Co. v. Brock, 180 N.W. 553, 555 (Minn. 1920).

87 Walker, 219 N.W.2d at 441 (Minn. 1974).

88 Bennett, 134 N.W.2d at 898 (holding that a non-compete agreement is enforceable where "the restraint is for a just and honest purpose, for the protection of a legitimate interest of the party in whose favor it is imposed, reasonable as between the parties, and not injurious to the public"); see also Walker Emp't Serv. Inc. v. Parkhurst, 219 N.W.2d 437, 441 (Minn. 1974) (holding that a non-compete agreement is invalid if, among other factors, it is injurious to the public).

89 Bess v. Bothman, 257 N.W.2d 791, 795 (Minn. 1977) (determining that a non-compete provision was not injurious to the public because it did not, for example, foster a monopoly).

90 Bennett, 134 N.W.2d at 899 ("[i]t is important to note that courts recognize a distinction between restrictive covenants as they relate to the ordinary commercial transaction involving business or property transfers and those which relate to employment contracts entered into by wage earners."). The court explained that "[a] different measure of reasonableness is used."

91 *See* Ikon, 22 Fed. Appx. at 649; Bess, 257 N.W.2d at 795.

92 Kunin v. Kunin, No. C0-99-206, 1999 WL 486814, at *3 (Minn. Ct. App. July 13, 1999) (holding that an eleven-year restriction on the president of a business which was sold was reasonable where the individual had the choice of collecting monthly payments and not competing, or foregoing the payments and competing); Lemon v. Gressman, No. C8-00-1739, 2001 WL 290512, at *1-3 (Minn. Ct. App. Mar. 27, 2001) (enforcing a non-compete clause prohibiting the sellers of a restaurant from participating as an owner or operator in any food service business for a period of five years within a one-mile radius of the current location of that business).

93 Schmit Towing, Inc. v. Frovik, No. A10-362, 2010 WL 4451572 (Minn. Ct. App. 2010).

94 Perez v. Super Maid, LLC, 55 F.Supp 3d 1065, 1078 (N.D. Ill. 2014).

95   Hilligoss v. Cargill, Inc., 649 N.W.2d 142 (Minn. 2002).

96   Western Forms v. Pickell, 308 F.3d 930, 933 (8th Cir. 2002) ("[T]his conclusion leads to the albeit strange result that the covenant not to compete began to run and eventually expired while [the employee] was still employed at Western, but this result is a direct consequence of poor drafting on Western's part.").

97   Burke v. Fine, 608 N.W.2d 909 (Minn. Ct. App. 2000).

98   Gavaras v. Greenspring Media, LLC, 994 F.Supp.2d 1006 (D. Minn. 2014).

99   See Sempris, LLC v. Watson, No. 12-2454, 2012 WL 5199582, at *3 (D. Minn. 2012).

100 Surgidev Corp. v. Eye Tech, Inc., 648 F. Supp. 661 (D. Minn. 1986).

101 Kirkevold, 87 F.R.D. at 336.

102 Nott Co. v. Eberhardt, Nos. A13-1061 and A13-1390, 2014 WL 2441118 (Minn. Ct. App. 2014).

103 JAB Inc. v. Naegle, 867 N.W.2d 254 (Minn. Ct. App. 2015).

104 GreatAmerica Leasing Corp. v. Dolan, No. 10-4631, 2011 WL 334829 (D. Minn. 2011).

105 Saliterman v. Finney, 361 N.W.2d 175, 178 (Minn. Ct. App. 1985).

106 See, e.g. GreatAmerica, supra.

107 Hydra-Mac Inc. v. Onan Corp., 450 N.W.2d 913, 919 (Minn. 1990).

108 *E.g.,* Medtronic, Inc. v. Hughes, No. A10-998, 2011 WL 134973 (Minn. Ct. App. 2011)

109 In *Gavaras v. Greenspring Media, LLC*, 994 F.Supp.2d 1006, 1012 (D. Minn. 2014), a Minnesota federal district court declined to blue-pencil a non-compete agreement. The court held that blue-penciling the non-compete agreement would not be appropriate because rewriting the agreement would require more than modifying the duration and territorial scope. The court stated that rewriting would require the court to divine the parties' intent at the time of contracting, seventeen years after the fact, and with a different employer.

110 Hruska v. Chandler Assoc., 372 N.W.2d 709, 715 (Minn. 1985) ("'he who seeks equity must do equity, and he who comes into equity must come with clean hands,' ... and equitable concerns influence whether a covenant not to compete should be enforced").

111 Fred O. Watson Co. v. U.S. Life Ins. Co., 258 N.W.2d 776, 778 (Minn. 1977).

112 *See, e.g.*, Berg v. Carlstrom, 347 N.W.2d 809, 812 (Minn. 1984) ("[U]nclean hands in a collateral matter is not a defense to equitable relief.").

113 Granger v. Craven, 199 N.W. 10, 14 (Minn. 1924).

114 *See* Edin v. Jostens, Inc., 343 N.W.2d 691, 694 (Minn. Ct. App. 1984) (holding that injunctive relief will not be granted where conduct has been unconscionable by reason of bad motive and refusing to enjoin employee under non-compete agreement where employer terminated a 50-year old employee with a diabetic condition and pushed him to the brink of physical and financial collapse).

115 Siebert v. Amateur Athletic Union of the United States, Inc., 422 F. Supp. 2d 1033, 1040 (D. Minn. 2006) (citing Schlobohm v. Spa Petite, Inc., 326 N.W.2d 920, 924 (Minn. 1982)).

116 Nave v. Dovolos, 395 N.W.2d 393, 397 (Minn. Ct. App. 1986).

117 Johnson Bldg. Co. v. River Bluff Dev. Co., 374 N.W.2d 187, 194 (Minn. Ct. App. 1985), Toombs v. Daniels, 361 N.W.2d 801, 809 (Minn. 1985).

118 Faust v. Parrott, 270 N.W.2d 117, 120 (Minn. 1978).

119 Cherne, 278 N.W.2d at 94.

120 B & Y Metal Painting, 279 N.W.2d at 817.

121 Gorco Constr. Co. v. Stein, 99 N.W.2d 69, 74 (Minn. 1959).

122 Kallok v. Medtronic, Inc., 573 N.W.2d 356, 363 (Minn. 1998).

123 Anderson v. Hunter, Keith, Marshall & Co., 417 N.W.2d 619, 628 (Minn. 1988) (quoting Hensley v. Eckerhart, 461 U.S. 424, 433 (1983)).

124 2015 O.R.S. 653.295.

125 Atl. Marine Constr. Co. v. United States District Court for the Western District of Texas, 134 S. Ct. 568 (2013).

126 *See* Amended Order dated Nov. 12, 2010 in *U.S. Superior Marketing v. Hoberg Shatto Group, Inc.,* Civ. File No. 69-DU-CV-09-616 (Floerke, J.) at p. 10, n.1 (citing *Miller v. Miller,* 222 N.W.2d 71, 78 (1974)).

127 "Fiduciary" derives from the Latin *fidere*, to trust, which is related to *fidelis*, faithful, and *fides*, faith, whence comes the word fidelity, the common dog's name fido ("I obey"), and the Spanish *fidel* (faithful). Perhaps then, the difference between a fiduciary duty and a duty of loyalty is the difference between faith and loyalty.

128 *E.g.,* Synergetics v. Hurst, 477 F.3d 949, 954 (8th Cir. 2007); NeoNetworks, Inc. v. Cree, No. A07-0729, A07-1578, LEXIS 565 (Minn. Ct. App. May 20, 2008) at *8.

129 Rehabilitation Specialists, Inc. v. Koering, 404 N.W.2d 301, 304 (Minn. Ct. App.1987). (emphasis added.); *see also* Sanitary Farm Dairies, Inc. v. Wolf, 261 Minn. 166, 112 N.W.2d 42 (1961).

130 Rehabilitation Specialists, Inc., 404 N.W.2d at 305.

131 *Id.* at 304; *see also* Sanitary Farm Dairies, 112 N.W.2d at 48–49.

132 But see Hearing Associates, Inc. v. Downs, No. A16-1317 (Minn. Ct. App. 2017), affirming liablity where, *inter alia*, two employees of an audiology practice allegedly contacted two satellite offices used by their employer about the possibility of renting space before leaving to start their own business.

133 Sanitary Farm Dairies, 112 N.W.2d at 49.

134 Hlubeck v. Beeler, 489, 9 N.W.2d 252, 254 (1943).

135 Bellboy Imp. Corp. v. Baghart, 2004 WL 2711052 (Minn. Ct. App. 2004).

136 Griep v. Yamaha Motor Corp., 120 F. Supp.2d 1196 (D. Minn. 2000).

137 Thompson v. Buhrs Americas, Inc., 2009 U.S. Dist. LEXIS 16592, *33 (D. Minn. 2009).

138 Hearing Associates, Inc., at 20.

139 *See* Loxtercamp, Inc. v. Belgrade Cooperative Assn., 368 N.W.2d 299, 301 (Minn. Ct. App. 1985); Rehabilitation Specialists, Inc, 404 N.W.2d at 305–06.

140 Rehabilitation Specialists, Inc., 404 N.W.2d at 305.

141 Signergy Sign Group, Inc. v. Adam, 2004 WL 2711312, at *1 (Minn. Ct. App. 2004).

142 *See* Minn. Stat. § 325C.01, subd. 5; Electro-Craft Corp., 332 N.W.2d at 899.

143 *See* Minn. Stat. § 325C.01, subd. 3; Electro-Craft Corp. v. Controlled Motion, Inc., 332 N.W.2d 890, 897 (Minn. 1983).

144 Minn. Stat. § 325C.03(a) (2013).

145 *See* K-Sun Corp. v. Heller Investments, Inc., 1998 WL 422182, at *4 (Minn. Ct. App. 1998) ("Damages cannot be a product of speculation or mere guess. They can, however, be supported by reasonable estimates based in fact. Damages need not be proved with certainty."). In *K-Sun*, the plaintiff was awarded damages based on evidence of its "out-of-product expenditures, projected sales, and anticipated profits." *Id.*

146 Minn. Stat. § 325C.03 (b) (2013); K-Sun Corp., 1998 WL 422182 at *4 (stating that the evidence supported the view that high-level executives of appellants deliberately engaged in a scheme to obtain relatively definitive confidential business information about K-Sun, its products, and its relationship with Epson, and its marketing potential to use to the economic disadvantage of, and that coupled with the fact that the scheme was carried out through a breach of an express confidentiality agreement, that the evidence satisfied the requirement that conduct be both willful and malicious to support an award of exemplary damages).

147 PepsiCo, Inc. v. Redmond, 54 F.3d 1262 (7th Cir. 1995).

148 Minn. Stat. § 325C.02(a).

149 E.g., Katch, LLC v. Sweetser, 143 F.Supp. 854 (D. Minn. 2015) (citing other cases).

150 Minn. Stat. § 325C.07.

151 18 U.S.C. § 1831. *See also* the Computer Fraud and Abuse Act, 18 U.S.C. § 1030.

152 Minn. Stat. § 609.52, Subd. 1 (6).

153 Hearing Associates, Inc., at 18.

154 *Id*. See Jostens, Inc., 318 N.W.2d at 702.

155 *Id*.

156 See Hearing Associates, Inc., at 20-21. Note: the Minnesota Supreme Court granted certiorari review of the Court of Appeals on this question but did not rule because the case settled. (The author represented appellants in that case.)

157 Jostens, Inc., 318 N.W.2d at 703.

158 John H. Matheson & Philip S. Garon, *Corporation Law & Practice* § 7.22 2d. ed., West, 2004.

159 U.S. Bank N.A. v. Cold Spring Granite Co., 802 N.W.2d 363, 381 (Minn. 2011).

160 Donahue v. Rodd Electrotype Co. of New England, 328 N.E.2d 505, 511 (Mass. 1975); Berreman v. W. Publ'g *Co.*, 615 N.W.2d 362, 367 (Minn. Ct. App. 2000).

161 Sundberg v. Lampert Lumber Co., 390 N.W.2d 352,357 (Minn. Ct. App. 1986) (citing F.H. O'Neal, *Close Corporations* § 1.02 (2d ed. 1971))" Berreman, 615 N.W.2d, at 368 (Minn. Ct. App. 2000).

162 Minn. Stat. § 302A.461, subd. 4(a)(1),(2).

163 Minn. Stat. § 302A.461, subd. 4(b).

164 Minn. Stat. § 302A.461, subd. 5.

165 Minn. Stat. § 302A.461, subd. 6.

166 U.S. Bank v. Cold Spring Granite Co., 802 N.W.2d 363, 381 (Minn. 2011).

167 *Id.*

168 Regan v. Nat. Res. Grp., Inc., 345 F.Supp.2d 1000 (D.Minn. 2004).

169 Triple Five of Minnesota, Inc. v. Simon, 280 F.Supp.2d 895, 900 (D. Minn. 2003).

170 McGrath, 2012 WL 6097116 at *11.

171 *Id.* at *14.

172 Pedro v. Pedro, 463 N.W.2d 285, 289-90 (Minn. Ct. App. 1990).

173 Henricksen v. Big League Game Co., No. Co-95-388, 1995 WL 550935 (Minn. Ct. App. Sept. 19, 1995)."

174 Sawyer v. Curt & Company, Inc., No. C7-90-2040, 1991 WL 65320, (Minn. Ct. App. 1991) at * 2.

175 Berreman v. West Publ'g. Co., 615 N.W.2d 362, 374 (Minn. App. 2000); Gunderson v. Alliance of Computer Prof'ls, Inc., 628 N.W.2d 173, 184 (Minn. Ct. App. 2001).

176 *Id.* at 1160 (quoting Justice Cardozo's famous admonition in Meinhard v. Salmon, 249 N.Y. 458, 164 N.E. 545, 546 (N.Y. 1928)); Gunderson, 628 N.W.2d at 185.

177 *E.g,* Sawyer v. Curt & Company, Inc.

178 Gunderson, 628 N.W.2d at 185.

179 McGrath v. MICO, Inc., 2012 WL 6097116 (Minn. Ct. App. Dec. 10, 2012).

180 Gunderson, 628 N.W.2d at 191.

181 *Id.* at 189

182 *Id.* at 190; Keogh v. John Henry Foster Minn., Inc., No. A07-0423, 2008 WL 1747936 at *6–7 (Minn. Ct. App. Apr. 15, 2008).

183 Haley v. Forcelle, 669 N.W.2d 48, 59–60.

184 Gunderson, 628 N.W.2d at 185.

185 Evans v. Blesi, 345 N.W.2d 775, 779 (Minn. Ct. App. 1984)

186 Regan v. Natural Res. Grp., Inc., 345 F. Supp. 2d 1000, 1012 (D. Minn. 2004) (citing *Gunderson*, 628 N.W.2d at 190).

187 Joseph W. Anthony & Karlyn Vegoe Boraas, "Betrayed, Belittled ... but Triumphant: Claims of Shareholders in Closely Held Corporations", 22 *Wm. Mitchell L. Rev.* 1173, 1175 (1996).

188 Minn. Stat. § 302A.751, subd. 1(b)(1).

189 Gunderson, 628 N.W.2d at 185.

190 *See, e.g.*, Crosby v. Beam, 548 N.E.2d 217, 221 (Ohio 1989); Gunderson, 628 N.W.2d at 185; Billigmeier v. Concorde Mktg., Inc., No. C4-10-324, 2001 WL 1530356, *4 (Minn. Ct. App. Dec. 4, 2001).

191 Powell v. Anderson, 2003 WL 22705878 (Minn. Ct. App. Nov. 12, 2003).

192 Advanced Commc'n Design, Inc. v. Follett, 615 N.W.2d 285, 290 (Minn. 2000) ("When conflicting opinions of expert witnesses have a reasonable basis in fact, the [fact-finder] must decide who is right."); Thomas v. Thomas, 407 N.W.2d 124, 126 (Minn. App. 1987) ("The [district] court is not bound by the opinion of any witnesses concerning values." (citing *Lehman v. Hansord Pontiac Co.*, 74 N.W.2d 305, 310 (1955))). The weight and credibility of expert testimony is for the fact-finder to determine. Shymanski v. Nash, 251 N.W.2d 854, 857 (Minn. 1977). The "opinions of expert witnesses are only advisory and the [fact-finder] may weigh such evidence in the light of all the facts and opinions presented to it and draw its own conclusions." Hous. & Redev. Auth. v. First Ave. Realty Co., 270 Minn. 297, 306, 133 N.W.2d 645, 652 (1965).

193 Anthony, *supra* note 187, at 1182.

194 *Id.* at 1185–86.

195 *See* Minn. Stat. § 302A.751, subd. 2; Minn. Stat. § 302A.473, subd. 7; Advanced Commun. Design, Inc. v. Follett, 615 N.W.2d 285, 290 (Minn. 2000).

196 Follett, 615 N.W.2d at 292–93.

197 *Id.* at 292; Powell v. Anderson, 2003 Minn. App. LEXIS 1389, 31, 2003 WL 22705878 (Minn. Ct. App. Nov. 12, 2003).

198 Anthony, *supra* note 187, at 1189.

199 *Id.* at 1189–90.

200 *Id.* at 1191.

201 *Id.*; Helfmam v. Johnson, Civ. No. A08-0396 (Minn. Ct. App. Feb. 24, 2009).

202 *See* Pooley v. Mankato Iron & Metal, Inc., 513 N.W.2d 834, 838 (Minn. Ct. App. 1994) (stating that application of a minority shareholder discount in the context of a court-ordered buyout is improper because the legislature enacted Minn. Stat. § 302A.751 to protect minority shareholders who have been unfairly prejudiced), review denied (Minn. May 17, 1994); Follett, 615 N.W.2d at 292 (declining to adopt a bright-line rule regarding the applicability of a marketability discount in the context of a court-ordered fair-value buyout under Minn. Stat. § 302A.751, and holding that "absent extraordinary circumstances, fair value in a court-ordered buy-out pursuant to section 302A.751 means a pro rata share of the value of the corporation as a going concern without discount for lack of marketability").

203 Minn. Stat. § 302A.751; Powell, 2004 WL 5135802 (valuation date is date of commencement of the lawsuit).

204 Haley v. Forceloe, 699 N.W. 2d at 58; Gunderson, 628 N.W.2d at 186; Fisher v. Jeddeloh, No. A07.0637, 2008 WL 933478, *4 (Minn. Ct. App., Apr. 8, 2008**).**

205 Anthony, *supra* note 187, at 1179–80.

206 Minn. Stat. § 302A.751, subd. 2.

207 Drewitz v. Walser, No. 300-1759, 2001 WL 436223, at *3 (Minn. Ct. App. May 1, 2001); Miller Waste Mills v. Mackay, 520 N.W. 2d 490 (Minn. Ct. App. 1994).

208 Gunderson, 628 N.W.2d at 193.

209 *Id.* at 187.

210 Dullea v. Dullea Company, No. 891-498, 1991 WL 271479, at *3 (Minn. Ct. App. Dec. 24, 1991).

211 Powell, 2004 WL 5135802.

212 Drewitz v. Motorwerks, Inc., 728 N.W.2d 231, 237 (Minn. 2007).

213 *Id.* at 238.

214 Minn. Stat. § 302A.751, subd. 2 (1998); Gunderson, 628 N.W.2d at 187.

215 *See, e.g.*, ICC Leasing Corp. v. Midwestern Mach. Co., 257 N.W.2d 551, 555 (Minn. 1977); Bolander v. Bolander, 703 N.W.2d 529, 541 (Minn. Ct. App. 2005).

216 Bolander, 703 N.W.2d at 541.

217 Gunderson, 628 N.W. 2d at 185.

218 *Id.*

219 Steele v. Great E. Cas. & Indem. Co., 158 Minn. 160, 162, 197 N.W. 101, 101 (1924). *Bolander*, 703 N.W.2d at 542.

220 Anthony, *supra* note 187, at 1182–83.

221 Sifferle v. Micom Corp., 384 N.W.2d 503 (Minn. Ct. App. 1986).

222 *Black's Law Dictionary* (10th ed. 2014).

223 Minn. Stat. § 363A.08, subd. 2.

224 Ellen Berrey et al., "Workers Wronged", *ABA Journal*, Nov. 2017, p. 39.

225 *Id.*

226 Minnesota attorney Marshall H. Tanick claims that the Pillsbury Company, which no longer exists but which was headquartered in downtown Minneapolis, invented the idea of a severance formula based on years of service in the early 1980s, which came to be known as the "Pillsbury Plan." *See* Marshall H. Tanick, "The Dough Boy's Devise: Severance Takes a Poke," *Bench & Bar of Minnesota*, Mar. 11, 2014.

227 Minn. Stat. § 269.192, subd. 1.

228 See also, Philip Berkowitz, "Non-Disparagement Agreements: Worth It?" poasted on Feb. 23, 2018 at www.littler.com. Note also that the Consumer Review Protection Act, 15 U.S.C. § 45(b) which prohibits non-disparagement clauses in certain consumer contracts does not apply to employment agreements.

229 29 U.S.C. § 621 et. seq.

230 Patrick Thornton, "CEO Receives $4 M *Award* for Defamation, *Minnesota Lawyer*, Aug. 5, 2011; Heron Marquez Estrada, "KSTP Hit with $1 Million Defamation Verdict," *Minneapolis Star Tribune*, Nov. 8, 2011.

231 See, e.g. Maethner v. Someplace Safe, Inc., No. A17-0998 (Minn. Ct. App. Feb. 12, 2018) (Holding that statements were not protected by a qualified privilege).

232 Frankson v. Design Space Int'l, 394 N.W.2d 140, 143 (Minn. 1986).

233 Stuempges v. Parke, Davis & Co., 297 N.W.2d 252, 257 (Minn. 1980).

234 McBride v. Sears, Roebuck & Co., 235 N.W.2d 371, 375 (Minn. 1975).

235 Hunt v. Univ. of Minn., 465 N.W.2d 88, 92 (Minn. Ct. App. 1991).

236 Conerly v. CVN Companies, Inc., 785 F.Supp. 801, 812 (D. Minn. 1992).

237 Harvet v. Unity Medical Ctr., Inc., 428 N.W.2d 574, 579 (Minn. Ct. App. 1988).

238 Lewis v. Equitable Life Assurance Society of the United States, 389 N.W.2d 876, 888 (Minn. 1986).

239 *Id.*

240 Michael K. Steenson & Peter B. Knapp, Minnesota Jury Instruction Guides—Civil § 50 (5th ed. 2006).

241 Weissman v. Sri Lanka Curry House, Inc., 469 N.W.2d 471, 473 (Minn. Ct. App. 1991).

242 Kallok v. Medtronic, Inc., 573 N.W.2d 356, 362 (Minn. 1998).

243 Restatement (Second) of Torts § 766A; *see also* Shafir v. Steele, 727 N.E.2d 1140 (2000).

244 Gieseke v. IDCA, Inc., 844 N.W.2d 210, 219 (Minn. 2014) (relying on the Restatement (Second) of Torts § 766(B)). Gieseke involved long-standing disputes between brothers with competing businesses. Although the Court explicitly reaffirmed that "tortious interference with prospective economic advantage is a viable claim in Minnesota," *id.* at 212, and "wrongful interference with the formation of a contract is no less actionable than a wrongful interference with an existing contract," *id.* at 213, it reversed judgment in favor of the plaintiff because he failed to identify and third parties with whom he had a reasonable expectation of a future economic relationship and failed to prove damages.

245 45 Am. Jur. 2d Interference Section 1.

246 Storage Tech. Corp. v. Cisco Sys., Inc., 2003 WL 22231544, at *2 (D. Minn. Sept. 25, 2003), affirmed 395 F.3d 921 (8th Cir. 2005).

247 *Id.*

248 *Id.* In *St Jude Medical S.C., Inc. v. Biosense Webster, Inc.*, 81 F.3d 785, however, the Eighth Circuit Court of Appeals clarified its decision in Storage Tech, noting "Minnesota law allows damages that would not be available in a suit on the contract itself," and held that in Biosense the district court, "correctly concluded that St. Jude could recover damages for lost profits based on Biosense's tortious interference." *Id.* at 790.

249 Kallok v. Medtronic, Inc., 573 N.W.2d 356, 363 (Minn. 1998).

250 *See, e.g.*, Cherne, 278 N.W.2d 81 (Minn. 1979) and Young v. Meyer, LEXIS 380, *3 (Minn. Ct. App. Apr. 4, 1989) (unpublished opinion) (referring to injunctive relief in cases also involving companion claims for breach of non-compete agreements).

251 Bankers Multiple Line Ins. Co. v. Farish, 464 So.2d 530, 533 (Fla. 1985).

252 Hospital Corp. of Lake Worth v. Romaguera, 511 So.2d 559, 561 (Fla. 4th DCA 1986).

253 *Id.* at 564.

254 Minn. Stat. § 549.20.

255 The Minnesota case of *Moore v. Hoff*, 821 N.W.2d 591 (Minn. Ct. App. 2012) is a good case study. The plaintiff sued a blogger known as "Johnny Northside" for defamation and interference with prospective advantage. The jury specifically found that the statements in the blog post were true and therefore ruled against the plaintiff on the defamation claim. But the jury ruled in favor of plaintiff on the interference claim, awarding him $60,000. The Minnesota Court of Appeals reversed, holding that plaintiff could not establish claim for interference based on publishing true statements on a blog.

256 *See* C.R. Bard, Inc. v. Worldtronics Corp., 561 A.2d 694, 235 N.J. Super. 168 (1989) ("Defendant's motive is not relevant to the determinations of this case ... It is not improper to give truthful information to a customer about someone else's product, and this is so even if the purpose is to interfere with an existing or prospective contractual relationship."). *See also* Restatement (Second) of Torts § 772 ("One who intentionally causes a third person not to perform a contract or not to enter into a prospective contractual relation with another does not interfere improperly with the other"s contractual relation, by giving the third person (a) truthful information, or (b) honest advice within the scope of a request for the advice.")

257 In Wal-Mart Stores, Inc. v. Sturges, 52 S.W.3d 711 (Tex. 2001), for example, plaintiffs asked Wal-Mart to amend the easement on tract of land it owned so that plaintiffs could finance and purchase tract to build a food store. A Wal-Mart manager said it would provide the amendment, but before it was completed, another Wal-Mart manager swooped in to purchase the property for a new Wal-Mart store. A jury awarded plaintiffs $1 million in lost profits and $500,000 in punitive damages on plaintiff's interference claim. The Texas Supreme Court reversed the verdict, noting, "In an economic system founded upon the principle of free competition, competitors should not be liable in tort for seeking a legitimate business advantage."

258 Sysdyne Corp. v. Rousslang, 860 N.W.2d 347 (Minn. 2015).

259 Acclaim Sys., Inc. v. Infosys, Ltd, No. 16-1770 (3rd Cir. Jan. 19. 2017).

260 Hester v. Case Western Reserve University, No. 105515, 2017 WL 123318 (Ohio Ct. App. Jan. 12, 2017.)

261 Nordling v. N. States Power Co., 478 N.W.2d 498, 505 (Minn. 1991).

262 *Id.*; *see also* Boers v. Payline Sys., Inc., 141 Or. App. 238, 243 (Or. Ct. App. 1996).

263 See Minn. Stat. § 181.961 (review of personnel record) and Minn. Stat. § 181.933 (true reasons letter.)

264 American Arbitration Association, 2017 Arbitrator Reference Manual, p. 13.

265 AAA Powerpoint, on file with the author.

266 Minn. Stat. § 181.171, Subd 3.

267 Minn. Stat. § 181.03.

268 Toyota-Lift of Minnesota, Inc. v. American Warehouse Systems, LLC, 886 N.W.2d 208 (Minn. 2016).

269 Minn. Stat. 325E.37.

270 Cherne, 278 N.W.2d at 92 (internal citation omitted).

271 Morse v. City of Waterville, 458 N.W.2d 728, 729-30 (Minn. Ct. App.1990), rev. denied (Minn. Sept. 28, 1990).

272 Hideaway, Inc. v. Gambit Invs. Inc., 386 N.W.2d 822, 824 (Minn. Ct. App. 1986); Hinz v. Neuroscience, Inc., 538 F.3d 979, 986 (8th Cir. 2008) (alterations in original).

273 Minn. R. Civ. P. 65.01 (emphasis added); Webb Publ'g Co. v. Fosshage, 426 N.W.2d 445, 448 (Minn. Ct. App. 1988); Sanborn Mfg. Co. v. Currie, 500 N.W.2d 161, 163 (Minn. 1993) ("A trial court may grant a temporary injunction if the party seeking it establishes that there is no adequate remedy at law and the denial of the injunction will result in irreparable injury."). Only "when it is clear that the rights of a party will be irreparably injured before a trial on the merits is held" should such an order be entered. Miller v. Foley, 317 N.W.2d 710, 712 (Minn. 1982); Sunny Fresh Foods, Inc. v. Microfresh

Foods Corp., 424 N.W.2d 309, 310 (Minn. Ct. App. 1988) (holding that order should issue only "in clear cases, reasonably free from doubt").

274 Cherne, 278 N.W.2d at 92.

275 City of Mounds View v. Metro. Airports Comm'n, 590 N.W.2d 355, 357 (Minn. Ct. App. 1999) (citing *Ecolab, Inc. v. Gartland*, 537 N.W.2d 291, 294 (Minn. Ct. App. 1995)). "The burden of proof rests upon the complainant to establish the material allegations entitling him to relief." Sunny Fresh Foods, Inc. v. Microfresh Foods Corp., 424 N.W.2d 309, 310 (Minn. Ct. App. 1988) (quoting *AMF Pinspotters, Inc. v. Harkins Bowling, Inc.*, 110 N.W.2d 348, 351 (Minn. 1961)).

276 Medtronic, Inc. v. Advanced Bionics Corp., 630 N.W.2d 438, 454 (Minn. Ct. App. 2001) (citing *Morse v. City of Waterville*, 458 N.W.2d 728, 729 (Minn. Ct. App. 1990)).

277 City of Mounds View, 590 N.W.2d at 357 (citing *Dahlberg Bros., Inc. v. Ford Motor Co.*, 137 N.W.2d 314, 321–22 (Minn. 1965)).

278 Dahlberg, 137 N.W.2d 314, 321-22.

279 Softchoice, Inc. v. Schmidt, 763 N.W.2d 660, 661 (Minn. Ct. App. 2009) (citing *Dahlberg*).

280 Sunny Fresh Foods, Inc.,424 N.W.2d at 310 (quoting *AMF Pinspotters, Inc. v. Harkins Bowling, Inc.*, 110 N.W.2d 348, 351 (Minn. 1961)).

281 Rosewood Mortgage Corp. v. Hefty, 383 N.W.2d 456, 459 (Minn. Ct. App. 1986) (citing *Eakman v. Brutger*, 285 N.W.2d 95, 97 (Minn. 1979).

282 Dataphase Sys., Inc. v. C L Sys., Inc., 640 F.2d 109, 114 (8th Cir. 1981).

283 Webb Publ'g Co. v. Fosshage, 426 N.W.2d 445, 448 (Minn. Ct. App. 1988) (citing *Menter Co. v. Brock*, 180 N. W. 553, 554-55 (Minn. 1920)); Cherne, 278 N.W.2d at 92 (Minn. 1979) (holding that an inherent threat of irreparable injury may be inferred from the breach of an otherwise valid and enforceable restrictive covenant, sufficient to invoke at least temporary equitable relief).

284 Thermorama, Inc., 125 N.W.2d at 845 (finding threat of irreparable harm significant where breach of covenant alleged); Medtronic Inc. v. Advanced Bionics Corp., 630 N.W.2d 438 (Minn. App. 2001) (same); Eutectic, 160 N.W.2d at 569, n.4 (Minn. 1968); Medtronic, Inc. v. Camp, No. 02-285, 2002 U.S. Dist. LEXIS 2206, at *4-5 (D. Minn. Feb. 6, 2002) (holding that irreparable harm may be inferred from a threat to misappropriate trade secrets or confidential information); Hypro, LLC v. Reser, No 04-4921, 2004 WL 2905321, at *5 (D. Minn. 204) (granting TRO and finding irreparable harm where defendants breached their contractual duties and were actively competing with plaintiff in the marketplace using plaintiff's confidential and proprietary information).

285 Minn. Stat. § 555.01.

286 *Id.*

287 *Id.* at § 555.02.

288 Gavaras v. Greenspring Media, LLC, 994 F. Supp. 2d 1006 (D.Minn. 2014) (citing *Seiz v. Citizens Pure Ice Co.*, 290 N.W. 802, 804 (Minn. 1940)).

289 Onvoy, Inc. v. ALLETE, Inc., 736 N.W.2d 611, 617-18 (Minn. 2007) (citing *State ex rel. Smith v. Haveland*, 25 N.W.2d 474, 476-77 (Minn. 1946)); Seiz, 290 N.W. at 804.

290 Gavaras, 994 F. Supp. 2d at 1006 (citing *Turner v. Alpha Phi Sorority House*, 276 N.W.2d 63, 66 (Minn. 1979)).

291 A version of this section originally appeared in *Minnesota Lawyer* on Feb. 7, 2017.

292 616 N.W.2d 732 (Minn. 2000).

293 Dan Jamieson, "Morgan Stanley Exits Recruitment Protocol," *Financial Advisor*, Oct. 30, 2017.

294 "Workers Say Wells Fargo Unfairly Scarred Their Careers," National Public Radio, Oct. 21, 2016 (story by Chris Arnold), available at https://www.npr.org/2016/10/21/498804659/former-wells-fargo-employees-join-class-action-lawsuit.

295 Anthony Youn, M.D., "Seriously? Doctors Think They Are Underpaid", CNN.com, May 1, 2012, available at http://thechart.blogs.cnn.com/2012/05/01/seriously-doctors-say-theyre-underpaid/comment-page-14/.

296 42 U.S.C.S. § 1395nn (§ 1877 of the Social Security Act); *see also* 42 C.F.R. §§ 411.350-411.389.

297 Michael Williams PhD and Betsy White Williams PhD, "The Disruptive Physician: A Conceptual Organization," 94 *Journal of Medical Licensure and Discipline*, No. 3, 2008, p. 12.

298 The Minnesota Court of Appeals addressed arguments that non-compete agreements for physicians should be non-enforceable due to public policy in *Albert Lea Clinic-Mayo Health System v. Waugh*, 1996 WL 70100 (Minn. Ct. App. 1996): "Waugh argues that a non-compete agreement applied to a physician should not be enforced because it is contrary to public policy. We disagree. In *Granger v. Craven*, 159 Minn. 296, 199 N.W. 10 (1924), the Minnesota Supreme Court rejected a similar public policy argument."

299 Granger v. Craven, 199 N.W. 10 (Minn. 1924). In analyzing the rationale behind the Granger decision fifty years later, the Minnesota Supreme Court suggested that the closeness of the patient-physician relationship is a reason non-competes may be necessary for employers: "[e]nforcement of restrictive covenants against professional employees is based on the relationship that is created, as for example, between a doctor and his patients. Once this relationship is formed, it is beyond question that a doctor's patients will seek his aid regardless of this doctor's employment situation." Walker Employment Service, Inc. v. Parkhurst, 219 N.W.2d 437 at 441 (Minn. 1974) (Walker did not involve a physician).

300 Freeman, 334 N.W.2d at at 630-36 (citing *Damsey v. Mankowitz*, 339 So.2d 282 (Fla. App. 1976)); Ellis v. McDaniel, 596 P.2d 222 (1979); New Castle Orthopedic Associates v. Burns, 392 A.2d 1383 (1978).

301 *See, e.g.*, Freeman (finding that a physician received no special benefits in exchange for signing a non-compete agreement and holding that mere continued employment was insufficient consideration to support the agreement); Burke, 608 N.W.2d at 909 (declining to enforce non-compete against cardiologist because underlying contract expired by its own terms).

302 Opinion 9.02, "Restrictive Covenants and the Practice of Medicine," available at http://www.ama-assn.org/ama/pub/physician-resources/medical-ethics/code-medical-ethics/opinion902.page.

303 *Id.*

304 Mass. Gen. Law ch. 112, § 12 (prohibiting any agreement or contract with a physician "which includes any restriction of the right of such physician to practice medicine in any geographic area for any period of time after the termination of such partnership.").

305 Tenn. Code Ann. § 63-1-148 ("This section shall not apply to physicians who specialize in the practice of emergency medicine.").

306 Colo. Rev. Stat. § 8-2-113(3) ("Any covenant not to compete provision of an employment, partnership, or corporate agreement between physicians which restricts the right of a physician to practice medicine, as defined in section 12-36-106, C.R.S., upon termination of such agreement, shall be void; except that all other provisions of such an agreement enforceable at law, including provisions which require the payment of damages in an amount that is reasonably related to the injury suffered by reason of termination of the agreement, shall be enforceable. Provisions which require the payment of damages upon termination of the agreement may include, but not be limited to, damages related to competition.").

307 *See, e.g.*, Valley Med. Specialists v. Farber, 982 P.2d 1277, 1282 (Ariz. 1999) (holding that the doctor-patient relationship is special and entitled to unique protection, that it cannot be easily or accurately compared to relationships in the commercial context, that the patients' rights to see the doctor of their choice is entitled to substantial protection, and that the employer's protectable interests of patients and referral sources in the case are comparably minimal).

308 *See, e.g.*, Intermountain Eye & Laser Ctrs., PLLC v. Miller, 127 P.3d 121, 132 (Idaho 2005) (holding that the restriction on the ophthalmologist's ability to engage in the practice of medicine exceeded the scope of the firm's legitimate business interests, because the ophthalmology firm's protectable interests "[are] limited by those patients' interest in continuity of care and access to the health provider of their choice" and that "[w]hile the public has a strong interest in freedom of contract, that interest must be balanced against the public interest in upholding the highly personal relationship between the physician and his or her patient."); Statesville Med. Grp. v. Dickey, 418 S.E.2d 256, 259 (N.C. App. 1992) (invalidating a non-compete agreement by a medical group against an endocrinologist, because it would substantially impede patients' access to their physician of choice, and impair their ease of access to second opinions). Courts have struck down non-compete agreements with doctors on other grounds as well. For example, in Indiana, the Indian Court of Appeals refused to enforce a non-compete agreement with a doctor, because the doctor was a specialist in a limited geographic area. Fumo v. Medical Group of Michigan City, Inc., 590 N.E.2d 1103, 1109 (Ind. Ct. App. 1992) ("Where a specialist offers services uniquely or sparsely available in a specified geographical area, an injunction may be unwarranted because the movant is unable to meet the burden of showing that the public would not be disserved."). The New Jersey Supreme Court invalidated a doctor's non-compete agreement on similar grounds. Cmty. Hosp. Group, Inc. v. More, 869 A.2d 884, 900 (N.J. 2005) (concluding that a restrictive covenant covering a 30-mile radius is injurious to the public where it would prohibit a neurosurgeon from practicing in an area where there was a shortage of neurosurgeons). In Arkansas, the Court of Appeals refused to enforce a non-compete agreement for a cardiologist, because the geographic scope was too broad. Jaraki v. Cardiology Assocs. of Northeast Ark, 55 S.W.3d 799, 804 (Ark. App. 2001) (holding that the geographic area in a non-compete clause prohibiting a cardiologist from practicing within 75-mile radius was too broad, and thus was not enforceable, where not all of area covered by clause was part of cardiology practice's referral base). In a unique and noteworthy situation, an independent agency of the federal government invalidated the non-compete agreements of ten cardiologists who were terminating their employment with Renown Health in Reno, Nevada in 2012. The Federal Trade Commission (FTC) invalidated these agreements, because they were concerned that Renown's strong monopoly position could destroy competition on price and quality.

309 St. Clair Med., P.C. v. Borgiel, 715 N.W.2d 914, 919 (Mich. Ct. App. 2006) (holding that a doctor violated his non-compete agreement, which prohibited him from practicing within seven miles of either of two medical clinics, because the agreement protected the former employer from unfair competition and therefore protected a reasonable competitive business interest, the agreement's geographic restriction was reasonable in relation to the former employer's competitive interest, the agreement was not unethical under the American Medical Association's principles of medical ethics, and the $40,000 in liquidated damages clause did not strike the court as unconscionable or excessive in relation to potential patient loss).

310 *Id.*

311 Mohanty v. St. John Heart Clinic, 866 N.E.2d 85, 99 (Ill. 2006) (holding the restraint on the practice of medicine was not greater than necessary to protect the employer's interests, because the restrictions on the physician's was in effect only within a narrowly circumscribed area of a large metropolitan area, and that the two- and five-mile restrictions would not cause the physicians any undue hardship, and does not suggest that a more narrowly drawn activity restriction would have been practicable).

312 West Penn Specialty MSO Inc. v. Nolan, 737 A.2d 295, 299-300 (Pa. Super. Ct. 1995) (holding that the doctor's departure signaled a significant loss of business opportunity and market advantage, because her employment with a new employer would put her old employer at a substantial competitive disadvantage).

313 Silvers, Asher, Sher, & McLaren, M.D.s Neurology, P .C. v. Batchu, 16 S.W.3d 340, 345 (Mo. App. W.D. 2000) (holding that where a neurologist set up a medical practice three miles from former clinic within one month after he was discharged, and he practiced medicine in violation of covenant until time of preliminary injunction, the trial court's enforcement of a two-year non-compete and territorial restriction from the date of injunction rather than date of termination was not inequitable).

314 *See* Correll v. Distinctive Dental Servs., P.A., 607 N.W.2d 440, 443 (Minn. 2000) (holding that a dentist in Winsted was barred from bringing a claim under the Minnesota Human Rights Act while trying to escape from the provisions of a non-compete agreement); Saliterman v. Finney, 361 N.W.2d 175, 177-78 (Minn. Ct. App. 1985) (holding that a non-compete covenant in an employment agreement between a family dental center and a dentist is assignable where it protects the goodwill of a business that is being sold, and that Minnesota has long recognized the uniquely vulnerable goodwill of patients which belongs to the owner of a medical practice).

315 E.g. Kari Family Clinic of Chiropractic, P.A. v. Bohnen, 349 N.W.2d 868, 869 (Minn. Ct. App. 1984) (finding no consideration for clause signed two months after chiropractic doctor started employment; Head v. Morris Veterinary Ctr., Inc., No. A04-2334, 2005 WL 1620328, at *5 (Minn. Ct. App. July 12, 2005) (blue-penciling non-compete clauses of two veterinarians from three years to one year where the record suggested that six months was an adequate time-period to train new veterinarians).

316 Minn. Stat. § 144A.72.

317 8 C.F.R. § 214.1(2).

318 *E.g.*, Melendres v. Soales, 306 N.W.2d 399 (Mich. Ct. App. 1981).

319 Pierre Michel Jeanneton v. Hilton Ina, 966 F.Supp. 133 (D. P. Rico 1997).

320 Varun Khanna v. Grandparents Living Theater, Inc., 1997 Ohio App. Lexis 4352, at *7; *see also*, Ran Geva v. Leo Burnett Co., 1990 Lexis 210 (N.D. Ill. Jan. 10, 1990) (finding H-1B visa petition for Israeli employee not to be a three-year employment contract).

321 Minn. Stat. Chapter 13.

322 Minn. Stat. § 43A.17, Subd. 9.

323 Patrick Condon, "Dayton Severance Payments to Three Officials Incur GOP Wrath," *Minneapolis Star Tribune*, Sept. 20, 2016.